Mastering
Employee development

Palgrave Master Series

Accounting
Accounting Skills
Advanced English Language
Advanced English Literature
Advanced Pure Mathematics
Arabic
Basic Management
Biology
British Politics
Business Communication
Business Environment
C Programming
C++ Programming
Chemistry
COBOL Programming
Communication
Computing
Counselling Skills
Counselling Theory
Customer Relations
Database Design
Delphi Programming
Desktop Publishing
Economic and Social History
Economics
Electrical Engineering
Electronics
Employee Development
English Grammar
English Language
English Literature
Fashion Buying and Merchandising
   Management
Fashion Styling
French
Geography

German
Global Information Systems
Human Resource Management
Information Technology
Internet
Java
Management Skills
Marketing Management
Mathematics
Microsoft Office
Microsoft Windows, Novell NetWare
   and UNIX
Modern British History
Modern European History
Modern United States History
Modern World History
Networks
Organisational Behaviour
Pascal and Delphi Programming
Philosophy
Physics
Practical Criticism
Psychology
Shakespeare
Social Welfare
Sociology
Spanish
Statistics
Strategic Management
Systems Analysis and Design
Team Leadership
Theology
Twentieth-Century Russian History
Visual Basic
World Religions

www.palgravemasterseries.com

Palgrave Master Series
Series Standing Order ISBN 0–333–69343–4
(outside North America only)

You can receive future titles in this series as they are published by placing a standing order. Please contact your bookseller or, in case of difficulty, write to us at the address below with your name and address, the title of the series and the ISBN quoted above.

Customer Services Department, Macmillan Distribution Ltd
Houndmills, Basingstoke, Hampshire RG21 6XS, England

Mastering
Employee development

Richard Pettinger

palgrave

First published 2002 by
PALGRAVE
Houndmills, Basingstoke, Hampshire RG21 6XS and
175 Fifth Avenue, New York, N.Y. 10010
Companies and representatives throughout the world

PALGRAVE is the new global academic imprint of
St. Martin's Press LLC Scholarly and Reference Division and
Palgrave Publishers Ltd (formerly Macmillan Press Ltd).

ISBN 0–333–97358–5

This book is printed on paper suitable for recycling and
made from fully managed and sustained forest sources.

A catalogue record for this book is available
from the British Library.

10   9   8   7   6   5   4   3   2   1
11   10 09 08 07 06 05 04 03 02

Printed and bound in Great Britain by
Creative Print and Design (Wales), Ebbw Vale

■ ⚈ Contents

Preface   ix

1   Introduction   **1**
Introduction   1
The broad context   2
Cost and charges   5
Cost–benefit analysis and employee development   8
Other contextual factors   9
Conclusions   11

2   How people learn   **13**
Introduction   13
Conditions   13
Preferred learning styles   17
How people learn   19
Other factors   23
Costs and benefits   26
Conclusions   26

3   Training needs analysis   **28**
Introduction   28
Individual performance appraisal   28
Self-assessment   30
Peer assessment   30
Subordinate assessment   31
Job assessment and evaluation   32
Organisational and managerial performance assessment   32
Group contributions   37
Strategic approaches to training needs analysis   37
Needs analysis, policy and direction   39
Monitoring, review and evaluation   40
Costs and benefits   40
Conclusions   40

4   Core training programmes and activities   **42**
Introduction   42
Universal programmes   42
Programme purposes   45
Costs and benefits   48
Conclusions   49

5 On-the-job training   **51**
   Introduction   51
   Working under guidance and supervision   52
   Expectations   54
   Generic programmes   55
   Frontline staff   56
   Multi-skilling   57
   Empowerment   57
   Flexibility   59
   Other factors in on-the-job training   60
   Costs and benefits   62
   Conclusions   62

6 Off-the-job training   **64**
   Introduction   64
   Opportunities   65
   Consequences   66
   Specific programmes   68
   Key factors   69
   Other factors   72
   Costs and benefits   73
   Conclusions   73

7 Projects and secondments   **76**
   Introduction   76
   Context   76
   Sources of project and project work   77
   Demands of project work   78
   Other approaches to projects and secondments   81
   Costs and benefits   86
   Conclusions   86

8 Monitoring, review and evaluation   **88**
   Introduction   88
   Basis   88
   Other factors   95
   Costs and benefits   97
   Conclusions   97

9 Designing training programmes   **99**
   Introduction   99
   Aims and objectives   99
   Process consultation   101
   Target audience   102
   Use of time   104
   Group size and mixes   106
   Costs and benefits   108
   Conclusions   109

10 Training and development equipment and resources 111
Introduction 111
Equipment and resources 112
Quality of training and learning environment 119
Costs and benefits 121
Conclusions 122

11 Mentoring, coaching and counselling 124
Introduction 124
Context 124
Qualities 126
Outputs 127
Nature of relationship 129
Characteristics 134
Costs and benefits 136
Conclusions 136

12 Organisation and employee development strategies 138
Introduction 138
A strategic approach 139
Raising expectations 141
The training and development environment 142
Strategic approaches to training needs analysis and appraisal 144
Other approaches 146
Continuous professional and occupational development demands 148
Costs and benefits 148
Conclusions 148

13 Organisational training functions 150
Introduction 150
Strategic position 151
Relating organisation strategy and the training function 158
Roles, functions and resources 160
Costs and benefits 161
Conclusions 161

14 Organisation development 164
Introduction 164
The development of positive culture, attitudes, values and beliefs 165
Generation of commitment 168
Coping with change and uncertainty 169
Barriers to change 171
Conflict 173
Costs and benefits 175
Conclusions 176

15 Management development 178
Introduction 178
The body of expertise 180

Management qualifications 182
Organisational and environmental expertise 183
Management development and product and service enhancement 186
Self-development 188
Succession and transformation 189
Costs and benefits 190
Conclusions 190

16 Government training and development policy **192**
Introduction 192
Problems 193
Cultural and social factors 204
Costs and benefits 205
Conclusions 205

17 The future of organisation and employee development **207**
Introduction 207
The European Union 207
Continuous professional and occupational development 209
Managing across cultures 210
Consultants and specialists 213
Costs and benefits 213
Conclusions 213

Bibliography 216

Index 218

■ ⍗ Preface

Training and development of those at work and going into work has always been a curiosity. Everyone agrees that it is a good and worthwhile thing, but (with notable exceptions) there is a collective unwillingness to accept responsibility for it.

Part of the reason for this is cultural. It always used to be assumed that education establishments prepared people with the skills, knowledge, attitudes and behaviour necessary for working life, and that organisations would simply show people what had to be done so that they could get on with it.

The other part is institutional. No clarity exists to this day about what organisation and employee development ought to be concerned with, who should do what, or who should pay for it.

The purpose of this book is to address each of these issues in turn. It also provides a concise and cohesive structure for the understanding of what constitutes employee and organisation development, and by implication, the foundations for an agreed and accepted body of expertise for the field. Everything is set in the context that expert, trained and developed employees contribute directly to successful, effective and profitable commercial and public service performance. Accordingly, needs analyses, core training and development requirements, on-the-job and off-the-job provisions, the use and value of projects and secondments, are each dealt with in turn. Structures for designing, monitoring, reviewing and evaluating events are proposed, discussed and illustrated. Attention is then paid to the enduring requirements to invest in, and manage, the development of organisations. The book finishes with a discussion of government training and development policy, and influences on the future.

At the end of each chapter there is an itemisation and summary of the costs and benefits that have to be considered in each case. Problems and issues that arise are also highlighted.

The book also concentrates on the prerequisites for all successful and enduringly effective training and development activities. These are: the need to address personal, occupational, organisational and professional demands; and the need to address and develop each aspect of behaviour, attitude, skill, knowledge, expertise and technological proficiency. There are illustrations of each aspect in practice and application; except where sourced, these are from the author's direct experience.

The book is intended as a foundation reader for all those who wish to understand the realm, role and function of organisation and employee development. It is an essential reader for those on foundation courses in personnel practice and other certificate level professional and management qualifications. It is of value to those on HND, HNC and undergraduate courses where there is a personnel or human resource management element. For many on the professional education scheme of the Chartered Institute of Personnel and Development, who are coming to this without prior knowledge of organisation and employee development, it is an essential pre-read, setting in context and providing the foundation for more advanced studies.

2002   **Richard Pettinger**

For additional support to this book, please see our website at www.palgrave_com/studyskills/masterseries/pettinger

■ ⩒ ▍ Introduction

'Give someone a fish and you feed them for a day. Teach them to fish and you feed them for life.'

Proverb

Introduction

UK organisations and their top managers have always exhibited an ambivalent attitude towards organisation and employee training and development. On the one hand, they have long bewailed the declining standard of school education, and the inability of young people to read, write, express themselves or do anything productive. This is then closely followed by complaints that school leavers exhibit a total lack of understanding of the world at large, the world of work, and the demands of particular jobs and occupations. People coming into work for the first time, so it is said, show a total lack of realism about what they are going to be asked to do, or how much they can reasonably expect to be paid (see Summary Box 1.1).

SUMMARY BOX 1.1   Unreasonable expectations

Many of these unreasonable expectations have been fuelled by business stories in the media placed by top managers themselves. The following are examples.

- **The internet:** a survey conducted by the Industrial Society in March 2001 concerning the expectations of school leavers found that many still expected to be able to draw up a simple web page and sell it on for a vast fortune either to an organisation, or else to shareholders on the stock exchange. The survey was commissioned after a member company of the London Chamber of Commerce and Industry was approached by a school leaver with his GCSE project – a website search engine. While it was clearly an excellent school project, it had little commercial application, and the company turned it down. Incensed, the school leaver used his technological expertise to vandalise the particular organisation's website. *(continued)*

On the other hand, there has been an institutionalised, almost cultural, refusal to do anything about changing these corporate attitudes. Above all, training and development are perceived to be very expensive and so industrial, commercial and public service organisations should not have to pay for it. In 1964, the UK government proposed a levy of 3 per cent of payroll in order to set up and establish a national training framework. This would be taken from all employers, for aid into industrial training boards and other bodies, and used to design and deliver training programmes to produce the required flow of expertise. However, during the consultative phase, the levy was reduced from 3 to 1 per cent. Moreover, provision was then made for companies to gain claw-backs and exemptions if they could demonstrate that they were doing their own rigorous, effective and planned training and development.

The broad context

Since 1981, when the majority of industrial training boards was abolished, there has been no statutory obligation worthy of the name that forces, coerces or encourages organisations to take responsibility for the development, enhancement and improvement of their workforce. The results of this are as follows:

- Training and development are not valued. The best organisations – and there are excellent companies in all sectors – take this on themselves, and train and develop their staff anyway. The worst are at least honest in that they make no pretence of having any form of coherent, cohesive or strategic approach to staff training and development – and this category includes many public service sector bodies, especially in health, education and social services. The mainstream either undertake or support *ad hoc*, unstructured training and development activities, often following a crisis or emergency which turned out badly because of the lack of trained or expert staff to deal with it.
- Training and development are both seen as costs and charges, rather than investment or capital expenditure.
- Training and development are seen as opportunities to overload frontline staff with new work (see Summary Box 1.2).
- Training and development are accorded low priority and status. Training and development budgets are among the first to be cut when organisations meet hard times, or are required to demonstrate savings and efficiencies to shareholders' representatives or governing bodies.

Empowerment programmes were originally supposed to be vehicles for the development of organisations through the enhancement of the skills and expertise of their frontline staff. At their best, the strategic purpose was that, by concentrating responsibility, authority and expertise at the frontline, it would be possible to reduce greatly the overhead expense of administrative and support functions, and managerial hierarchies.

This was extremely successful at *Harvester* restaurants. Supported by extensive staff training programmes and enhanced pay, terms and conditions of employment, and organisational support, the company was able to reduce its non-frontline staff by a quarter at exactly the same time as sales and reputation were enhanced.

Other organisations found this purpose diluted. A major mortgage lender used its empowerment programme to increase production targets placed on its call centre and cashier staff. The empowerment programme was supported only by software; there were no tutorials, seminars or management support. The performance targets, which included a requirement to average handling 15 calls per hour for call centre staff, and to generate sales of financial products in 20 per cent of those calling at cash desks, were underpinned by disciplinary rather than training programmes.

- Training and development are offered on a distributive rather than an integrative or a strategic basis. In the worst cases, this is accorded on the basis of rank, status and patronage rather than need. Senior staff use their influence to attend their own preferred training and development events; and they use their position to ensure that favourites, their personal staff and assistants, are chosen to go to events also. In some cases, they will send junior staff to 'senior management functions' just to make sure that they are not missing out on anything (see Summary Box 1.3).

When she was Dean of the Harvard Business School, Rosabeth Moss Kanter produced a series of programmes for BBC television's *Management Matters*. She also quoted the prevalence of sending junior staff on senior management courses, so that top managers and directors would be certain that they had not missed anything. She went further, as follows:

- She stated that the practice gave those senior managers a perverse status, in that top management programmes were only considered worthy of attendance by their assistants.
- The practice was used to enhance favouritism and patronage, rather than organisational or staff development.   (continued)

- Wherever this was offered on a distributive (i.e. one person would go at the expense of another) rather than an open basis, the effect on the rest of the staff was demotivation and demoralisation. This inevitably led to declines in productivity, and increases in turnover, especially of capable staff.

Source: R.M. Kanter, *Management Matters*, BBC2 (1997).

- Those who go into training and development as a profession or occupation are accorded low status, at least informally. Training and development are regarded as *cul-de-sac* jobs, or places where people go to die. People who go into these functions cannot be any good, otherwise they would remain in the mainstream. Above all, the greatest insult is that training and development represent a retreat from 'the real world' into an 'ivory tower' – what is delivered by organisational training and development functions bears little relation to how things are in the real world (see Summary Box 1.4).

SUMMARY BOX 1.4   Ivory towers

The accusation that those who go into training and development (and also further and higher education) are retreating into an ivory tower is often true. In the past, this has, in many cases, been reinforced when teachers, trainers and lecturers have preached or delivered courses and seminars in isolation from reality.

Present standards of delivery are now generally much higher and much more in accordance with reality. However, the ivory tower accusation still persists and this is because:

- people working in highly stressful jobs and situations have invested a lot of energy and enthusiasm (and in many cases grief) in making a success of them – if they are then faced with the prospect of someone telling them that life can be both more productive and less stressful, this can be taken as devaluing past and present exertions;
- people are, in any case, used to their ways of working, and the patterns of life that they have built around them – offering development and enhancement, while overtly positive, again calls into question the integrity of the present and past exertions.

All of this can be – and is – very personally and occupationally confrontational. In many cases, where there is a demonstrable direct relationship between theory and practice, this is most confrontational of all – because people who have used great amounts of energy and commitment are now being told plainly that there are better ways of doing the job.

- Training and development are only required by those who are useless at their job. This is reinforced in many organisations, occupations and professions where there are cultural and behavioural barriers against asking for advice and guidance. This is reinforced when strong and dominant personalities are understood, believed or perceived to expect their staff to know and be able to do everything. This is then compounded when staff are confronted with the attitude that something is 'only common sense', or 'if you don't know that then you cannot be up to much' (see Summary Box 1.5).

SUMMARY BOX 1.5   'You are useless': examples from South-East England in January 2001

- A doctor at a major London teaching hospital took a chance on a drug dosage in spite of the fact that he had not been able to relate the drug's brand name to anything with which he was familiar.
- A lecturer at a major London university spent a day and a night making a computer program work, rather than asking a colleague for help; had the colleague demonstrated the particular program, this would have taken a matter of minutes only.
- A supermarket cashier spent 20 minutes working out how to give a refund rather than calling the supervisor for the third time in half an hour.
- A railway company ticket salesperson insisted to a regular user that the fare that they had requested was not available; again, this course of action was preferred above and beyond speaking to the supervisor.
- A light aircraft crashed, killing all of its occupants, because the pilot did not want to be seen by his friends to check the precise location before going into land.

Sources: University College London/University College Hospital; Metro Newspaper (1–31 January, 2001).

This is an immensely difficult cultural and behavioural barrier in many circumstances, and one that has to be addressed at an organisational, professional, operational and strategic level if there is to be real progress in the field. It is in many cases reinforced further still by organisations that can afford to do so, paying premium wages and salaries for rare expertise.

Cost and charges

Historically, as stated above, UK organisations were, and remain, collectively unwilling to pay for training and development. This is because they are not sure what they will be getting in return. They are therefore equally unsure about whether this is what they want or need. There is no quantifiable return on investment. This contrasts with the perceived certainties of investing in production service and technological advances which are normally based on projections and forecasts in their support, and which can then be comfortably engaged because they are 'bound' or 'certain' to produce positive results (see Summary Box 1.6).

Not all organisations are this bad. For example:

- **Nissan:** when the Nissan car company first established its factories in the USA and UK, it spent an average of £12,000 per employee on initial induction, orientation and job training before production lines were switched on.
- **Body Shop:** the cosmetics and gift company, requires all employees to undertake training and development programmes. These are negotiated with the employees. In addition, all employees spend one day a month carrying out some form of community service.
- **Ernst & Young:** the management consultancy, requires its employees to spend 10 per cent of their working week in some form of business, organisation or staff development activity.
- **Canon:** the camera and photocopier company, requires all its managerial and sales staff to attend an intensive three-week induction and orientation programme; and employment is conditional upon passing this.
- **Lucas CAV:** pays for all its staff to attend evening classes. The only stipulation is that they must take part in something.

Of course, all organisational management and employee development has to be paid for, and the starting point – the need for returns on the investment of both money and time – is correct. It is also clear that a great deal of what passes for organisation and employee development is not easily quantified. However, this should engage the view that: 'We don't know, so we'll find out', rather than: 'We don't know, so it cannot be any good'.

Within this context, it is usual to identify the following:

- **Absence costs:** the costs of having members of staff on the payroll while they are elsewhere being trained and developed.
- **Replacement costs:** the costs of hiring temporary staff to carry out work while others are away being trained and developed; or the costs of overtime incurred as the result.
- **Training expenses:** the costs of the particular event, plus subsistence and travel expenses when necessary.
- **Books, stationery, equipment:** as required and/or as demanded by particular staff and for events (though in practice many employees, especially junior, are required to supply these themselves).
- **The hiring of consultants, experts, facilitators, tutors and trainers:** where these are required for in-house work.
- **The use of organisational rooms and facilities:** for which an overhead is incurred.
- **Implementation costs:** incurred when the trainee needs time, resources and support to put into practice what has been taught, or to carry out a project or assignment.

- **Opportunity costs:** whatever has been foregone as the result of going to the particular course or event, or making expenditure on specific training and development activities at the expense of others.

All this can be estimated with varying degrees of accuracy. Prices for consultants and course fees are normally clearly stated. Absence costs may have to consider the amount of work and output not achieved, and stresses, strains and overtime demands placed on those left behind, as well as the hiring of temporary cover.

The end result is something that is fairly accurate, and at this stage, that is the best that is available (see Summary Box 1.7).

SUMMARY BOX 1.7   The Professional Education Scheme of the Chartered Institute of Personnel and Development

From 1986 onwards the Chartered Institute of Personnel and Development (CIPD) ran a compulsory case study question on all of its final examination papers. In many cases, these questions asked for accurate costings based on information that, because of examination constraints, was normally presented as approximately one page at the most.

The problem was with accuracy. It should be apparent from the text above that complete accuracy of costing is not possible in any organisational circumstances in the real world, let alone on an examination case study. However, the fact that the question was asked, did at least require candidates to think about the costs, prices and charges that surrounded human resource management work in general, and employee and organisation development in particular.

The overwhelming problem is that costing training and development looks messy, drawn as it is from a variety of sources. To the more specialist senior or general manager, it also looks expensive when it is all added up. It is therefore necessary to look at the reverse of the coin, the costs and charges incurred through not incorporating training and development. These include the following:

- Recruitment and replacement costs as employees lose faith in the idea that their organisations have their best interests at heart. These can be quantified with a fair degree of accuracy by looking at employment agency and recruitment advertising bills, and staff turnover and absenteeism figures.
- Medium and long-term loss of market share and competitive edge as the organisation goes on in the same old ways, and is gradually overtaken by others (e.g. as the influence of the Sieff family declined at Marks & Spencer, so did the company's commitment to training and development for all staff – and so did turnover and profit volumes and margins). This is not easy to quantify, and may not become apparent when it does start to happen, as company accounts are produced and published at least a year in arrears.
- Decline in employee commitment and therefore effectiveness. Again, this is difficult to observe and quantify at best, and in other cases extremely

nebulous. It should however be the start of a 'what if?' enquiry by senior and general managers, using the phrase: 'What if we do make the connection between enhanced training and development, and employee commitment and involvement?' What are the costs – and benefits?

Cost–benefit analysis and employee development

A cost–benefit analysis is normally carried out by making specific enquiries along the following lines (see Figures 1.1 and 1.2).

ACTION CHOICES	PRIORITIES	INITIATIVES
TIME FRAME SHORT MEDIUM LONG-TERM	STRATEGIC ASPECTS	RISK
RELATIVE VALUATION	INCOME EXPENDITURE	VALUE

Figure 1.1 Cost–benefit analysis model

ACTION CHOICE	PRIORITY	INITIATIVE
• size • capacity • projected length of useful life	• buy/lease of trainers • critical for staff attitudes	• market aimed at • ability and propensity to pay
SHORT-TERM • familiarity, confidence LONG-TERM • market size	STRATEGY • niche • competition from other holiday packages • returns on volume sales	RISK • local publicity • accidents and tragedies both to this venture and others would cause loss of overall confidence and demand
RELATIVE VALUATION • low to consumers, part of very high choice sector • critical in staff capability	INCOME • steady, long-term EXPENDITURE • high initial • steady long-term	VALUE • ability to brand and differentiate • perceived value

Figure 1.2 Example: cost–benefit analysis model for staff training on a cruise liner

It is then possible for all involved, including senior managers, to have an informed debate and come to a supported judgement and conclusion as to whether something is worth doing or not, and what the opportunities and consequences are as the result. It demonstrates an active corporate and managerial responsibility. From this emerges a wholesome and supportive corporate attitude to training, in which it is clear to all:

- who does what, when, where, why and how;
- who pays for what (including employee commitments) and under what circumstances;
- any other financial or resource commitments, including the content of formal training agreements and retainer clauses.

Other contextual factors

The context of organisation and employee development is dominated by debates about costs, charges, benefits and who pays. There are other factors that have to be considered as follows.

Organisational policy and direction

Organisations involved in mergers, take-overs, restructuring, business process re-engineering, total quality management and technological re-equipment and refurbishment invariably ignore or downgrade the employee development aspects. This is partly because the broad direction looks so straightforward on paper (if it did not, it would not be acceptable to top managers and directors), that it is easy to assume that it will be straightforward for the staff. It partly arises out of fear – if the plans are put to the staff, they are certain to ask awkward questions (they will certainly want to know where they stand in the future). It may indicate places where the new idea is likely or certain to fail. It is also necessary to consider 'group-think' – if a senior management and consulting group or think-tank has come up with such proposals then they *must* be good, especially considering the expense involved.

Opportunities of internet and computer-based training

The corporate attraction here is founded on pure expediency in many cases. The line of reasoning is that, if material is available on the internet (especially their own), then staff can use it at any time, and rather than paying course fees, or having to give people time off, they can simply log on to specific websites, or into particular programmes when it suits them. Intranet and e-mail systems can be used to provide instant tutorial support as and when required. The only additional charges that may be incurred are the purchase of particular software and virtual courses, and these are a lot cheaper than giving people time off (see Summary Box 1.8).

Continuous professional and occupational development

Continued membership and ability to work and practise in many professions,
professional bodies and occupational groups in many cases depends on carrying
out prescribed minimum periods of continuous development and updating each
year. This is universally expected of professions such as medicine and the law –
everyone wants and expects treatment and advice based on current thinking,
requirements and expertise, rather than that which is now obsolete. This is
also the case in many managerial associations and bodies, and it is usually
straightforward for organisations to implement, because managers themselves
create the context in which this is possible.

Problems arise further down the line. For example, many health authorities
require nurses to carry out their continuous professional development and
updates in their own time and without funding, and this also applies to school
teachers, and in the private sector, to engineers, salespeople, financial advisers
and other crafts people.

A by-product of continuous professional and occupational development is the
continuous development of attitudes and behaviour. If people are required to do
this themselves, in their own time and at their own cost, they inevitably become
identified with the occupation rather than the organisation, unless there is some
overriding reason for doing things this way.

It is always best if organisations accept continuous professional development
as a universal obligation and apply it to all their staff. This is so that the frontline

staff become actively committed for example to food processing, customer relations (retail, call centres), tree and shrub developments (horticulture). By offering training and development in this way, organisations are requiring their staff to commit to their business or activities, and providing the groundwork and support for doing so. This approach contributes extensively to individual and collective continuous attitudes and behaviour as well as skills development – and therefore long-term enduring organisation stability, profitability and effectiveness.

Staffing mixes

This part of the context of employee development concerns the following:

- Whether training and development should be made available to all and if so, on what basis. What of those who do not wish to be developed? Body Shop, Nissan and Lucas came to their own clear views on this; employee development was not optional, and they were not prepared to carry unproductive, unmotivated and obsolete staff. The clear answer is therefore to make opportunities available to everyone, bonded by a common set of rules and guidance under which people undertake particular activities.
- Whether it is best to train your own staff or to buy in ready expertise from outside. The clear answer in practice is that both are essential, and should form part of the strategic approach to employee development (see below, Chapter 12). No organisation can afford to become too inward-looking by ignoring outside expertise; nor can it afford to continually deny the potential of its existing staff by always buying in key expertise from outside.

Many organisations still remain fearful that if they train their key staff, these people will leave to better themselves elsewhere. They will certainly do this if they do not get the opportunities to put into practice what they have learned, or if they feel that they are being left behind in the expertise stakes.

Conclusions

The context in which organisation and employee development is to take place clearly requires a long, hard appraisal by senior and general managers. They need to be clear where their own particular attitudes and approaches to this aspect of management lie. They should be clear that their staff fully know and understand the corporate attitudes to employee development. Especially, they will know whether it carries a price or a value, whether it is universally available, or the province of the chosen few.

It is also important to recognise that all staff form their own view of the context of employee development. Especially where they are required to carry out professional and occupational development in their own time, the clear message is that this part of working life is unvalued or undervalued by the organisation and its senior managers.

QUESTIONS

1 Find out the costs and charges for:
   - an MBA programme;
   - a continuous professional development programme put on by a professional association.

   What messages are given out by organisations that require their staff to study each of these and require staff to pay for them themselves? Compare and contrast this with organisations that pay everything and provide full support to their staff.

2 Consider the pros and cons of paying for evening classes for all employees.

3 For an organisation with which you are familiar, make an initial assessment of the attitude to employee development. How far does this extend, and – initially – what changes should the organisation be considering?

4 Make an initial assessment of the best and worst uses of the internet as an employee development vehicle.

5 Why do so many organisations over-pay for expert staff? What are the consequences of this for existing members of staff?

▪ⵉ 2 How people learn

'*Nobody ever does anything perfectly. The important thing for this company is that everyone learns – from their successes, from their failure, from their mistakes. Only by doing this have we improved in the past, and will we continue to improve in the future.*'

Konosuke Matsushita, founder of The Matsushita Corporation

Introduction

No effective organisation or employee development can take place unless it is first established how people learn. This is quite complex. It is all too easy to get drawn into preferred learning styles and learning cycles before considering the conditions that must first exist if effective learning – and therefore development, enhancement and advancement – are to take place.

Conditions

Capability

Those involved must be capable of learning. They must be pre-qualified to undertake whatever is proposed (see Summary Box 2.1). Many trainers and teachers coming to groups for the first and perhaps only time run pre-qualification assessments as the first session of their courses and then do their best to tailor the material accordingly. They commit themselves to supporting anyone who is likely to struggle with the course, development material or standards.

SUMMARY BOX 2.1   Capability and pre-qualification

Some pre-qualification standards are overtly straightforward, e.g. undergraduate qualifications as a pre-qualification for postgraduate study, or periods of employment and therefore organisation and environmental familiarity as a precursor to professional education or professional body membership schemes.

Others are less clear and require more careful consideration. For example, there are no absolute pre-qualifications required to be an airline pilot. The tendency therefore is to look for desired personality traits of tenacity, courage, calmness and responsiveness as the foundation for the development of occupational capability.   (*continued*)

Others still draw on assumed connections between qualifications and capability. For example, it is assumed that a university degree in medicine is an adequate pre-qualification for medical training; or that five-years' frontline experience is adequate pre-qualification for organisationally based supervisory or management training.

This therefore clearly requires at least brief consideration in each case and the questioning of assumptions about pre-qualification and capability.

If it is plain at an early stage that someone is not going to make the grade or does not have the basic capabilities required, they should be counselled to remove themselves from the course, event or activities. If individuals insist on going ahead and participating, then they should be supported throughout to ensure that they get as much out of it as they possibly can. It is both morally wrong, and also repugnant from the point of view of shear humanity, to accept someone for something that they cannot possibly do on their own (however much they may insist on it themselves), and then abdicate responsibility or leave them to flounder.

Willingness

People must want to learn and develop. This motivation – as with all – is formed on a partnership or joint venture basis. Organisations are well within their rights to expect staff to attend training and development events and activities provided that they create effective conditions and support. Employees are entitled to expect opportunities for training and development provided that they themselves are committed to attendance, participation and involvement – and the opportunity to put into practice what they have learned (see Summary Box 2.2).

SUMMARY BOX 2.2   Unwillingness to learn

Where unwillingness to learn exists, it is necessary to establish the reasons. These may be:

- lack of known, believed or perceived support;
- the knowledge or understanding that the partnership between employer and employee is heavily loaded on the employer's side;
- lack of work-based support – normally either the training has to be done in the employee's own time without any reciprocal support, or the employee has to pay for it and will only be reimbursed after completion or a period of post-completion service;
- the job-related workload expected still remains the same and there is little, or no, flexibility to accommodate this;

- lack of knowledge or understanding of the benefits on offer through the training itself, or upon completion;
- known, believed or perceived lack of benefits or opportunities to put into subsequent practice what is to be learned;
- the training and development are part of a wider restructuring, re-engineering or empowerment programme, the purpose of which is known, believed or perceived to put more stress and strain on frontline staff.

Commitment

Closely related to motivation and willingness is commitment. Again, this is a partnership. Organisations and their managers commit staff to extended periods of training and development, and these are subsequently called into question, clearly downgraded or downvalued, through later changes in managerial staff, reorganisations, or alterations in organisational, departmental, divisional, functional and political direction and priorities.

Conversely, commitment may be all on the member of staff without organisation support (see Summary Box 2.2 above). Managers and supervisors may – and do – resent the opportunities given to their staff. Many such managers still see trained, qualified and expert staff as a threat to their own position; and they may use this fear to undermine the development of their own people.

The balance of commitment has to be examined in each individual case. Sometimes there is a custom and practice on which to fall back, for example:

- all persons on course x will get time off and their fees paid;
- all people on event y will get time off and their fees paid but have to pay their own expenses;

and this is always valuable.

Rewards

Both organisations and individuals quite legitimately expect rewards and benefits to accrue as the result of being supported and undertaking particular training and development activities. Organisations expect increased output and loyalty. Staff expect increased pay, opportunities, career and occupational development; and the specific chance to put into practice what they have learned.

Again, problems arise when the balance goes awry. Organisations quite rightly resent staff who use organisational-driven opportunities to get jobs elsewhere; and staff resent their organisations taking all the benefits while they themselves get none (see Figure 2.1).

Problems arise because:

- as stated above, the relationship between expectations and rewards is heavily loaded in the employer's favour;

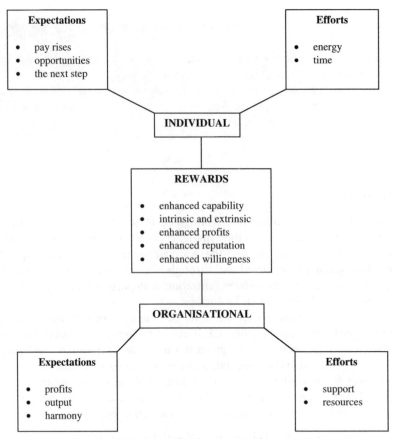

Figure 2.1 Training development and expectations

- the rewards actually available do not meet expectations (and this applies to both parties);
- the efforts and commitment required are out of proportion or harmony with the expectations and rewards;
- rewards promised to individuals are not delivered;
- rewards expected by organisations are not immediately apparent.

Equality

For an effective learning and development environment to be created and maintained, the principle of fundamental equality of opportunity and treatment for all is essential. It is also required that the equality of partnership between the organisation and individual is maintained, so that the balance of capability, willingness, commitment and rewards is known, clearly understood and acceptable to all.

Equality of treatment, opportunity and value is also a central element of all effective organisation practice, as well as a legal requirement. Every organisation and employee development activity therefore requires a fundamental equality and evenness of appraisal, assessment, delivery and evaluation, regardless of the race, gender, religion, ethnic origin, marital status or age of those attending events, or participating in development programmes.

Once the context is understood, specific attention can be paid to preferred learning styles and how people learn.

Preferred learning styles

Learning is the process by which skills, knowledge, attitudes, behaviour and expertise are formed and developed. Learning takes place as the result of education, training, socialisation and experience. It also occurs as the result of conditioning and restriction, whereby the individual is persuaded to adopt, and ultimately accept, guidance, regulation, conformity and compliance in particular situations.

Individuals learn at different rates, times and stages in their lives. Some people acquire new knowledge, skills and qualities easily, while others struggle to learn the very basics of the same things.

Much of this is because individuals have preferred learning styles. Some people have very strong preferred learning styles – they can only learn in one particular way and other methods have little effect; others find that they can adapt themselves effectively to many ways in which things are taught.

Honey (1986) identified four preferred learning styles as follows (see Figure 2.2):

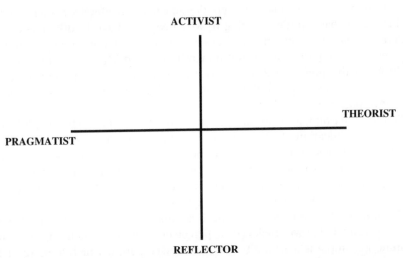

Figure 2.2 Preferred learning styles. This spectrum was devised by Honey and Mumford to identify the preferred learning style. By completing a questionnaire and plotting the results the respondent would: (a) identify those activities likely to be most and least beneficial; (b) identify those areas which needed working on, so that full benefit from all activities could be gained

- **Activist:** concentrating on learning by doing, via direct experience and through considering the results of trial and error so that performance may be improved next time.
- **Pragmatist:** concentrating on that which is possible, practical and of direct application to given situations.
- **Theorist:** concentrating on why things are as they are and investigating theories and concepts that form the background to this.
- **Reflector:** concentrating on assessment and analysing why things have turned out in particular ways, and using this as the basis on which to build understanding.

Honey and Mumford (1992) designed a questionnaire the purpose of which was to identify under which of these four headings an individual's preferred learning style fell. The results would then be used to ensure that individuals understood why they tended to learn some things better than others; to seek out those activities that were best suited to preferred learning styles; and to develop lesser and least preferred areas of learning styles to enhance their total learning capability.

Other aspects of preferred learning styles may be identified as follows.

- the influence of rewards and outcomes;
- peer, professional and social group expectations;
- the nature of the material and the means by which it is taught or learned;
- the quality of the teacher;
- time factors.

There are also clearly some absolutes. For example, someone who wishes to learn how to drive a car will have to sit in a car and drive, however much of a theorist they may be. Similarly, it is not possible to be an effective leader of people if there is no basic understanding of why people behave in different ways in different situations (and different ways in the same situation), however much of a pragmatist the particular person may otherwise be. This underlines the need to broaden the preferred learning style into an individual learning style that can accept effective input and information from as wide a variety of sources and means as possible.

Preferred learning and working styles are models and archetypes. While they give a good indication of what satisfies, and are sympathetic to individuals, and what they are most receptive to, the approach is not an end in itself. Those who wish to develop as much as possible, and maximise their opportunities, work on their non-preferred learning styles so that they gain full benefits from these activities when they are confronted with them.

The preferred learning style approach is transcended when the need, want or drive to learn is known, believed or perceived to be overwhelming. The most common example is learning to drive a car (see above) which is more or less universally carried out on the road in a dual-controlled car, whatever the learner's preferred learning style. This applies to other universal life skills – cooking, home management, parenting, money management; and also to many jobs and occupations, for example:

- nursing, where there is a combination of university and college input which is reinforced by on-the-job training on the wards;
- airline piloting and other public transport driving including heavy goods vehicle, again with plenty of simulation, but finished off in the real situation under supervision;
- architecture and design, supported in many ways during training with discussions and examples concerning space usage and aesthetic aspects of appearance; but again judged finally on the number of buildings put up, or products put on shelves (see Summary Box 2.3).

SUMMARY BOX 2.3   Failure to transcend the preferred learning style

A dress designer made a national reputation for producing high-quality, stylish and expensive clothes. This she achieved through a combination of:

- extensive travel in order to study the use of materials in other parts of the world;
- extensive shopping around for materials;
- extensive experimentation in the combination of materials before finally producing the finished product.

She was able to sustain this for the production of exclusive single items for wealthy customers. She had great difficulty producing for mass markets because she was unable to adapt her preferred learning and working style to the financial and timescale strictures that these imposed.

Preferred learning styles are therefore also something to be managed and developed. They are an individual responsibility in particular sets of circumstances. This does not indicate an abdication of responsibility in this area on the part of trainers and facilitators. If the best, expected or most convenient way of putting things across does not accord precisely with someone's preferred learning or working style, then there is a joint responsibility to see that the job is completed to everyone's satisfaction.

How people learn

It is necessary to understand three basic approaches as follows.

Behaviourist

The behaviourist or stimulus response (S-R) approach states that series of actions and movements are learned as responses to particular stimuli. Learning is (in part at least) a form of conditioning, reinforced by feedback. Feedback may either be positive and rewarding, or negative and punitive. The effect of positive feedback is to increase desired behaviour. The effect of negative feedback is to reduce undesired behaviour. For example:

- **Positive:** if employees receive praise for doing good work, they tend to do good work as often as possible in order to receive the praise as often as possible.
- **Negative:** if managers are angry every time work is poor or late, employees will tend to do good work and on time in order to avoid the anger.

The result may therefore be very much the same – that good work is done on time – but the means by which this has been learned (as well as the attitude and approach) are very different. The overall view is that people learn and repeat behaviour that has positive and favourable consequences. They avoid that which has negative and undesirable consequences.

The behaviourist approach is extremely useful in:

- on-the-job training, especially concerning the use of machines, computers and technology; and in dealing with customer queries, responses and complaints;
- establishing effective emergency procedures and ensuring that these are followed.

For the approach to be effective, reinforcement – both positive and negative – must be consistent and continually applied. For example, emergency procedures such as fire drills and building evacuations only remain effective if regularly practised and rehearsed.

Cognitive

The cognitive approach takes a broader view. It states that learning occurs as the result of different responses to the great variety of queues and stimuli that are present. To be effective, learning must take account also of individual personality, perception and motivation. These all contribute to the disposition of the individual to learn.

The operation of feedback, rewards and punishments is also more complex than that indicated by the behaviourist approach. The key lies in the volume of value and information available to the individual and the ways in which this is received, understood and processed. Rather than a conditioned series of movements, behaviour is learned through mental processes and retained in the memory. It is reinforced by expectations, and the anticipation of rewards and achievement. It is adaptable in that knowledge and skills learned from one situation can be reprocessed in order to understand and be effective in others. The cognitive approach also recognises creativity, invention and imagination as elements present in learning.

The cognitive approach is especially effective in training and development in:

- leadership skills;
- product and service design, development and improvement;
- marketing and public relations;
- problem-solving activities.

Conditioning

The conditioning approach to learning takes the view that any behaviour in a particular setting or context that is rewarded or reinforced in some way will tend to be repeated in that context. For example:

- if someone is complimented on their appearance, they will tend to maintain that appearance;
- if someone is complimented on presenting work in a particular way, they will tend to continue to present work in that particular way;
- if employees lose money for turning up late for work, they will arrive on time.

Conditioning approaches to employee development are especially useful in the development of:

- pre-programmed sets of activities, especially the production of goods and information;
- the establishing of timetables and schedules, in order to give structure to working activities;
- culture and behaviour development in terms of reporting relationships, modes of dress and address.

Other factors

As stated above, people learn at different rates, times and stages in their lives. Other factors that need to be considered are as follows:

- The desire and motivation to learn brought about by the individual's own needs and drives, usually in the expectation that this will bring success, rewards, enhanced potential and expertise, and also increased esteem, respect, value and status.
- Pressure to learn placed on individuals by others, including organisations, to enable them to acquire the knowledge, skills and qualities required and also to adopt the attitudes, values and behaviour necessary in order to be comfortable in particular situations.
- Specific drives and requirements such as the need for continuous professional and occupational development and enhancement.
- Individual attitudes and dispositions to acquire new skills, knowledge and qualities.
- Personal preferences and choices.

The result is to increase the range, depth and interactions of thoughts, ideas and concepts, as well as skills, knowledge, attitudes, behaviour and expertise; to increase the ability to organise and reorganise these; and to order them in productive and effective activities.

The learning cycle illustrates the importance of the relationship between behaviour, action and experience. It also emphasises the need to reinforce abstract learning with practice and performance (see Figure 2.3).

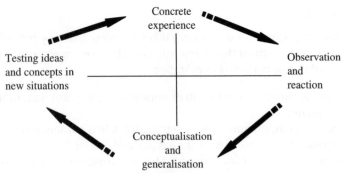

Figure 2.3 Learning cycle. The cycle illustrates the importance of the relationship between behaviour, action and experience. It also emphasises (testing and
experience) the need to reinforce abstract learning with practice and performance.
[*Source*: Kolb (1985)]

Retention

The ability to retain and internalise that which has been taught and learned is
based on a combination of the following factors:

- The ability to practise and use the skills and qualities acquired.
- The value of the new skills and qualities once they have been taught and
  learned; and it is important to recognise that this may be different from their
  perceived or anticipated value before they were learned.
- The regularity and frequency with which the new expertise is to be put to use.
- The rewards that are to accrue as the result.
- The punishments and threats that occur if learning and development does not
  take place. This is especially important in the acquisition of attitudes, values
  and behaviour, and in conforming to rules and standards.

This process is called *reinforcement*. Reinforcement may be:

- continuous, in which case the learning is soon internalised;
- intermittent, in which case it is likely to become important from time to
  time only and may lead to the need for revision, retraining and refresher
  courses;
- occasional, in which case the learning is likely to have been of general or
  marginal value only;
- tainted, when it becomes apparent that the learning and development was of
  no value whatsoever.

More generally, learning, acquiring and becoming proficient in new skills and
qualities normally leads to enhanced feelings of personal confidence and self-
respect. It enhances flexibility of attitudes and approaches. It is also increasingly
likely that this will bring greater general perceptions of worth and value to the
organisation.

Feedback

Feedback is essential on all aspects of performance leading to enhanced general levels of understanding, confidence and support. It is best in the following circumstances:

- It should be positive rather than negative, enhancing the general concept of progress to which learning is supposed to contribute. Negative feedback is best used only as a nuclear deterrent (i.e. it is present but never to be used). It is normally only applied to persistent failure to accept and conform to necessary rules, rather than because of failings in skills and knowledge.
- It should concentrate on processes as well as results, so that individuals both know their results and also understand why they have succeeded or failed.
- It should be delivered as near to the conclusion of the learning as possible and then followed with opportunities to apply that which has been learned.
- It should be continuous, so that any problems with what has been learned can subsequently be rectified.

Other factors

Developing the whole person

People both have a much more positive attitude and approach to training and development, and also learn better if they know, believe and understand that they are receiving the broadest range of opportunities available in the circumstances. All effective employee development addresses the four factors of organisational, occupational, professional and personal development needs, wants and requirements (see Figure 2.4).

Organisational

This refers to training and development for present occupations and activities; initial and continuing job training; training required as the result of re-equipment and technological changes, new systems and procedures; induction, and the establishment and reinforcement of the desired and required activities, behaviour and demeanour. Organisations have a right to insist on this provided that it is adequately and effectively valued and supported.

Occupational

Occupational training is a joint venture between organisation and individual. The need for occupational training for the present may become apparent as the result of performance appraisal, training needs analysis or operational shortfalls (e.g. increases in reject rates or customer complaints, inability to work the information system to its full capacity), and once established, this too is normally obligatory.

Other occupational training is designed to ensure future as well as present effectiveness. Occupation-based training and development therefore includes:

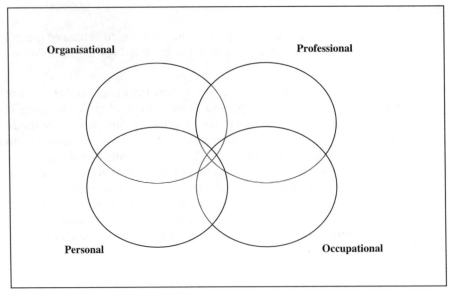

Organisational   Professional

Personal   Occupational

Figure 2.4   The training and development mix

- training for full or maximum possible flexibility;
- training for known developments in present occupations;
- training for the next occupation;
- training for likely or potential future jobs and occupations;
- training for promotion;
- and training for redeployment.

Professional

As stated above, undertaking prescribed periods of continuous professional development is, in many cases, a condition of being allowed to continue to practise. However, this also has to be seen as an active joint responsibility.

The professional person must be supported through their obligations. This is a condition and obligation of employing this kind of expertise.

It is also true when employing less 'obvious', yet highly qualified, staff. For example:

- hairdressers must be trained in how to use, handle and store new dyes and bleaches when they come on the market, and how to do new cuts when they become fashionable and in demand;
- civil engineers regularly have new safety procedures, structural forms and materials mixes to contend with, and have to be able to implement these when required by clients;
- secretaries have to be trained in new word processing and information management processes and packages when these are adopted by organisations.

This is all legitimate and obligatory continuous professional development and needs to be both conducted and also valued as such.

Personal

In the long-term, people only learn effectively if some consideration is given to their personal priorities and preferences. This does not mean organisations acting as unconditional sponsors for employee whims. It does mean recognising and acknowledging that all employees have their own legitimate interests in their future development and career paths as well as in personal development. Part of the complete picture of how people learn and their motivation for this therefore lies in understanding that a part of employee development is concerned with 'employability elsewhere' in the labour market (see Summary Box 2.4).

SUMMARY BOX 2.4   Employability

The term 'employability' was coined by Rosabeth Moss Kanter during a series of talks in 1994 for the BBC. Her hypothesis was:

- It was legitimate for employees to understand that organisations could not guarantee them a future, and therefore to enhance their own prospects by maximising or optimising their development from their own self-interest.
- It was legitimate for employers not to be able to promise to accommodate every employee for life. After all, redundancies had taken place at the time in the army and Church of England as well as (incredibly) teaching and nursing. Also some organisations simply do not have the scope to offer full career and professional development and fulfilment.

There is, in any case, a strong marketing and presentational issue, as well as the question of organisation and employee development. Organisations that provide extensive training and development quickly gain a reputation for this. They are therefore much more likely to find it easier to attract and retain good people, and to get the best out of them, even if the staff subsequently move on.

Source: Rosabeth Moss Kanter, *Business Matters*, BBC2 (1994–96).

The BASKET approach

The acronym BASKET is used to indicate the full range of training and development required. It applies in all situations where there is any form of teaching, instruction, learning and application. BASKET stands for:

- **Behaviour:** the development of the required patterns of behaviour among all employees; the development of behavioural standards of interaction within, and between, groups of employees and occupations.
- **Attitudes:** the development of positive, collective and individual attitudes; the removal of negative, collective and individual attitudes.
- **Skills:** the development of skills for the present and future.
- **Knowledge:** job, organisational, environmental, professional and occupational knowledge and awareness.

- **Experience and expertise:** the development of performance from adequate, to competent, to expert through periods of planned training, job and work enhancement and the provision of opportunities.
- **Technology:** the development of proficiency on all equipment required; the development of proficiency in equipment and technology which employees and groups may be required to use at some time in the future.

In practice, there are overlaps between each. Each also feeds off the other. Attention to the behavioural aspects reinforces confidence, capability and willingness in job performance. Attention to the technological and skills aspects reinforces positive attitudes and behaviour as well as developing experience and expertise. The more thoroughly and extensively training and development activities are carried out, the greater the reinforcement in each of these areas.

Costs and benefits

The costs and benefits of understanding how and why people learn are summarised in Table 2.1.

Conclusions

The primary purpose of employee development is to enhance skills, knowledge, qualifications and expertise through the use and application of the great variety of means and methods available. If this is to be profitable and effective for all concerned, then how people learn must be understood. This requires full consideration of the context in which people are expected to learn and develop, and an understanding of the ways in which they may respond to particular activities and initiatives.

It is especially important to understand that attention to workplace attitudes helps employees to adopt and find the place required of them in their environment. This helps to provide a clear mutual understanding between organisation and employee, and is one of the cornerstones of the working environment, as well as of effective training and development. Above all, as organisations strive for ever-greater levels of flexibility and responsiveness, understanding how these characteristics are built and developed is essential.

Table 2.1   Costs and benefits

Costs	Benefits
• Minor fixed cost element only • Possible need for attitude shift	• The ability to address the full range of needs • The ability to maximise the full potential, interest, capability and willingness of everyone • Enhanced commitment and motivation

QUESTIONS

1　Discuss the view that as everyone has their own individual preferred learning style, structured induction programmes are a waste of time.

2　What lessons may be learned by organisations providing training and development programmes for their staff from the providers of universal training and development such as driving schools?

3　Produce an outline training and development programme for yourself for the next 12 months. This should include aims and objectives, training methods, learning outcomes, and provide clear attention to organisational, occupational, professional and personal development.

4　In your experience, what are the key drives and restraints on learning and development? What are the main lessons to be learned by organisations and their managers from this?

◼ ☑ **3** Training needs analysis

'An expert can do in an hour what any fool can do in a week.'

Neville Shute, *Beyond the Black Stump*, Pan (1960)

Introduction

Everything in all organisations is capable of development and improvement. Everything is also susceptible to strategic, operational, competitive, technological and occupational pressures to be developed and improved in order to reinforce the organisation's standing, position, effectiveness and profitability in its markets. The purpose of training needs analysis is to assess organisational, departmental, divisional, group, occupational and individual performance from the point of view of:

- identifying gaps and shortfalls in performance in each of these areas;
- identifying which of these can be addressed and overcome through organisational and employee development activities, and which cannot.

Organisation and employee development needs may become apparent by chance, or as the result of investigating a problem where a strategic, operational or technological solution was previously clearly indicated. Otherwise, organisation and employee development needs become apparent through the use of the great range of tools and techniques that are available and in use.

Individual performance appraisal

A great many organisations use performance appraisal extremely effectively and build long-term, sustained and productive employee development programmes and activities as the result. The key is a continuing active and responsible relationship based on mutual visibility, knowledge and understanding, and punctuated with formal review sessions every three to four months.

Problems arise when the appraiser–appraisee relationship is not honest, or if the scheme is known, believed or perceived to be a bureaucratic or punitive exercise (see Summary Box 3.1).

SUMMARY BOX 3.1 Problems with individual performance appraisal schemes

To be effective and successful all performance appraisal must be conducted in the following ways:

- It must be against preset and pre-agreed aims and objectives, fully and clearly expounded, and understood by all concerned. These should additionally be given priority and deadlines for achievement. Performance targets should be realistic and achievable. If they are not, they will be ignored. If they are too easy or straightforward, they set a wider agenda for the lowering of performance standards.
- Appraisal is a process, consisting of both a series of regularised formal reviews at which targets and objectives are to be assessed for success and failure; and a continuous relationship between appraiser and appraisee that ensures a mutual and continuing confidence.
- The performance measurement must be flexible and dynamic and part of the wider process of ensuring that the organisation's strategy and purpose are achieved.
- It must be a participative process between appraiser and appraisee to ensure that the wider behavioural objective of mutual commitment is achieved.
- Formal reviews should take place at least every 6 months. Ideally, this should occur every 3–4 months (see text above). If they are less frequent than this, it becomes very difficult to conduct an adequate or genuine review of what has been done.

Particular organisational appraisal schemes may seek to provide:

- merit and performance-related pay awards;
- the identification of potential;
- the identification of occupation–person match and mismatch;
- the identification of wider organisation development prospects;
- the identification of areas of excellent, adequate, satisfactory, poor and substandard performance;
- the identification of actual and potential problem areas.

Appraisal schemes fall into disrepute for the following reasons:

- they are not believed in or valued;
- they do not contribute to the wider success of the organisation;
- they are bureaucratic or mechanistic, in that schemes and their paperwork are important, rather than the process;
- reviews are too infrequent or missed altogether;
- what is promised in the scheme (e.g. pay awards, training promotion, variety) are not delivered in practice.

Some schemes also suffer from performance criteria being identified in general terms only. This leads to inconsistency in application and unfairness in the award of such things as merit pay rises and places on training courses.

Conducted properly, this approach to performance appraisal and measurement allows issues to be raised early and discussed in a non-adversarial manner. New directions and development proposals are committed fully because they are the result of prior consultation and joint agreement.

Self-assessment

Self-assessment places the onus for development on the individual. Individuals have to undertake to be honest and self-critical enough to know where the gaps genuinely lie. Their superiors have to be honest enough to use open and frank admissions of failure or shortfall as an indicator of development needs, rather than poor performance, negligence or incompetence. Indeed, as soon as it becomes apparent that the self-assessment process is being used against them, individuals will draw attention only to their strengths; and this remains true whether self-appraisal is the main form of review or analysis, or part of a wider process.

For those with sufficient influence, self-appraisal may also be used to indicate personal preferences in development whether or not this is what the organisation actually requires. It is damaging to the whole training-needs' assessment process when it comes to be known, believed or perceived that individuals are using the system for their own ends.

Peer assessment

Conducted effectively, peer assessment is likely to draw attention to shortfalls in particular aspects of departmental, divisional or functional performance. This then leads to a positive debate among peers as to which needs and gaps are best filled with training and development activities, and which require other approaches.

The main problems here centre on the potential for victimisation. A particular department, division or function emerges, often by accident, as the perceived cause of everyone's problems and becomes the focus for scrutiny to the exclusion of all others. This is sometimes known as spotlighting (see Summary Box 3.2).

SUMMARY BOX 3.2   The parable of the spotlight

People who can get themselves behind the spotlight can decide where it is to be shone. Spotlighting is normally a toxic and tainted activity, and becomes very powerful and influential where standards and patterns of wider organisational behaviour are not maintained. The result is the ability to shine spotlights on other people, departments, divisions and functions, and by doing so, draw attention away from the workings of one's own department. The purpose is to create a view of the victim department in the spotlight that is negative, at the same time creating an aura of greater darkness around one's own department in the position behind the spotlight, in which consequently it may be seen so clearly.

Subordinate assessment

Sometimes known as 360 degree appraisal, this involves asking junior and frontline staff to rate the performance of their superiors and their departments. Knowing that they are to be assessed in this way places great responsibilities on managers to do things as well as possible and to recognise and attend to staff and operational priorities.

The main issues that have to be recognised, understood and accepted are:

- where serious problems are raised by many or all staff about the performance of a particular manager or supervisor, there is, at the very least, a perceived or believed need and the organisation is therefore committed to doing something about it;
- it often takes great courage for employees to speak out in this way, and also for managers and supervisors to place themselves in this position;
- there are real potential problems of victimisation; in the wrong overall environment, this again leads to scapegoating a particular individual for the entire ills of the department (see Summary Box 3.3).

SUMMARY BOX 3.3   Pauline Mortimer

Pauline Mortimer was the office manager in a university department. The department itself was highly successful. It expanded rapidly, drawing in new teaching, research and administrative staff. It gained research projects and a high volume of students from all backgrounds. In particular, the number of administrative staff rose from two to six in one year.

Two of the administrative staff made themselves a line to the head of department, bypassing their own manager, Pauline Mortimer. This was subordinate assessment by any other name. However, it was tainted and corrupted by the fact that:

- it was unofficial;
- it was not discouraged by the head of department;
- it was used to discuss personal and personality issues as well as professional matters.

By common consent, Pauline was not easy to get on with, nor was her performance perfect. However, she became the department's victim, and after several months, she was eased out to another department.

Within two days of the departure of Pauline Mortimer, the two administrative staff had found their next victim. He was a lecturer in his late fifties, who had been filling in for a colleague on paternity leave.

Job assessment and evaluation

A slightly different approach to needs' analysis is taken through job and work assessment and evaluation. Normally conducted as a structured exercise, it is nevertheless likely to indicate organisational and employee development needs in terms of:

- the effectiveness of the job in terms of the present and immediate future;
- the potential effectiveness of the job in terms of the medium to long-term future;
- specific changes envisaged in terms of priorities, technology and expertise changes;
- assessing the potential of the actual and potential job holders;
- and the extent to which any gaps identified could and should be filled by training and development. This is likely in most cases, and more or less certain where job and work evaluation is related to organisational, departmental or divisional restructuring and resizing.

Organisational and managerial performance assessment

Measuring organisational and managerial performance normally consists of regular strategic and operational reviews, product and service effectiveness – profitability, viability, positions on the product and service lifecycles, speed of new products and services to market, reliability and accuracy of forecasting and projections. This too can be turned into project secondment and job development work, and is especially effective where precise targeting is combined with a remit to look at wider issues if, and when, they become apparent (see Summary Box 3.4).

Measuring organisational, occupational, business and managerial performance is certain to bring to light areas for strategic and operational development where resources and investment are required, and where collective attitudes, behaviour and performance are falling short. Some of this assessment clearly therefore does not produce training and development gaps or needs. This is a completely legitimate function of all training-needs' analysis approaches.

However, precise forms of enquiry into specific activities and incidents are as equally certain to produce needs and opportunities for organisational and individual development. It is usual to look at these as performance gaps and critical incidents.

Performance gaps

Performance gaps exist:

- where something is done quite well but can be improved;
- where a small but critical element is missing or neglected;

- where there are repeated occurrences of specific issues (e.g. customer complaints about a single product; customer complaints about a speed of response);
- where there are no single occurrences of a wide range of different issues, many or all of which appear to come from the same source or cause. Such things as late deliveries, bad packaging, inability to contact locations by telephone, unavailability of staff, inability of staff to respond to questions, should all at least give cause for enquiry into managerial and supervisory development, and may lead, in turn, to further demands for staff development.

Critical incidents

Critical incidents are assessed as follows:

- key features, aspects and milestones in product or service delivery;
- key activities and expertise performance;
- key relationships with suppliers, distributors, consultants and subcontractors;
- customer, client and supplier liaison.

For these, it is usual to define as accurately as possible the components of the critical incident. Livy (1990) uses the criteria of difficulty, frequency and importance to define critical incidents as follows (see Figure 3.1).

If the only area to be remedied is that of importance or value, then this is a strategic issue, a matter of policy and priority. Difficulty and frequency have more direct implications for training and development (see Summary Box 3.5).

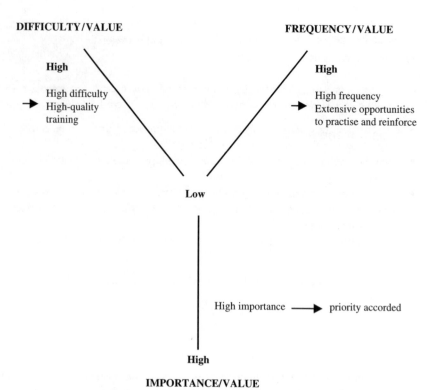

DIFFICULTY/VALUE

High

High difficulty
High-quality
training

FREQUENCY/VALUE

High

High frequency
Extensive opportunities
to practise and reinforce

Low

High importance ⟶ priority accorded

High

IMPORTANCE/VALUE

Figure 3.1   Critical incidents. [*Source*: Livy (1990)]

SUMMARY BOX 3.5   The application of critical incident approaches

Critical incident approaches may be applied to specific and functional areas, each of which have training and development implications as follows.

Human resource management

- The numbers of strikes, disputes and grievances.
- Movements in numbers of disciplinaries and dismissals.
- Movements in numbers of accidents and injuries; movements in numbers of self-certificated absenteeism.
- Movements in staff turnover; movements (especially decreases in organisational, departmental, divisional and functional staff stability).
- Increases in administration of support functions at the expense of frontline operations; the mechanisms, stability and morality of pay awards, promotions and other enhancements.
- The ways in which performance-related pay are known, believed and perceived to be operated.

Critical incident analysis in staff and human resource management may lead to identifying needs for training in staff management skills and techniques, understanding the operation of procedures, communication skills, and specific activities such as manual handling and environment awareness.

Production and service output

- Production targets, especially where production output bears no relationship to targets.
- Production volume and quality, especially where these fall short of projections, or are wildly over-projection.
- Increases in customer complaints about one aspect of product and service performance.
- Increases in customer complaints about total product and service performance.
- Increases in customer complaints about specific areas of the organisation.
- Difficulties in use of production service and information technology.
- The extent and prevalence of internal disputes between those in different parts of the supply, production, service and output chain.
- The extent and prevalence of blockages, what causes them, and their effects on total effectiveness.

Critical incident analyses in these areas may lead to needs being identified in: induction, initial and continuous job training-needs; customer service and care needs; communication skills; and improvement in quality awareness.

Marketing and sales

- Currency and effectiveness of marketing information and research.
- Organisational perceptions of good value.
- Benefits to customers perceived by producers are not/no longer perceived to be benefits by customers themselves.
- Lack of full market knowledge and understanding.
- Poor public relations.
- Required and desired images and identity, and those not generated by marketing and advertising campaigns.
- The effectiveness of the public relations function.

Critical incident analyses in the areas of marketing and sales may identify: public relations training needs; the need for effective market analyses related to staff and organisation capabilities. More generally, it may be necessary to train marketing and sales staff better in information gathering, analysis and evaluation activities. In these areas there may also be a derived recruitment and selection implication relating to the quality of staff when they are taken on, and the qualities and qualifications required of individuals in these activities.

Both critical incident and also training needs analyses are certain to identify requirements in each of the following areas.

Communications

- Quality and volume of written, oral, formal and informal communications; the balance of each.
- Extent and nature of communication, blockages and misunderstandings.
- Frequency and value of team, group, department, division and functional meetings; their agenda; outputs and outcomes.
- Effectiveness of formal and established communication systems – especially consultation, participation and access to information.
- Organisational and operational confidentiality; perceived organisational and operational confidentiality.
- Language used – the simpler and more direct this is, the more likely it is that what is said will be understood.
- Integrity of communications – the extent to which they mean what they say and say what they mean; the extent and prevalence of hidden/secondary agenda.

Organisational

- Lack of adequate consultation.
- Increases in awards against the organisation by employment tribunals, the Health and Safety Executive, Trading Standards.
- Lack of autonomy on the part of those working away from head office.
- Bad/negative/adversarial management style – often compounded by priorities on administration and procedural efficiency rather than operational success.
- Lack of clarity of overall purpose; lack of attention to over-arching and sub-ordinate goals, aims and objectives.
- Inaccessibility of managers and supervisors; lack of communication and coordination between functional and operational groups, departments and divisions.
- Complexity/simplicity of procedures; accessibility and understanding of procedures; time taken and resources used in their operation.
- The extent and balance of crisis management; the matters that fall into the 'crisis' area.
- Attention to work patterns and methods; extent of alienation and divisive work practices; attention to job and work improvement methods.
- Extent and prevalence of *them and us* divides between – head office and outlying functions; primary and support functions; managers and staff.
- Organisational politics – identifying where real power and influence lies; why; whether this is appropriate; the extent and influence of dominant personalities and departments.

Each of these elements represents a key feature of effective supervisory and management training, as well as attention to universal development of attitudes, values and behaviour.

Group contributions

Organisational working groups are also likely to identify training and development needs as a part of their genuine functioning. All group development requires attention to group processes, performance targets and output. These groups include:

- working improvement groups, quality improvement groups, and quality circles;
- project groups, concerned with both internal and external development, and also client-based activities;
- peer groups and professional and occupational clusters;
- *ad hoc* groups, including canteen and social gatherings.

In each case, their effectiveness in identifying and analysing training needs is dependent upon their fundamental integrity, openness and honesty, and the degree of candour with which they can report their findings within the organisation at large. They become both ineffective and tainted if they concentrate wholly on process at the expense of task, or vice versa, or if results are then used against the individuals and groups identified.

Strategic approaches to training needs analysis

Each of the areas indicated above have great value in identifying individual, group and collective needs. The weakness of individual approaches is the lack of overall rigour that may be required, and the differences in value placed by departments, divisions, functions, managers and individuals on the process. To ensure that whatever is in place is as effective as possible, a strategic approach is required. This means:

- Establishing and enforcing the priority of training needs analysis. This must be especially at formal performance appraisal times and intervals. It requires the ability, willingness and flexibility to accommodate issues raised in both this and other approaches.
- Identifying those areas required. It is usual to consider the absolute standards required in skills, knowledge, attitudes, behaviour, expertise and performance, and to provide structures for identifying and remedying shortfalls in each, though many organisations concentrate only on skills and knowledge.
- Having the flexibility and responsiveness necessary to address other areas when these become apparent. This especially refers to the ability to deal with: shortfalls in the usage/potential/capacity mix of technology; and weaknesses and divisions in organisation culture, cohesion, unity and clarity of purpose.
- Taking a strategic approach to organisation and individual training and development needs. This requires consideration of: whose needs; what needs; why they are needs; why this is considered the best possible approach in the circumstances; and what else has been considered.
- Taking a strategic approach when a universal general or widespread need has become apparent (see Summary Box 3.6).

SUMMARY BOX 3.6   Early retirement at Boots

Some years ago, Boots, the high street chemist and department store chain, found itself to be (perceived itself to be) over-staffed. It accordingly asked for volunteers to take early retirement.

The company was shocked when it was swamped with volunteers. Notoriously, the youngest volunteer was 38 years old. The individual concerned had worked for 20 years at the company, and if allowed, would have been able to retire on half pension.

The company quickly re-thought its strategy. It allowed early retirement for those within two years of normal retirement age. To the company's credit it also engaged an extensive strategic programme of training needs analysis and employee development. This ultimately led to requirements on the part of all staff to undertake training and development of some form or another. All new starters were put through a designed strategic induction and initial job training and development programme. Subsequently, those who wished to do so, were encouraged to gain national validation through the NVQ scheme.

By taking a linear approach to a perceived problem, the company was able to identify a far more serious issue of widespread demotivation and demoralisation. It managed to address these problems in the long-term through engaging in a much more extensive programme of strategic employee and organisation development.

- Committing to this direction long-term in the certain knowledge that the benefits afforded:
  (a) are likely not to become apparent in the short-term and may take years to become fully realised;
  (b) may lead to teething troubles when initially implemented, as the staff come to understand that changes are to take place;
  (c) may be diluted initially by confrontational staff responses, especially if there is an adversarial staff management style or history of bad or ineffective human resource management and industrial relations in practice.
- Committing to resource it fully, in terms of both finance and expertise; and this means according it a priority sufficiently high enough to ensure that it is not given away, diluted or cancelled in subsequent strategic reviews before it has had time to work. This also means committing the organisation to budgeting for the collective group and individual training and development activities that subsequently become apparent and required. It is clearly no use in identifying the needs if there exists no commitment or provision to meet them. The need to meet professional, occupational and personal demands, as well as those of the organisation (see Chapter 2 above), must be understood; and this also applies to the demands of standard and universal programmes (see below).

Beyond this, structured approaches to training needs analysis depend for effectiveness on:

- a clear policy and direction;
- a clear and acceptable set of rules;
- universally applied framework questions and demands;
- monitoring, review and evaluation mechanisms, at both senior and operational management levels.

Needs analysis, policy and direction

A needs' analysis, a policy and a direction are required to ensure that overall standards of conduct are universally known and understood. To be effective this requires a unified approach, addressing everyone and everything in the same basic ways, combining the overall standard with sufficient flexibility and responsiveness to allow particular departmental, divisional, group and individual quirks to emerge. There must also be absolute standards of equality of treatment and opportunity. Demonstrable relationships between organisational, occupational, professional and personal demands and priorities, and commitment to support whatever is implemented to the same standards (e.g. if one activity is fully paid for, all should be; if no activities are paid for, there should again be no exceptions).

Clear and universally applied sets of rules

These are notified to all staff. These rules must ensure that:

- All training and development needs are recorded and filed, and used as part of the broader employee development process. If proposed activities are implemented, then there is a starting point for understanding why these were thought necessary or desirable. If they are not implemented, then the reasons for this (including legitimate changes in circumstances or priorities) can also be assessed accurately.
- The overall approach is non-adversarial and non-punitive. It reinforces the point made earlier (see Chapter 2 above) that all employee development is a joint venture and responsibility. If an adversarial or punitive approach is adopted, the whole process becomes corrupted and therefore useless.

Rigorously applied framework

The ideal approach is a universally applied format used as part of the overall appraisal process, filled in and signed jointly by appraiser and appraisee. This applies to all approaches indicated above. This should indicate: what is going well; what needs to be remedied over the coming period and future periods; plans for action over the coming period; outline proposals for future activities in subsequent periods.

These forms should be no more than a single sheet of paper. This is in the interests of clarity, usefulness and precision. This is then used at the next formal review.

One key question to be addressed at subsequent reviews is whether apparent training and development needs were actual training and development needs. Another is whether the activities proposed and undertaken actually addressed the intended problem or issue. Successful evaluation of these sharpen up the operational aspects of training needs analyses.

Monitoring, review and evaluation

Monitoring, review and evaluation takes place at strategic and operational levels. At a strategic level, training needs analysis is assessed in line with organisational progress and development, and against particular performance indicators relating to the effectiveness of products, services and support functions. At an operational level, this is undertaken as part of developing the effectiveness of relations between appraisers and appraisees, and to ensure that the process continues to work and does not just become a form-filling exercise. This latter discredits the whole process if it becomes known or perceived as such, and simply gets institutionalised as a paperwork nuisance.

Costs and benefits

The costs and benefits of structured and organised approaches to training needs analyses are as summarised in Table 3.1.

Conclusions

The whole purpose of effective training needs analysis is to identify the learning and development priorities and commitments of the organisation as a whole, and of the individuals who work within it. If it does not do this, it should be scrapped and reconstituted.

Once it is committed to, it is essential that whatever is produced is addressed. This means committing sufficient resources on a strategic rather than *ad hoc* or first come first served basis – or worst of all, on a distributive, competitive

---

Table 3.1   Costs and benefits

Costs	Benefits
• Fixed-cost elements in gaining acceptance of this as a priority, and in carrying it out • Possible variable-cost elements in hiring processing staff to set up the organisational basis	• Full range of needs becomes apparent • Mutuality of interest • Greater employee expectations • Greater employee commitment • Enhanced rewards to individuals • Enhanced total awareness of potential

or lobbied approach. Everything therefore requires prioritisation, costings and structure, as a precursor to delivery, implementation and review. From this point of view, training needs analysis is the first step of the total organisation and employee development process.

Whatever is produced by training needs analysis must never become the basis for recourse to disciplinary or poor performance procedures. Where performance appraisal indicates or demonstrates negligence, incompetence or some other fundamentally unacceptable approach, this must be dealt with *away* from this part of the staff management process. Disciplinary procedures must never be commenced during performance appraisal.

The other point to note is that it is very easy to become drawn into a fundamentally negative way of thinking. This is, after all, concerned with identifying areas for improvement, and the consequence of this is that attention is concentrated on the imperfections rather than the good things. This must be recognised as a potential pitfall.

It is also necessary to note the broader context of the totality of organisation performance. Extensive training needs may be presented in very high performing organisations that want and need to ensure that their success continues. Low performing organisations may have fewer such needs on the other hand, because there are fundamental structural and strategic weaknesses that no amount of organisation and individual development can resolve.

QUESTIONS

1 Work in pairs. Produce a set of performance criteria for (a) yourself; (b) your partner. From this, briefly assess each other's performance. Identify those gaps in performance that can and cannot be filled by training and development activities. Produce an outline development programme for the coming period.

2 What strategic approach to organisational and individual development needs analysis should be taken by:
   • a sole trader corner shop;
   • a low-cost/low-budget airline;
   • a top professional football club?
   Give reasons why you have identified this approach for each?

3 Assess the effectiveness of training-and-development needs analysis at your own organisation, or one with which you are familiar. What recommendations would you make to improve these and why?

4 Under what circumstances may an effective and rigorous training needs analysis identify very few training needs? In general, what should happen as the result?

▮ ⌄ 4 Core training programmes and activities

'Everyone knows what to do in an emergency. Training and development in emergency procedures are simply not necessary.'

Un-named director, Townsend–Thoresen Car Ferries, February 1987, three weeks before the *Herald of Free Enterprise* disaster

Introduction

All organisations are required by law to have standard procedures in place for the management of staff, health and safety, and emergencies. These have to be made available to all staff who must know and understand how and why they are operated. It is therefore essential that provisions exist in all organisations for this form of training.

It is important to recognise that, at their core, they are sufficiently important, as well as legally required, to transcend preferred learning styles, though specific programmes for particular occupations may take more account of this.

It is important to recognise that shortfalls in standard programmes may become apparent as the result of training-needs' analyses, as well as accidents, emergencies, disasters, pollution scares and staff management crises resulting in employment tribunals, compensation claims and allegations of bullying, victimisation and harassment. It is also important to recognise that these programmes must be delivered to particular standards of content and presentation. This leads, in turn, to a first consideration of the role and qualities of in-house trainers.

Universal programmes

The programmes required in all organisations, whatever their size, status and location, are:

- **Induction:** introductions; getting to know you; setting basic standards; indicating required attitudes, values and behaviour; ways of working; meeting colleagues; meeting key staff with whom they interact; where appropriate, meeting key suppliers, customers and clients; general organisational and environmental familiarisation.

- **Emergencies:** becoming familiar with building and other premises layouts; training and briefing in emergency evacuation procedures; patterns of behaviour required; regular fire drills; the availability and use of protective clothing; other emergencies such as security, information systems crashes, supply and customer crises.

- **Healthy and safe working practices:** general rules and regulations, again including emergency and evacuation procedures; setting and maintaining required standards of healthy and safe performance; strict adherence to statute and directive requirements; specific environmental health and safety matters; setting and maintaining the right attitudes and behaviour.

- **Equality of treatment and opportunity:** ensuring that staff are aware of legislation; ensuring that staff are aware of their rights and duties; instilling universal standards of attitude, value and behaviour; intolerance of discrimination, bullying, victimisation and harassment on grounds of race, ethnic origin, gender, marital status, age or occupation; reinforcing these with day-to-day practice; applying these universally throughout organisations; reinforcing the message each time it is necessary (e.g. when activities are to be opened up in a new location with a different culture; when staff from a particular group are to be engaged for the first time).

- **Human resource management procedures and practices:** staff management requirements and expectations; disciplinary, grievance, dismissal and redundancy procedures; establishing and reinforcing equality of opportunity and treatment; standards of behaviour – especially including those which are not acceptable (vandalism, violence, bullying, victimisation and harassment); training opportunities; other things to do with contracts of employment and terms and conditions (e.g. hours of work, pay, rewards, expenses, overtime); custom and practice; consultative and participative activities; other industrial relations matters; team and group briefings (see Summary Box 4.1).

SUMMARY BOX 4.1   Lessons from Japan (1)

One major platform of the manufacturing industrial revolution brought to the West by Japan in the 1970s and the 1980s was the extensive attention paid to core training programmes and activities. Acutely conscious of the fact that they were seeking to bridge a cultural divide, Japanese companies establishing operations in the West went to a great deal of trouble to ensure that all staff understood the cultural, behavioural and performance requirements of their new company.

Attention was paid to every area – operations, marketing and sales; human resource and staff management; industrial relations; and attitudes, values and behaviour. Companies also introduced pre-training – getting the staff on site months in advance of opening and ensuring that they were fully trained in all aspects before activities were commenced.   (continued)

Managerial staff were (and continue to be) placed on extended intensive induction programmes concentrating on each of the above areas, and with a very strong emphasis on individual managerial responsibility. The problems that arose in the manager's domain were expected to be resolved without recourse to procedures. Disputes and grievances were to be kept to an absolute minimum. The manager's highest priority was to be long-term, enduring and high-quality product sales and service performance. Everything else was subordinate to that.

- **Attendance and absence including sickness absence:** paying specific attention to operational and behavioural factors; drawing attention to procedures; ensuring that all staff are briefed in procedures.
- **Operational procedures and practices:** including establishing patterns of behaviour and performance; ensuring that all staff understand what to do in cases of emergency, breakdown and crisis; adhering to procedures when there are supplier or customer complaints.
- **Initial job training and orientation:** again including custom and practice; getting used to established patterns of work; dealing with regular institutionalised practices such as hand-overs, inter-departmental liaison, and customer and supplier relations.
- **Continued job training and development:** including the development of the present job and occupation; job rotation, enrichment and enhancement; development of activities and procedures; training and development for the next job and future opportunities; reinforcing the required attitudes and patterns of behaviour (see Summary Box 4.2).

SUMMARY BOX 4.2   Lessons from Japan (2)

Japanese companies establishing operations in Western Europe and North America were extremely strong on the cultural and behavioural aspects as key components of long-term, enduring, profitable performance. They understood that their major source of competitive advantage at the time derived from the establishment of effective work patterns and relationships, and attention to detail. Much of the initial training and development effort was concentrated on this. It was essential that everyone who was to be employed needed to understand why they were required to do things in certain ways, as well as the fact of the matter.

During the radical transformations of manufacturing led by (among others) Sony, Matsushita, Nissan and Toyota in the 1960s, staff loyalty was engaged through the premise of 'high value work for high levels of income and satisfaction'. The leaders of those companies understood at the time that it was necessary to pay attention to every aspect of work practice and environment if this were to be achieved. The full environment needed to be managed, not just operational practice. These companies also understood that, while it was possible to engage in short-term high levels of productive activity through attention to the financial reward only, long-term and sustainable output was only possible if the staff received high levels of intrinsic value and esteem.

- **Handling complaints:** from both internal and external sources; making complaints; recourse to grievance procedures; customer and supplier empathy; positive and high standards of behaviour, attitudes and values.
- **Management and supervisory development:** identifying potential; identifying and responding to ambition; planned periods of development; training for present and future managerial and supervisory jobs; equality of opportunity.
- **Culture, attitudes, values, behaviour and standards:** what is tolerated and what is not; what is rewarded and what is not; what is punished and what is not; modes of dress and address; rank, status and trappings.
- **Waste and effluent disposal:** general attitudes and demeanour in the management of waste and effluent; attention to the working environment; wider responsibilities to the environment as a whole; safe handling practices where appropriate; liaison with waste and effluent contractors.
- **The training and development priorities of the year/period:** making opportunities available; designing core training programmes; pre-planned staff and management development activities; the priority accorded; and the availability, or otherwise, of opportunities.

The length of each activity, and whether each is considered as a separate issue or rolled up into one, depend quite legitimately on the nature of the staff, the work to be carried out, and the complexity, or otherwise, of the working environment and relationships. For example, many organisations quite legitimately do not make a separate issue of culture, values, attitudes, behaviour and standards, instead ensuring that these are clearly articulated and understood during induction and reinforced during each of the other activities.

Programme purposes

It is essential that staff know and understand what really happens, how they are really expected to act and behave. For example, if the stated starting time is 8.00 am, but in practice everyone arrives by 7.45 am, this needs to be made clear. If it is stated that in the case of an emergency a bell will sound, but in practice it is a siren, then this too must be made clear (ideally, the written form will be amended, but this does not always happen). If something needs to be signed for, but in practice never is, then everyone involved needs to understand the full consequences of this, and a current corporate view established.

Beyond this, each of these core programmes has the following generic purpose, aims and objectives:

- To establish and develop the required attitudes, behaviour and values. It is critical to realise that where these programmes are skimped or sloppy, staff arrive at their own interpretation of the required and present attitudes, behaviour and values.
- To establish and develop patterns of behaviour that are engaged by the staff as a condition and consequence of their employment. This ranges across:

- the extreme: how to behave in an emergency; what to do if there is a fight;
- the commonplace and ordinary: how to address colleagues; how to dress; how to answer the phone;
- the standards of organisational and operational patterns of behaviour: logging on; clocking in and out; use of tachographs, logbooks, progress reports;
- skills and expertise: applying these in the ways required by the particular organisation, department, division or function; to begin to develop these for the future; and to identify potential.

- To relate and harmonise individual, group, organisational, occupational and professional needs; and/or to recognise that where this is not possible, or not fully realised, then there are enduring problems of dysfunction, frustration and dissatisfaction.
- To continue to develop absolute standards in each area for the present and future.
- To continue to develop individuals, groups, departments, divisions, functions and the organisation for the future.
- To solve problems; to increase the operational capability of all; to maintain, develop and improve performance and output overall; to develop greater effectiveness of resource utilisation, and greater effectiveness of professional and occupational output; to develop a reputation for high levels of quality and customer satisfaction.

Training programme quality

These purposes are only achievable so long as the quality of the standard training programmes is assured. This reflects:

- The priority placed on each by the organisation as a whole and by individual managers and supervisors; if they are not valued highly, then the quality and content are invariably poor.
- The content of each is reinforced in practice.
- The content of each sets specific standards of attitudes and behaviour, as well as performance; where these are not achieved, the steps for improvement are undertaken with recourse to disciplinary and poor performance sanctions where appropriate.
- People are trained in how to use the programmes themselves, and how to maintain standards of attitudes, behaviour and performance. This is more important for management and supervisory development. In many cases, as greater responsibilities are placed on frontline staff for basic supervisory, managerial and administrative activities, this is also of increasing universal importance. In all cases, people need to understand why and how things are important, as well as the fact that they are.
- People are trained in how to deliver and respond to the programmes as a whole, and also participative aspects in which they may have good or expert knowledge.

- People are trained in monitoring, reviewing and evaluating the effects of what is done, and constantly and actively seeking ways of building on successes and strengths, and addressing weaknesses and gaps.

Feedback

All people must be trained in giving and receiving feedback. This is a key and universally required skill and attitude.

Organisations have to be big and receptive enough to acknowledge their own strengths and weaknesses. Strengths should be a matter of pride and honour but not arrogance. Provided that this holds good, they are entitled to be credited by their own people, and also by others, for things that they do well. This is an excellent and highly responsible organisational and senior management discipline.

Weaknesses require acceptance, evaluation and remedy. At the very least, if someone has described any organisational activity as a weakness, then it is essential to establish the facts of the matter, and/or why and where this perception has arisen. Where this is clearly a matter of substance, then remedial action is required. It is also essential that the organisation addresses this from the point of view of putting it right, rather than looking for scapegoats. The following points should be noted:

- All individuals need to be able to comment accurately and fairly on their own performance and that of others. Ideally, this is confined to processes and outputs, and where the desired or required aims and objectives were met. Where these were not met, all individuals should be capable of giving an informed explanation of the reasons. Ideally also, it is essential to be able to acknowledge weaknesses as a precursor to engaging in a collective effort with the organisation, department, division, function and superior to put it right (see Summary Box 4.3).

SUMMARY BOX 4.3   The practice of giving feedback

In theory, everything is gained from an open, honest, assertive and informed approach. In practice, in a great many cases, this is simply not possible.

In the wrong situation, an honest acknowledgement of weakness or failure simply results in dismissal, downgrading, loss of reputation or loss of performance bonuses and increments. Staff that acknowledge weakness are victimised and come to be known and viewed as weak and ineffective. This is a more or less universal cultural factor in the corporate and head office functions of multinational corporations, public service bodies and other large or heavily bureaucratic organisations.

Staff that acknowledge weakness come to be blamed for all the failings of their department and colleagues. When things go wrong, there is no need to look further and so nobody does – both the cause and perpetrator are already identified.

This is expedient and morally repugnant. It also causes long-term damage to organisation and departmental morale, stress for the particular individual, and dilution

(continued)

of the effectiveness of training and development activities, and the monitoring, review and evaluation that is so critical a part. The consequence is that a conspiracy emerges so that when people are asked for their own weaknesses they respond with: 'I find it impossible to leave my desk/workstation easily'; or 'I find it impossible to shut off from work completely'. This leads directly to a failure to address institutional weaknesses, or to give organisations and their employees the opportunity to put matters right in an atmosphere of harmony and cooperation.

- All individuals should be capable of receiving accurate and positive praise, criticism and appraisal of their own performance. This must concentrate on work and must never become known, believed or perceived to be adversarial, punitive or leading to bullying, victimisation and harassment.

  Again, in practice, it very often does happen that criticism is negative, contemptuous or personalised. The instant remedy for this is recourse to the grievance procedure. In the long-term, it is essential that when senior managers do get to understand that this is going on, they engage attitudes, behavioural and value standards that are going to get over this. This often takes a long time in practice. It is compounded by the fact that senior staff in many cases either do not understand the importance and value of this, or else have forgotten it.

- Everybody must also be able to engage in open dialogue that enables faults and imperfections to be noted and tackled at the earliest possible moment. This is so that serious issues are kept to an absolute minimum. Again, if the right attitudes are created at induction and maintained in practice, this is straightforward. If not, then no such productive dialogue is possible. Whenever there are attempts to raise things in this way, they become diluted at best and otherwise lost altogether.

Costs and benefits

The costs and benefits of conducting standard and core training programmes and activities in these ways are as summarised in Table 4.1.

Table 4.1   Costs and benefits

Costs	Benefits
- Paying for managerial, supervisory and staff time and resources - Opportunity costs: those involved cannot be doing anything else - Short-term stresses on daily workload - Prioritised use of resources - Costs involved in training staff - Costs involved in accrediting staff (if appropriate)	- Clear common standards - Areas of shortfall in practice easily identified - Early and effective remedies - Non-existence of behavioural costs – declining attitudes, values and morale

Conclusions

The contribution made by core training programmes to both immediate, and also enduring, organisational professionalism and effectiveness should be clear. The effect is to set standards of behaviour and performance, and to reinforce the working environment so that all staff can concentrate on delivering their own expertise or occupation to the highest possible standards.

The reverse is also true. If these programmes are not delivered effectively, this is either because they are not valued or else because the organisation's top managers simply do not understand the contribution that would be made, and therefore do not allocate sufficient priority or resources (see Summary Box 4.4).

SUMMARY BOX 4.4   Co-Steel Sheerness Plc

Co-Steel Sheerness Plc is situated on the north coast of Kent in the town of Sheerness on the Isle of Sheppey. It breaks all the rules of operations management. It is not located near to the sources of its required inputs – ore and energy fuel. Nor is it located near to its markets. Road access between the organisation and the wider world is by a single bridge linking the Isle of Sheppey with the mainland County of Kent. There is a sea ferry terminal in the town of Sheerness which links with Vlissingen, The Netherlands, 8 hours away.

During the 1980s and 1990s, the company was both successful and profitable. It concentrated on its inherent strengths. The top managers of the company generated a culture and ways of working that transcended the operational issues that had to be faced. This culture was reinforced with staff policies of organisation and continuous development, a fully effective core training programme, and continued attention to the behavioural aspects of performance. High levels of motivation and commitment were generated through the enduring effectiveness of the core programme and extensive job training.

The company was sold by its owners to a Canadian multinational in 1994; and was subsequently sold on again in 1998. Each of the corporate buyers lost the key message, that maintenance and investment in the core training programme lay at the core of the company's success. Matters came to a head when the company declared large losses in the year 2000. The core training programme was cancelled, and redundancies announced. The company continues to make losses.

It is also apparent from this example that once effective core training programmes are fully integrated into organisational activities, they quickly become unvalued. To the unwary (as with Co-Steel's new owners) they are a potentially soft and easy target for short-term resource cuts.

Finally, it is universally accepted in principle that well trained, capable, informed and motivated staff give much better service to customers and clients. They are also much more likely to remain with the organisation for longer, take less time off sick, and work to sustainably higher performance levels over the long-term. Committing to, and using, core training programmes in these ways is therefore a key step towards sustainable profitability and effectiveness.

QUESTIONS

1 Over what period of time, in your view, should companies and organisations expect to see positive results accruing from long-term and sustained investment in core training and development activities?

2 If a company can attract and recruit staff, but not retain them, what does this suggest to you about the effectiveness of training and development activities? What remedial action should be taken?

3 Produce a fully-costed health and safety training programme for the organisation of your choice. How will you measure the effectiveness of this?

4 Produce an outline induction and core training programme for each of the following groups:
   - school students on work experience placements of two weeks at a bank branch;
   - supervisors going into their first jobs in a call centre;
   - managerial staff at a car manufacturing plant with declining levels of production and output, and increasing levels of sickness absenteeism;
   - a new senior manager at a water company that has just been fined £500,000 for dumping effluent in the river.

Address the following questions for each: content; addressing preferred learning styles; length of programme; cost; required and desired outputs.

■ ⋎ 5 On-the-job training

'I used to practise everyday. If I won, I practised. If I lost, I practised. If I was fresh, I practised. If I was tired, I practised. If I was jet-lagged, I would still practise.'

Christine Evert, former tennis champion

Introduction

Those who do not value organisational and individual training and development point to a perceived (indeed, in some cases) real lack of relationship between what is taught and what is required in practice. The 'unique selling point' of on the job training is that it instantly gets over this particular barrier (see Summary Box 5.1).

SUMMARY BOX 5.1   Effective on-the-job training

The key elements of effective on-the-job training are as follows:

- training must be for actual practice rather than an ideal;
- training meets best practice standards whatever the sector or occupation.

For example:

Lifting

Nurses and social care staff are given extensive training in lifting. This is essential because many patients and social service clients are heavy, disabled or immobile, and therefore difficult to move into ideal positions. 'Best practice' in these sectors requires universal availability of lifting equipment and staff training in its usage. In practice, most hospitals and residential social care facilities do not have sufficient lifting equipment. Because of shortages of both equipment and staff in these occupations, the training therefore bears little resemblance to actual practice.

It has to be properly prioritised and structured, and conducted rigorously and effectively. At its best, on-the-job training works as follows:

- it teaches people a series of tasks and activities required of them in their daily work, and in their context and environment;
- it draws a direct relationship between what has been learned elsewhere and how it is now to be applied as required and in context;
- it establishes and reinforces the required attitudes, values, behaviour and approaches to work;
- those concerned see a direct relationship between what they have been taught and the output that they produce (see Summary Box 5.2).

SUMMARY BOX 5.2   On-the-job training at its worst

At its worst, on-the-job training is rushed, scrappy, incomplete and inadequate. The result is that new starters arrive at a view of:

- the value of their work;
- the value of themselves to the organisation;
- their own commitment to the present which either leads to a determination to make the best of it until they can find something else; growing and developing the job in their own interests which may, or may not, coincide with those of the organisation; leaving as soon as possible.

This is compounded when it is known or understood that the organisation concerned has given training and development a low priority as a matter of policy rather than accident. However the matter has arisen, there is no basis for a long-term and mutually effective working relationship. Moreover, it is compounded in many situations by lumbering the least assertive, experienced or capable employees with the responsibility of initial job training for new starters or incomers.

On-the-job training should be a cornerstone for the development of commitment, as well as capability, and the best organisations use a wide variety of methods to do this.

Working under guidance and supervision

This is the most commonly and universally applied method. It is valuable in all situations, organisations and occupations. The keys to success and effectiveness are:

- the demeanour, commitment, attitudes, values and beliefs of the trainer;
- the capability and willingness of trainers to teach, supervise, assess, correct and reinforce – and the approaches that they use in each of these areas;
- the amount of time and energy that the trainer can commit to these activities; and the amount of time and energy that they are prepared and willing to commit;
- the attitudes taken to the fact that people learn at different rates and speeds. This especially applies to known or perceived quick and slow learners.

It is especially important to bear in mind the deadline by which individuals are required to be proficient at their job. There are perceptual problems around:

- Those who learn very quickly – leading to perceptions of halo effects on the part of the organisation, complacency on the part of both trainer and trainee. This may also lead to medium to long-term decline in individual performance if the trainee is either doing work that is far too easy, or doing it imperfectly.
- Those who apparently learn very quickly, who give the overwhelming impression that they are grasping and applying the required skills, knowledge and expertise (see Summary Box 5.3).

SUMMARY BOX 5.3   Learning very quickly: example

Helen Marcus was a middle manager at a train operating company. She was assigned an urgent project with very high priority that involved designing a new passenger timetable implementation system in a very short period of time in response to specific demands from the rail regulator.

Helen worked 18-hour days for a period of many months. She worked weekends, and as the result, destroyed her home life. However, the project was completed on time. Her bosses were congratulated by railway chiefs, and the regulator pronounced himself satisfied.

Shortly afterwards, she had her performance review with her manager, David Pears. The meeting was extremely short. Helen filled in her own performance appraisal form and took it along to David's office. She sat down. David looked at her across the desk and said: 'Helen, I have not filled in your performance review. Generally speaking, you have been working well and everyone is very grateful that you carried out the timetabling project so effectively. However, this has had an effect on your personal presentation and demeanour. You do not dress to the standards required of this organisation, and as such project a bad image to the rest of the world. Moreover, you drink far too much coffee and leave dirty cups on your desk. It has also been reported to me that when you have been working late at night you have been bringing hamburgers and other fast food into the office. I also strongly suspect you of smoking. As you know, both of these are strictly against company regulations. As the result of this, I am unable to give you anything more than an average to adequate review. In fact, if it wasn't for the delivery of the project you would be the subject of poor performance review and this would probably lead to dismissal.'

The outcome of the project gained the train operating company an increase in revenue over the coming six months of £35 million. Shortly after the review, Helen left the company to join one of the new budget airlines.

- Those who apparently learn very slowly. This impression is often either given off or else reinforced by a calm or quiet disposition.
- Those who do learn very slowly and require constant reinforcement and support. This may be because of a lack of aptitude, fear, a nervous disposition, over-eagerness to please, rushing at the job – or unwillingness, incompetence or negligence.

The role of the trainer here is to recognise which of these is present, and deal with it. If it is any of the last three, it should be handed on to those in charge so that poor performance review or other disciplinary action can be undertaken. This should be a matter of serious concern when there are questions of particular individuals passing or failing probationary work periods. Not to do so is unfair to those in work, to those who try very hard and produce good to average performance, and to those who are genuine slow learners.

It therefore becomes clear that both trainer and trainee need clear guidelines under which to work so that there is a full mutual understanding of what has to be taught and learned, and what each may expect of the other in terms of output and support (see Summary Box 5.4).

SUMMARY BOX 5.4   Sprite Soft Drinks

Sprite Soft Drinks is a family business that makes and distributes soft drinks for the whole of southern England. It has expanded rapidly in recent years and now manufactures Coca-Cola under licence to that company.

Sprite Soft Drinks has always had a very high turnover of machine minders and other unskilled staff involved on the production side. The company is comfortable with this. Ian Chester, the Managing Director, states: 'There is no intrinsic interest in lemonade manufacture. So we don't try to make any. We simply ensure that we have a steady supply of labour. The average length of stay is between 4 and 6 months.'

Accordingly, the company provide very little on-the-job training. The work is deskilled to the point at which a new starter can become proficient as a machine operator in ten minutes. Other than loading the ingredients, the only other main duty is to clear away any of the plastic bottles in the production process that either do not fill properly, or else overfill and explode. The production areas are kept at constant temperatures through the use of electric industrial fans.

One day representatives of the Coca-Cola company were due to come and inspect the premises. This was part of the contracted arrangement. As the delegation arrived, the operative in charge of the Coca-Cola line was clearing a blockage. Pressed for time, he threw the debris at the bin, rather than carrying it. It slipped out of his hand and flew into the fan. This fused the entire factory.

Even where there are no pressing requirements for anything other than basic training, this illustrates that it can still be extremely expensive if basic standards and requirements are not established and reinforced.

Expectations

Trainee

The trainee is entitled to expect full and complete instruction in what to do, how to do it, and why things are done in particular ways. Training should also be delivered in such ways as to demonstrate the contribution that the operation or activity makes to the totality of organisational, departmental and divisional performance. Where operations and activities are carried out in isolation, the reasons for this must also be made clear. Boundaries defining what individuals can and cannot do, and the reasons for these, must be given. Where someone is bringing a professional qualification or expertise with them (see Summary Box 5.3 above) they must still be trained in ways of working and how the expertise is to be applied in the particular situation.

This is an especially important part of induction programmes and initial job training when the new member of staff will have as many uncertainties about how they are expected to behave and act as with what they are required to do.

Trainer

The trainer is entitled to expect willingness and commitment from the employee commensurate with the full context of the job. Problems are always faced by job trainers where it is known, believed or perceived that frontline work is undervalued, undemanding and boring; and the problem is compounded when the staff involved are understood to be overloaded.

The trainer is responsible for developing a productive and positive relationship with the employee. Provided that they do this, they are entitled to expect a reciprocal positive attitude and steady development in job expertise. If they do not do this, then they must expect problems (see Summary Box 5.5).

SUMMARY BOX 5.5   'You can't get good servants these days'

Many organisations go to great lengths and expense in their recruitment and selection processes to get people with the required skills, knowledge and expertise. Many organisations then damage or ruin the whole process by paying insufficient attention to the quality of initial and continuing job training.

Where recruitment and selection processes are thorough, the negative effect on individual new starters and bad job training is compounded. This is because expectations have been raised that are extremely high by the thoroughness, rigour and professionalism of the recruitment and selection activities. These are then dashed by the sloppiness or incompleteness of initial job training.

Many organisations then compound the error by addressing the recruitment and selection part of the process again, rather than looking at the ability to retain initially highly motivated new staff.

Generic programmes

Each of the generic programmes outlined in the previous chapter must be at least partly carried out on the job. Emergency procedures must be regularly rehearsed. Health and safety practices must be reinforced in the doing, and this includes the use of equipment and protective clothing, and following any specified procedures. Introductions to disciplinary, grievance and other staff management procedures and practices are reinforced through understanding the context in which they are to be applied.

The organisational approach to induction and orientation establishes the overall basis of attitudes, behaviour and mutual commitment. Induction that is slapdash, unstructured and which provides no clear or sustained job training reflects diluted, unvalued and (invariably) low standards and expectations. It also reinforces any destructive and adversarial aspects of staff management and industrial relations. The lack of initial and continuing on-the-job training may then become reflected in subsequent performance appraisals and unwary organisations find themselves downgrading, undervaluing or even getting rid of otherwise willing and capable staff, simply because they provided no adequate initial commitment in this area.

Frontline staff

Those who work on supply side, production and service output, or directly with customers and clients, are the key to enduring organisational profitability and effectiveness. This should always be the main driving force behind on the job training for staff in these occupations. Key elements of on the job training should therefore always be:

- meeting and becoming familiar with suppliers, customers and clients; understanding their needs, pressures and demands (see Summary Box 5.6);

SUMMARY BOX 5.6   'The customer is not your enemy'

This slogan was displayed at a call centre when it was opened. The centre handled bank account and Visa card enquiries. The message was designed to reinforce the job training given to all operatives which clearly stated that:

- they were to work through all calls to the satisfaction of the customer;
- they were to confirm by question that the customer was happy with the outcome;
- they were to ask if there was anything else required.

It is certainly possible to debate the literary merits of the slogan itself! However, its purpose and the prominence with which it was displayed ensured that everyone never lost sight of the priority of the centre.

This may be contrasted with a similar centre in the same building. This was owned by a large clearing bank. The job training was very similar also. However, staff were additionally required to deal with an average of 22 calls per hour. Failure to do this over specified periods always led to poor performance reviews. This meant that the staff involved concentrated on the volume of calls rather than quality of service. Some staff also used to get friends and family to call in with standard requests. Additionally, staff members carried their own mobile phones into work so that in periods of extreme stress they would either phone each other – or themselves.

- learning the content and delivery of product and service quality and excellence;
- becoming familiar, and subsequently expert, with technology and equipment;
- learning the ways in which they were to do their jobs including patterns of behaviour;
- understanding their position (if any) when customers and clients complain about something.

The best job training programmes also encourage (if not formalise) staff suggestions and the search for operational and procedural improvements so that the staff attitude is positive, dynamic and productive rather than reactive and responsive.

Multi-skilling

Job training for multiple and varied capability has the great benefit of ensuring that staff are as productive as possible over extended periods of time. It is also appropriate in some cases in job rotation, enrichment, enlargement and enhancement programmes, where people are moved from one job to another on a regular and formal basis in order to:

- enhance their level of interest, and therefore commitment, to the work and organisation;
- prevent them from becoming stale or bored in one job;
- enhance their employability;
- bring out potential;
- develop and enhance overall positive attitudes and behaviour;
- remove the causes of alienation, and the staff management and industrial relations problems that are certain to accrue as the result.

Multi-skilling was viewed as the answer to union-imposed demarcation and restrictive practices operated in many primary and secondary industries and public services. In truth, most organisations and their managers were happy with the traditional approach because it meant that they were able to operate within familiar and well-understood boundaries. It was not until Japanese manufacturing and other production processes transformed the competitive basis for that work through paying high levels of wage for full multi-skilling and flexibility that UK, European Union and North American organisations addressed these issues seriously (see Summary Box 5.7).

Empowerment

Empowerment is a current managerial fad and buzzword. Multi-skilling and wide-ranging on the job training are carried out with a view to developing the qualities of responsibility and accountability, as well as occupational expertise, in frontline staff. It works extremely well when it is supported with (see Summary Box 5.8):

SUMMARY BOX 5.7   Nissan and job training

As stated above (see Summary Boxes 4.1 and 4.2), Japanese manufacturing organisations have always understood the value of effective staff training, and the direct relationship between the priority given to this, and product quality and effectiveness.

This Nissan company opened a truck manufacturing plant in Smyrna, Tennessee, USA, and Washington, Tyne and Wear, UK in the early 1980s. At each plant, the company spent an average of £12,000 per member of staff on job training before opening the factory for fully commercial operations. Staff were to be paid high levels of wages (the highest in the car manufacturing sector) in return for fully flexible and multi-skilled patterns of work, and the abolition of traditional demarcation lines.

In the UK, the company continues to expend an average of £6500 per member of staff per annum on initial, continuing and job related training, and opportunities for project work, secondment and development. Other than one factory in Tokyo, Japan, and another in Seoul, South Korea, the Nissan factory at Washington is the most productive car plant in the world in terms of output per member of staff. In the year 2001, it was producing cars at the rate of 115 cars per member of staff per annum.

SUMMARY BOX 5.8   Harvester Restaurants – and banking

Harvester Restaurants Ltd was one of the first companies to introduce a successful programme of staff empowerment. The company was able to abolish two tiers of management through:

- giving chefs the freedom to design their own menus, and resources to make purchases;
- giving collective responsibility to all staff for the maintenance and upkeep of a high quality restaurant environment, including the ability to request decoration and maintenance;
- providing both visible and telephone support around the clock.

All staff were given 15 per cent pay rises at the inception of the programme. Subsequently, a profit-sharing arrangement was introduced on top of this. The organisation found that its effectiveness was enhanced through the ability to address and resolve operational issues and customer problems quickly, through the increase in expertise of a reduced number of staff. It also ensured that the company focussed strategically on the frontline, rather than support staff and administrative procedures.

This may be contrasted with the attitude towards empowerment of clearing banks. The major UK clearing banks now require all their cashier and customer services staff to attempt to sell financial products to members of the public who come to them. Because the process is conducted in isolation and because it is reinforced by head office edict only, it is demoralising for staff, and irritating for customers.

- adequate levels of resource;
- organisational commitment to back the judgement and decisions of the empowered staff;
- continuous job training (rather than learning through empowerment programmes and leaving these as ends in themselves);
- continued visible managerial support;
- round the clock access to managers and organisational resources in the case of crises and emergencies.

Flexibility

Multi-skilling and flexibility are overtly very similar. However, full flexibility of work is only to be achieved if there is a corporate and collective positive attitude and commitment to the full range of responsibilities that are present as a consequence. These include the following:

- High-priority and high-quality on-the-job training.
- High levels of staff value, including high levels of pay and rewards.
- Fully integrated performance appraisal carried out positively and continuously.
- Fully supportive and visible managerial and supervisory style; and this has to include acknowledgement of the needs, wants and demands of those working on non-standard work patterns and locations (see Summary Box 5.9).

SUMMARY BOX 5.9   On-the-job training and flexible working arrangements

The key issues that have to be faced here concern:

- staff on short and regular hours arrangements (e.g. those on evening shift work at supermarkets, call centres and databases);
- staff on long and irregular hours arrangements (e.g. flight and ferry crews; health and social care professions; some further and higher education);
- staff working away from home and the organisation for extended periods (e.g. civil and other engineering, construction, computer project work);
- staff working from home (traditionally direct sales staff; now with the availability of technology, this is extended to many administrative, human resource, finance and other support functions);
- subcontractors, specialists and consultants hired for specific reasons. This used to mainly concern building, civil or other engineering. It now also includes management consultants, change agents, IT specialists, and those working on specific subcontracted tasks for predetermined periods, jobs and projects. In all these cases, the host organisation is legally, as well as morally responsible for core and generic induction, training and briefing to ensure that absolute standards are met and maintained.

- Fully integrated core and generic training programmes, so that all those working in these ways adhere to the same absolute standards of behaviour as well as performance. It is very easy for staff on non-regular patterns to be missed or avoided. The effect of this is to dilute the effectiveness of core staff. It then becomes known, believed or perceived that there are double or multiple standards. Much of the effect is then lost, and other problems, especially disciplinary, grievance and unevenness of work output, start to become apparent.

Other factors in on-the-job training

The other areas that those responsible for job training provision have to be aware of including the following.

Time serving

Many occupations, professions and NVQ programmes insist on minimum periods of planned job and work experience with the trainee signed off at the end by a qualified, competent or experienced member of staff. This applies to:

- those in nursing and healthcare;
- engineering at apprenticeship and professional entry levels;
- other apprenticeships (e.g. chef, hairdresser);
- and to those following accredited vocational education and training paths.

There is an absolute responsibility for all organisations employing these staff to prioritise their supervision and support (see Summary Box 5.10).

SUMMARY BOX 5.10   Nursing

The final year of nursing training is spent on a variety of different placements, both in hospital and also elsewhere.

Because of acute staff shortages in hospitals, the on-the-job training and support are rarely effective. Final-year student nurses are regularly used as night and weekend staff, rather than receiving the planned and supported experience required. The result of this has been:

- to put pressure on existing expert and experienced staff during times of staff and resource shortage;
- to put pressure on final-year students who are, in many cases, having to teach themselves rather than being supported or guided;
- to put pressure on the totality of the service provided.

The result is declining staff and student morale, exits from the profession, and extreme difficulties in recruitment and retention.

These general lessons must be learned by all organisations and managers with responsibility for on-the-job training. If trainees in any field are given inadequate support, facilities, direction and guidance they will not stay in their job.

Planned experience

At its best, planned experience is applied, and opportunities given, to all staff, at all levels. The purpose is to develop as much expertise in all tasks and occupations as possible. It also inevitably reinforces perceptions of mutual value, esteem and commitment. It ensures that all staff involved become familiar over pre-planned periods with everything that may be required of them, and with the ways in which work is to be carried out. The process is reinforced where it is formalised through the use of logbooks and integrated appraisal and other performance evaluation approaches; and reinforced further where it is accredited by independent bodies, e.g. the National Council for Vocational Qualifications and its successors; and universities and higher and further education colleges (see Summary Box 5.11).

SUMMARY BOX 5.11   Planned experience and management development

The effective development of management and supervisors is dependent on high-quality off- and on-the-job training. On-the-job training consists of:

- Familiarity and initial experience of as many functions as possible within the planned period. This is normally reinforced through work shadowing and project assignments, as well as supportive responsibility for particular tasks and activities during the period of planned experience.
- Dealing with problems as they arise, especially staff management, customer and supplier care issues.
- Attending management meetings as both observer and participant.
- Working on developing specific tasks, activities and procedures.

Again, this requires corporate will and effective support if it is to be fully effective. It is also essential to give as much space as possible in any such programme for individuals to develop and implement their own preferred approaches and solutions to specific issues and problems.

Continuous professional development

Many professional and occupational bodies require minimum periods of continuous professional development (CPD) as a condition of continued membership. Many organisations also make their staff do this as a condition of employment (a high-profile current example is the insistence by Body Shop that all their staff work within the community for one day per month). The main problem is to ensure that there are adequate resources and institutional support. Whether for a professional body or organisation demand, all such activities are only fully effective if the enduring results are valued.

Technological training

Familiarity and training in the use of specific equipment is essential if returns on investment are to be optimised. All too often, this part of the use, application

Table 5.1 Costs and benefits	
Costs	**Benefits**
• Disruption of regular work flows and patterns • Variable cost of training instructors • Fixed costs in terms of priority and attitude shifts	• Immediate full familiarisation with work content and environment • Learning is directly linked to doing • Immediate apparentness of job development opportunities

and exploitation of high-quality and expensive technology is diluted because insufficient attention is given to this aspect. This is a waste of resources. In the worst cases, this can lead to undue protectionism and influence on the part of those who do happen to be able to use particular equipment to its full advantage.

Costs and benefits

The costs and benefits of effective on-the-job training are summarised in Table 5.1.

Conclusions

Effective on-the-job training is dependent upon the level of corporate priority and support given. Otherwise, while primarily concerned with the application of skills and expertise to tasks and work, it should never be forgotten that this also reinforces attitudes and values in the priority that it is afforded, and the ways in which it is carried out.

It is essential to recognise the value of having staff able and willing to carry out on the job training for incomers and new starters. It is relatively straightforward to teach basic instructional and teaching techniques. Basic and foundation courses are normally a maximum of two days. The ability to teach and instruct comes more easily to some than others. However, basic principles can be taught, learned and applied by most people. In most organisations, there are plenty of opportunities for these to be applied, reinforced and developed by a wide variety of staff.

It is also essential to recognise the direct relationship between effective job training and performance development, and organisational profitability and success. Everyone prefers to deal with expert, qualified and motivated staff. Product and service quality is higher, and service delivery is quicker and with fewer queries and complaints. This, in turn, reinforces both individual and collective morale as well as security of employment.

QUESTIONS

    I Identify the key skills required of an effective on-the-job trainer. Identify a programme for developing these in yourself. State how you are going to measure this for success or failure, and how and under what circumstances you will be able to put it into practice.

2 Produce a simple instruction sheet to be used as an aid by someone coming to use a piece of technology or equipment for the first time.

3 What initial and continuing job training should be given to:
- university graduates coming to work in a bank for the first six months of their employment?
- factory shift supervisors in their first job?
- evening and weekend shift supervisors at supermarkets?
- call centre staff who have specific requirements to deal with an average 22 calls per hour?

4 How would you measure the effectiveness of generic and job training programmes for subcontractors working on a three-month computer project installation?

5 Consider the nursing example (Summary Box 5.10) above. What investment is required to improve the quality of this job training provision? How, when, where and by whom should this be measured for success and effectiveness?

■ Ṿ 6 Off-the-job training

> *'I used to practise batting using a golf ball and a stump. That way, when I had to use a bat against a cricket ball in games, everything was much easier.'*
>
> Sir Donald Bradman

Introduction

Off-the-job training and development are anything that provides organisational, occupational, professional, group or individual learning away from the place of work. There is a great range and variety of methods available and each brings its own opportunities, advantages – and consequences (see Summary Box 6.1).

SUMMARY BOX 6.1   Off-the-job training methods, techniques and opportunities

- **Classroom:** lectures, talks, seminars, day release, block release and full-time study. These are good for demonstrating expectations, cultural soundness and giving regular information and updates. They are limited by spans of attention, preferred learning styles, suitability of material, and the capacities and capabilities of the teacher.
- **Laboratory and workshop:** for the development of precise, practical and scientific skills and the ability to practise or apply these in a safe situation. Limited by availability of equipment and information, and capability of tutors.
- **Projects:** for the purposes of solving problems and developing the capabilities and experience of staff undertaking them. Limited by the scale and scope of particular projects, and the capability, interest and commitment of those who supervise them.
- **Secondments:** for the purpose of developing and broadening the experience of staff, and to ensure a regular supply of fresh ideas in different activities. Must be integrated to the day-to-day operations. For the members of staff involved, secondments should be linked to other activities, skills development and projects with clear targets and objectives.
- **Competencies training:** specifically targeted at the 'can do' elements of work. Many vocational and management training programmes have been written in this way in order to concentrate on the skills, expertise and technological capability requirements.

- **Open and distance learning:** whereby students are given frameworks or objectives to work to, and set their own agenda, timetable, goals and learning methods within the programme. This is limited by preferred learning styles and the quality of support available.
- **Computer-aided and website-based learning:** useful in both technical and managerial areas, especially in the areas of decision-making, design, systems operations and 'what if?' type scenario evaluation. Limited by the quality of the interactive elements of the website or programme; and by the capability and willingness of the organisations to support it physically.
- **Mentoring, coaching and counselling:** the development of one-to-one relationships with key employees for the purpose of developing them into high performers in their professional or occupational fields. This is extremely time and resource consuming. It requires both capability and willingness on the part of the named coach, counsellor or mentor (see below, Chapter 11).
- **Role plays and case studies:** these give the opportunity to generate discussion, evaluation and analytical skills and capabilities; and to build on past experiences of real organisations and situations.
- **Outward-bound:** generally perceived to be of greatest value in the assessment and development of leadership, strategic and operational characteristics; and in the formation of confidence, trust and mutuality in work groups and teams. Limited by the integration of the outward-bound activities into other organisational and individual development activities.
- **Skills updates:** in all technical, professional and occupational areas. Skills updates are also generated when there is substantial change in technology; and this approach may be used as part of a broader organisation development programme.
- **High-cost seminars and professional association programmes:** the creation of a forum where persons from similar occupations or organisations can meet and exchange ideas supported by a modicum of structured input, especially from experts in the particular field.

There is a great range of material and opportunities available to all those concerned with the development of organisations and individuals. All methods used should be related to individual and collective development requirements and approaches. The use of off-the-job training methods should be viewed as part of a process to be built on so that both staff and the organisation are developed and improved in a structured and orderly (and profitable and effective) fashion.

Opportunities

Off-the-job training gives the opportunity to develop ideas and concepts in a safe environment. This includes the opportunity for creative thinking, organisational, occupational and professional daydreams, and brainstorming problems and key issues.

It gives the opportunity to learn key and critical skills, knowledge and expertise in a safe environment. An obvious example is the use of flight simulators to train military and airline pilots; others include model offices and retail training centres run by organisations and further education colleges. Some organisations have their own colleges and education and training centres (e.g. civil service college, police training colleges, construction industry training centre).

Removing people from the place of work enables those involved to step outside environmental and operational pressures and to get a better view of the context in which their activities are taking place. When involved with others from different departments, divisions and functions in the organisation, a better, fuller and broader understanding of operational priorities, pressures and constraints is achieved. When an event is with people from other organisations, fresh and uninhibited ways of looking at matters often become apparent (see Summary Box 6.2).

SUMMARY BOX 6.2   Action learning

The approach taken by Reg Revans in the development of action learning aimed to build on the abilities of outsiders to see organisational and operational problems and issues from this broader perspective and apply it to resolving these matters.

Action learning sets and clinics consisted of people from different organisations. They were brought together on a regular basis. The priorities, problems and issues were then thrashed out in full among the set members. In many cases, set members would go into their colleagues' organisations to support and sometimes implement change and development programmes.

Each set appointed its own facilitator and this role was critical to success and effectiveness. The facilitator was required to steer, arbitrate, provide resources and contacts, and act as a sounding board. Ideally, facilitators of action learning sets have no power of veto regarding anything that is proposed and agreed by set members. However, in practice it is often necessary to ensure that all proposals are fully worked through before being laid in front of particular organisations.

It encourages fresh and independent input and ideas. This applies especially to taught courses. People are exposed to expert and informed knowledge, research and techniques. They receive the benefit of others' skills and expertise. Above all, they develop a much broader and deeper understanding through interaction, debate, involvement, as well as the use of libraries, books, periodicals, the internet and other resources. Those who attend courses can (and should be prepared to) suspend pre-judgement and operational environment pressures on any matter whatsoever.

Consequences

The consequences of sending people off-the-job to learn and be developed also have to be understood. It may become clear to trainees that what they thought they were going to get is not being delivered. It may become clear from interactions with others on events that things could be done differently at their own place of work. Trainees may find that they are being under or over-paid, or that their terms and conditions of employment are better or worse relative to similar occupations in other organisations. Off-the-job events provide a fresh set of networking opportunities (see Summary Box 6.3).

SUMMARY BOX 6.3   Networking

Professional education schemes

Those who attend the professional education schemes of bodies, such as the Chartered Institute of Personnel and Development (CIPD), the Institute of Administrative Management (IAM) or the Institute of Chartered Accountants, start to build their own network of contacts. This, in turn, influences the ways in which they think about, and begin to develop, their general professional practice and particular job or occupation. This may, or may not, be in harmony with the ways in which their organisation or department presently functions.

While on professional education schemes, it is usual for employees to begin to attend, and become familiar with, the branch and networking structures of the particular professional body. This is a further general support and development opportunity, and most branches of professional bodies provide regular guest speakers and seminars to attract, retain and develop general interest as well as specific current issues.

High-cost seminars

Those responsible for designing and delivering these events understand that they have to build in extended tea, coffee and lunch-breaks so that those attending have good networking opportunities. Attendees will have been initially attracted by the overt value of the event, e.g. subject matter, product or service demonstration, and key note speaker. However, when they get there, they expect opportunities to meet with their professional colleagues as well as value from the event itself. In many cases, attendees will have rescheduled busy and pressurised work patterns just in order to be able to do this. Failure to make this provision on the part of event designers always leads to attendee frustration.

Attending off-the-job events also reflects real and perceived levels and value in which the individual and the training are held. This is dependent on the organisation context in which programmes are offered. In general, the following apply:

- Organisations that are prepared to fund and support individuals normally place positive value on both the individual and the training.
- Organisations that are not prepared to do this, do not normally value either as highly as those that do.

- Organisations that insist that their staff attend events are normally setting their own distinctive standards (which may be positive or negative, and will not be acceptable to everyone).
- Organisations that distinguish between those members of staff who may and may not attend relevant events on the basis of status, seniority, occupation or influence are not normally wholesome in the first place, and this approach tends to reinforce it.

Specific programmes

Many organisations offer specific, predesigned and predetermined programmes of off-the-job training. Many staff, occupations and professions insist that this is provided in the interests of developing both the capability of the individual and also the profession itself. Staff in key occupations can also insist on this in order to maintain and develop their own employability. Some organisations insist that employees undertake and pass specific programmes as a condition of continued employment. This normally falls into the following categories:

- Induction and initial job training programmes reinforced by directed private study (either self-set or through such bodies as NCVQ, Open University, colleges of higher and further education), so that a validated, known and understood body of expertise can be assumed.
- Professional education schemes of such bodies as CIPD, IAM and CIM. The benefits to the organisation are retention for the specific period of study, together with the opportunity for supported project and assignment work. This also enables the individual to be developed along understood and more or less universal professional lines. It brings current thinking, learning, expertise and ideas from the particular profession or occupation at large into the organisation. Also where organisations do insist that individuals stay on for a contracted period upon qualification or success, there are further opportunities to develop and assess future potential.

Other areas may also be considered as follows:

- Apprenticeship, occupation and technological training so that individuals in particular areas (e.g. catering, engineering, technology and information systems) receive a combination of off-the-job education and training, and direct application on the job.
- Day release (e.g. HNC in general, vocational and specific subjects) either as a precursor to professional and occupational development studies, or as a component of general employee development.
- Open, directed or private study. Where this is the case, the level of study required should be made clear and, if necessary, discussed with staff affected, because it is certain to affect their private and social lives (this also applies to many professional, occupational education and development schemes).

Again, whatever is required is underpinned by the overall organisational attitude and approach. The greater the level of support and flexibility offered, the greater the perception of value and priority placed both on the training, and also the individual (see Summary Box 6.4).

SUMMARY BOX 6.4   Support and flexibility

It is important not to mistake support and flexibility for dilution of standards. Two neighbouring universities in London offered (and continue to offer) part-time postgraduate studies leading to Masters degree qualifications. The target market of each is similar – those in managerial positions in international corporations wanting to develop their expertise and potential with the qualification as a mark of success, value and achievement.

One of the universities is rigid about attendance and output. It requires one day attendance per week for two years. It makes no allowances for job pressures when setting course work, assignments or examinations. It will not extend programmes of study, or allow attendees to further spin their studies out.

The other university is much more flexible and open and will consider each student case on its merits. While the notional full length of the course is exactly the same (one day per week for two years) students may choose to extend this at any time. They may defer modules, coursework, assignments and exams if they choose. The university takes this approach because it understands the pressures that its students are under at their places of work and it can take steps to accommodate them.

The first university has a negligible drop-out rate and a pass rate of 90 per cent of those who start the course. The second has a drop out rate of 40 per cent and a pass rate of 35 per cent of those who start the course.

Key factors

As stated above (see Summary Box 6.1) there is a great range of opportunities available; and anything can be turned into a learning or development opportunity. The important factors include the following:

- The relationship between the particular activity and what students, trainees and attendees are supposed to learn, and why. Demonstrable capability and proficiency achieved on a course or in a project does not prove workplace expertise – this has to be related directly to willingness to perform. This then, in turn, has to be reinforced by the ability to practise and develop at work whatever has been learned off-the-job.

  This capability and proficiency must satisfy at least one of the four requirements of personal, professional, occupational or organisational interest. If it does not, then the effort is wasted. It also reinforces beliefs and perceptions about the disparity between theory and practice so beloved of those who denigrate off-the-job training (see Summary Box 6.5).

- **The relationship between theory and practice.** Anything that is overtly academic or esoteric must have some demonstrable relationship with current practice and the ability to apply. The delivery of bodies of knowledge and background on taught courses must be made relevant to the current state of affairs and development of the particular subject or discipline. For example, to be an expert engineer requires extensive mathematical expertise; yet if the teaching of the mathematical body of knowledge loses sight of this, then the overall purpose and direction are lost. Similarly, those studying business and management normally have to become familiar with the Hawthorne experiments (in a nutshell, the effects on factory output of a series of management initiatives); yet it is essential that these are related to the present if the full lessons are to be understood.

- **The relationship between course and attendee.** Organisations are legitimately entitled to expect their employees to attend events provided that they are being given full support and that there is a positive mutual interest in doing so. Beyond that, events must satisfy at least one of the personal, occupational, organisational or professional criteria.

    It can also happen that (often with the best will in the world) the value of the event is diluted by personal and professional clashes between training providers, attendees and their organisation. This may be for reasons beyond everyone's control, e.g. other pressures on attendees, the constraints of the body of knowledge, understanding and expertise to be taught; or it may be that, for whatever reason, the event does not gel on a human or cultural level.

- **The relationship between the event and the environment in which it is delivered.** It is possible to deliver excellent, high-quality courses in bad surroundings and with inadequate equipment, but this depends utterly on the capability and energy of the teacher or trainer, and the willingness of attendees to depend totally on this expertise. Otherwise an environment suitable for everyone has to be created, with general support, comfort, equipment and facilities – and this includes the expertise of teacher or trainer. This environment normally includes a full range of support functions and mechanisms, both directly from the event and also back at the place of work.

- **The relationship between off-the-job training and on-the-job opportunities.** This applies to both present and future opportunities, and reinforces the required elements of identifying and developing future potential and preferences. It also applies to pre-occupational school, college and university courses (see Summary Box 6.6).

SUMMARY BOX 6.6   Pre-occupational courses

Pre-occupational courses include the following:

- Planned work experience carried out by schoolchildren or back-to-work returners in order to become familiar or re-familiar with the working environment.
- Secretarial and clerical courses run by colleges of further education and some school sixth-forms. People on these courses normally take a range of prescribed qualifications run by national examination boards (e.g. RSA, LCCI).
- Technical and occupational training courses in catering, hairdressing, engineering, construction, motor and other mechanics, electrical engineering and plumbing.
- Undergraduate courses in civil and structural engineering, applied physics and chemistry, business studies, computer science; and pre-professional training such as teaching, medicine and nursing.
- Some postgraduate courses, e.g. diplomas in town planning, management studies, architecture, surveying, hotel and retail management.

There are responsibilities and obligations on schools, colleges and universities that provide these, as well as employers, trade federations, professional bodies, examination boards and political institutions, to ensure that what is provided is of present and future value to all concerned, and also to develop and enhance the body of skills, knowledge and expertise in the particular field. It is extremely demoralising for trainees, and frustrating for employers, where there are serious discrepancies between what is anticipated and what is actually essential and desirable in practice.

- **The relationship between what is provided and general perceptions of value.** It is a lot harder to gain a reputation for excellence and quality than lose it; and extremely hard to rebuild or regain a good reputation once this has been lost. Staff sent on courses where the providers are known, believed or perceived to be of poor reputation, themselves feel unvalued. This is compounded if it becomes clear that trainers and teachers are not expert or enthusiastic and committed.

Perceptions of value are diluted when the student or attendee is expected to undertake full responsibility for their own future without any organisational or institutional support, and when no reciprocal benefit is known or implicit.

Perceptions of value are diluted when it is known or believed that what is being provided is a cheap substitute for doing the job properly. This applies to many interactive computer-based website, video and workbook programmes that are not given adequate physical or expert support. The problem is compounded when students and attendees are required to work to mechanistic, one-dimensional or general programmes in the interests of completion rather than development and enhancement (see Summary Box 6.7).

SUMMARY BOX 6.7   Teacher training and mathematics tests

All those who wish to train to become schoolteachers are required to take a computer-based mathematics test. Students have a limited period of time in which to work through a computer program. They are given no feedback on individual or collective answers. They simply complete the program, and some time later the result is returned to them. There is no indication of where things have gone right or wrong, nor is there any 'human' debrief. The problem is compounded because this test is widely perceived to have little value in the development of a basis for expert practice in school teaching. There is also no support or justification offered by the Department for Education and Employment, or teacher training institutions.

Other factors

Support

The key factor is long-term support for planned, ordered and prioritised off-the-job events related to organisational, professional, occupational, personal, group and individual development. This, above all, means contextual support – the willingness to create and develop, in turn, an organisational and managerial culture and style that enable the maximisation of all off-the-job events that people attend. It follows from this that it is essential that there is a collective corporate reasoning for sending people on events to which everyone can subscribe and which is clearly understood by all. This is the basis on which all effective employee and organisation development, strategies, policies and procedures are then produced (see Chapter 12 below).

Where the converse – i.e. a lack of organisational and managerial support – exists, this must also be made clear. Then, when they do attend events, individuals and groups at least understand that the onus and responsibility rest with themselves to maximise the opportunities, skills, knowledge and expertise provided.

It is also necessary to ensure a basic unity, fairness and equality of approach and opportunity. If the organisation has an open, positive and supportive attitude to training and development, individual managers and supervisors that refuse or make it difficult for staff to attend events, must be brought to book. Conversely, in an unsupportive environment, collective resentment is certain to be generated by those managers and supervisors that do enable their staff to attend events; and this is compounded when it is known, believed or perceived that this ability is based on status or presence and influence at head office.

Process

Individual and collective attendance at off-the-job events needs to be planned and part of a collective, individual and organisation development process. To be fully effective this needs:

- research into the quality and currency of event providers, this includes universities and colleges of further and higher education, as well as consultants and private training centres;
- scheduling of events in harmony with the present state of personal, professional and occupational development of individuals and groups;
- the identification of organisational key and core skills, knowledge and expertise;
- the effective appraisal and training needs analysis approaches (see Chapter 3 above) so that elements can be identified and addressed through planned attendance at events;
- effective monitoring, review and evaluation approaches (see Chapter 8 below) so that a full assessment of the immediate and enduring quality and applicability of particular events are understood;
- where people are sent on events as part of their reward package, or in order to network, the value of the reward or network continues to be assured and have currency.

Costs and benefits

It is necessary to understand the full range of costs and benefits that off-the-job training brings – as summarised in Table 6.1.

Conclusions

To be of enduring benefit, off-the-job training requires scheduling, prioritisation, support and a clear rationale. All this is enhanced, in turn, if it is a part of the organisation's overall product and service strategy. It also helps if the organisation has its own library and other general resources in support.

Organisations in any case, are beginning to be required to accept a much

Table 6.1   Costs and benefits

Costs	Benefits
• Course and event fees	• New skills, knowledge and expertise
• Resources and expenses	• New attitudes and behaviour
• Replacement costs (where required)	• Derived skills, knowledge and expertise
• Opportunity costs (individuals on courses cannot be doing anything else)	• Organisational and collective enhancement
• Overtime	• Motivation and commitment
• Salary and other fixed costs	• Identification of potential and opportunities
• Costs of frustration when what has been learned cannot be put into practice	• Development of potential into capability
	• Development of capability into expertise
• Costs of dysfunction when attendees come back with new attitudes and behaviour as well as skills and knowledge	• Boosts and speeds up development processes
	• Reflection of value
• Strains on those remaining at work	
• Resourcing of process and organisational obligations	

greater share of responsibility for the development of all employees, and this increasingly reinforces the genuine mutuality of interest and commitment that is supposed to exist. Many occupations now have statutory or regulated continuous professional development requirements, and off-the-job training and seminar attendance form a core, and often required, part of this.

Many other occupations have *prime facie* continued professional and occupational development requirements and these can be both complex and wide-ranging. As current examples:

• hairdressing and the use of dyes and chemicals is now much more heavily regulated;
• health and hygiene regulations that all professional chefs following courses of study are required to know and be examined in;
• managers and crew in the airline industry understanding the causes, symptoms and treatment of deep vein thromboses in long-haul passengers.

Off-the-job training normally concentrates on the development of skills, knowledge, expertise and technological capability. However, behaviour and attitudes are reinforced positively or negatively, depending on the quality of the provision, organisational and managerial support, and the ability to practise and enhance at work that which has been taught elsewhere. This may be carried out directly as part of the job, and/or reinforced through further development in project work and secondment.

QUESTIONS

    1 What value, and to whom, would a half-day seminar entitled 'Marketing on the Internet' have?

2 Consider Summary Box 6.4. Why is the one university so much more successful than the other?

3 Itemise the costs and benefits involved in sending a junior member of staff on a two-year HNC programme. What conclusions can you draw?

4 Why are outward-bound and paint-balling events, and the like, attractive to organisations and their staff? What conclusions can you draw? What conditions have to be present to ensure that they are indeed successful in delivery?

5 An employee is given two weeks' study leave before his/her final professional exams. The week before the exams there is a crisis at work. The employee is ordered back to work. The organisation cannot do without him/her. How can this matter be resolved to the satisfaction of all concerned? Should there be any difference in approach if the employee was: a senior manager; a school leaver; a technology trainee?

■ M **7** Projects and secondments

> *'All projects lead to other things. The improved steam engine that James Watt designed and patented in 1776 is the event which for most people signifies the advent of the industrial revolution. Actually, Watt until his death, saw only one use for this steam engine: to pump water out of coal mines. It was his partner, Matthew Boulton, who saw that the improved steam engine could be used in other ways.'*
>
> Peter F. Drucker, *Management Challenges of the 21st Century*, HarperCollins (2000)

Introduction

Projects and secondments are two sides of the same coin. In organisational and employee development project work, individuals or groups are given a specific task to carry out, a task that has a finite time span and a discernible and understood beginning, middle and end. They may carry this out so that it sits within their present occupation and tasks; or they may be seconded away from their current activities to give it their full attention. Secondments may also be applied or given to individuals (much more rarely to groups):

- as part of programmes of planned development and experience;
- as part of professional and occupational training (e.g. police officers may be seconded to CID, forensics, traffic division early in their employment for short periods of time);
- or because an opportunity for development presents itself, and the particular individual is both capable and willing (e.g. a highly capable but inexperienced undergraduate successfully revamped and updated Reckitt & Coleman's entire corporate induction programme on a two-month secondment on his four-month internship).

Context

The context in which successful organisation and employee development project work and secondments take place is as stated elsewhere. It requires institutional resources, commitment, support and backing; a basis in organisational strategy, drive and priority; tangible results; and effective monitoring, review and evaluation. Those on projects and secondments additionally require the following:

- Named, capable and willing points of reference to whom they can turn on specific issues as and when required.
- A named mentor, buddy, guide or support with whom overall progress and specific issues can be discussed in full confidence; and where there is a complete mutuality of respect, value, regard and confidence (see also Chapter 11 below).
- Adequate resources to carry out the work successfully and effectively. Part of most projects and secondments normally involves resources gathering. However, this should never be an excuse for deliberately starving what is supposed to be a positive, productive, profitable and effective venture.
- Organisational openness to results. If the organisation desires or requires a particular result at the outset, this should be made clear, together with reasons; and this also applies to ways of working and the conduct of the project or secondment. In particular, if there are operational, behavioural or political barriers and confines within which people are going to be required to work, then these too must be made clear.
- Evaluation of the real, believed and perceived success/failure of the venture. This must be carried out fully, whether successful or a failure. It must be non-punitive and (except where there is clear evidence of negligence or wilfulness) the basis for learning, development and improvement (see Summary Box 7.1).

SUMMARY BOX 7.1   Attitudes to success and failure

Panasonic, the Japanese electrical goods giant, had just won planning approval to extend and enlarge one of its factory sites in the UK. This followed extensive project and piloting work, and was to lead to the creation of 1400 new jobs. The local Chief Executive was asked the following.

Interviewer:
'So then – you don't make mistakes. You get everything right first time, every time?'

Response:
'Of course we make mistakes. I make them – lots of them – everyday. So does everybody else. The important thing – the reason why we are so successful – is that we acknowledge them and learn from them.'

Sources of project and project work

In organisational and employee development, project work comes from the following:

- Identification of real issues to be researched, evaluated and written up as part of staff members following professional and occupational education schemes and other formal qualifications.
- Sudden vacancies or gaps in skills, knowledge and expertise that lend themselves to the approach. This may only become apparent as the result of evalua-

tion of other aspects of human resource and staff management such as job or work re-evaluation or when a vacancy or gap occurs, or is first recognised.

- Outside demands and influences. These include: changes in market conditions; changes in staff and skills availability; sudden increases in price or loss of ready availability of key resources.
- Feasibility, pilot and pre-feasibility and pre-pilot studies as the result of new product, service or process developments, or when moves into new markets, locations and activities are being considered.
- Laboratory and other 'safe' projects in which ideas and hypotheses are tested and pre-tested in safe conditions using computer simulations and other data to model likely and possible outcomes.
- Feasibility, pre-feasibility and other initial studies when organisations, departments, divisions, functions are contemplating structural or cultural changes, including the use of change agents and consultants, business process re-engineering and total quality management programmes.
- Self-generated by teams, groups or individuals in the pursuit of their own development and enhancement.
- Generated as the result of work improvement groups, quality improvement groups, quality circles.
- The need to prove or disprove some hypothesis.
- The need to illustrate something in detail which is presently only dimly or generally understood.
- The need to solve specific problems which may come from anywhere within the particular organisation and its environment.
- *Ad hoc* and by chance.

Whatever the source, the project will only be successful:

- if the individual or group is capable and willing to carry it out and see it through;
- if the organisation, and its managers and supervisors, are prepared to support it;
- if it is seen as part of a process leading on to further activities.

Demands of project work

The key demands are as follows:

- There must be a real issue to tackle, which is known and understood to be of value.
- The matter must be of current or potential concern, and not obsolete by the time it is delivered.
- There must be a real structure for the work, including precise terms of reference, brief or remit. This, above all, means a set timescale and agreed ways of working, often with a series of 'dates by which' being inserted into the process (see Summary Box 7.2).

- **Title:** Mass Customisation in the Clothing Industry.
- **Duration:** six months.
- **Terms of reference:** 'The purpose of this project is to investigate and illustrate the feasibility of customising mass produced casual clothes using the internet as the medium'.
- **Methodology:** book and desk research; customer survey; selection of organisation case studies.
- **Limitations:** time factors; had to be fitted in with other work.
- **Data search:** identification of case studies; including write-up (six weeks).
- **Determination of further investigations:** including pilot investigation, evaluation, analysis and lessons (by end of month three).
- **Determination of final organisation:** as substantial case study (allow one month; to be completed by end of month four).
- **Draft write-up:** by end of month five.
- **Final write-up and presentation:** by end of month six.
- **Other matters:** agree brief, schedule and meetings with supervisor; arrange regular contacts with supervisor (at least once every two weeks); making formal feedback and support arrangements; further and double checks by institution and individual.

Source: Costas Pringipas, 'Mass Customisation in the Clothing Industry', UCL (2001).

- The work must be rigorously structured and fully investigated within the time, environment and resource constraints present. This inevitably means that it is not possible to carry out a full investigation of all sources or full survey of the particular field of inquiry. Those who commission project work need to understand this.
- Timescales must be realistic so that what is to be done can be done adequately and effectively.
- A methodology or way of working – what is to be done, when, why and how – must be agreed, and this includes timescales, boundaries and limitations. It is unfortunate that the use of the term 'methodology' tends to complicate a part of project and research work that is self-evidently required, and which is, in fact, completely straightforward.
- The ways of working sometimes need modifying as the result of pilot or initial investigations, and these should then be agreed along the lines of: 'What *else* is to be done, when, why and how?' Again, this requires agreement, acceptance and resourcing.
- A presentation format needs to be agreed. It is usual to present project work in writing. In many cases also, an oral presentation is required both with work carried out as part of a college course, and also in-house projects (see Summary Box 7.3).

Written

The structure should reflect the work that has been done. Written presentations should always include: terms of reference or project brief or purpose; how, when and why the work was carried out (the methodology); an analysis and evaluation of the findings; conclusions; recommendations if these are required.

Some projects, especially those associated with college courses, require a certain word limit. This should reflect the size and scale of the investigation and should never be an excuse for padding or waffle.

Conclusions and recommendations (if appropriate or required) should follow directly from the main body of work. If there is a required end result, then work carried out should support this. If, as the result of the work, the desired end result is not possible, then this too should be made clear. If the project commissioner then wants to go ahead anyway, they at least know the pitfalls and limitations.

The project should always be fully written up, even if the commissioner only requires a short or executive summary, or recommendations. That way, if support for a point of view is ever required in the future, it is readily available.

Oral

Oral presentation of projects should always be kept short unless there is a minimum time requirement. It is always possible to convey the essence of a project through:

- handing out a short, written summary prior to the presentation;
- sticking to a formal presentation of no more than 10–15 minutes, and concentrating on the key stages of the work, and main findings, conclusions and recommendations;
- knowing and understanding the material in full so that when the audience comes back with questions these can be answered fully;
- having full details available in writing in case anyone wants them (the project commissioner usually will).

Oral presentations should never be used to tackle minute, statistical or organisational information unless this is specifically requested.

- Serious flaws and imperfections in the work must be acknowledged and brought to the attention of the project commissioner. This is normally perfectly acceptable, and in many cases, more or less certain to occur because of time and resource constraints. Clearly therefore, the work is not going to be perfect and all that is necessary is that this is recognised. If then things do go wrong in the future, there are points of further investigation immediately apparent.
- Projects and secondments lead to other things. It is often very difficult personally, professionally and occupationally for individuals and groups to return to their previous status quo after involvement in pioneering

organisational and employee development work. Moreover, if they have been away for a long time (e.g. a period of months) the status quo will itself have changed and those concerned will effectively be returning to a new environment.

- It is not possible for organisations to ignore or un-learn what has been learned. Knowledge, understanding and evidence that something needs attention or is/is not going to work cannot rationally be discounted or ignored (see Summary Box 7.4).

SUMMARY BOX 7.4   'Care in the Community'

'Care in the Community' was a major social services initiative designed to remove vulnerable, disturbed and at-risk members of society from public institutions and have them professionally cared for in their homes where possible, and in smaller units otherwise.

The pilot project for this was undertaken by Kent County Council in the mid 1980s. The issue, environment and scale of undertaking were extensively researched, fully evaluated and written up. The conclusions were:

- the proposed venture was socially desirable;
- it would enhance the quality of life of vulnerable people;
- it would cost more than the present provision because of the need to recruit extra expert staff.

The report was duly presented to the Social Services Secretary.

The response of the Secretary of State was brief. The answers produced by the project were wrong. In denial of the evidence, the Social Services Secretary stated that:

- care in the community would be cheaper than the present provision;
- the property base of the big institutions in which people had hitherto been housed would be sold off (despite the then property slump);
- the government was, in any case, going ahead (which it did).

Subsequently, everything that the Kent County Council pilot project showed came to pass. The programme quickly became a byword for a lack of care for vulnerable and at-risk members of society and, in many cases, this was reinforced by the knowledge and perception that some people who were a danger, both to themselves and others, were at large and largely unsupervised in the community.

Other approaches to projects and secondments

Action learning

A key approach to the management of project work in organisation and employee development was the work of Reg Revens (see Summary Box 6.1). The benefits include the following:

- A bias for action and not a procedure, and a drive for tangible and useful results, rather than 'more work needs to be done'. This is reinforced by the fact that set members are responsible for implementing their own proposals. Organisations involved in action learning also expect progress, development, enhancement and change rather than endless procedural meetings.
- The ability to use involvement in action learning as a catalyst for further change and development elsewhere in the organisation. Project work always has implications and spin-offs for functions related to the area in which it is conducted. Secondments (whether to action learning or anything else) always result at least in current issues being seen through fresh pairs of eyes.
- It helps to concentrate on primary purposes rather than support functions. Even where process or administrative streamlining is the particular action learning remit, concentration is on serving the organisation better as a whole (see Summary Box 7.5).

SUMMARY BOX 7.5   Action learning and recommendations

The key lesson for everyone concerned with project work is to note the structure required of those making recommendations in action learning programmes or sets. The approach taken is:

- **Recommendations for what:** the identification of a priority order for what now needs to happen, when, where and why.
- **Recommendations to whom:** identifying those responsible for authorising, implementing and evaluating what is to be carried out.
- **Costs:** as precise and detailed a statement of costs and charges that are to be incurred, and the benefits that are to accrue as the result of making this expenditure.
- **Time:** specific dates by which each of the recommendations has to be implemented.

This draws a sharp contrast with 'recommendations' produced in many other situations. These are invariably written in language based on 'should', 'could' or 'might' – and these effectively amount to little more than a general statement of intent. The action learning approach requires acceptance and action.

Back to the floor

'Back to the floor' is the title of a television series in which senior and other non-frontline managers return to the cutting edge of their organisation's activities. In the series, these secondments were for one week, but other periods are clearly possible and in many cases, suitable. The benefits of the approach are:

- to restore to senior managers a real understanding of what it is actually like to work in the particular frontline and to (in many cases) re-learn the pressures, constraints, opportunities and consequences inherent in these activities;
- to identify and understand the actual nature of staff, supplier, customer and client demands, needs and wants;

- to note shortfalls and take steps to improve product and service delivery;
- to note shortfalls and take steps to improve the working environment and quality of working life (see Summary Box 7.6).

SUMMARY BOX 7.6   Back to the floor: Sandals

Sandals is a luxury holiday package tour operator. It prides itself on the quality of all of its facilities. Its flagship activity is the provision of a full wedding service for couples wishing to get married in exotic and luxurious locations.

Stephen Garley, the Chief Executive of Sandals, was filmed going *Back to the floor* for one week at the company's luxury resort on the West Indies island of Antigua. During his secondment, he carried out all of the frontline functions required of a wedding assistant. He then returned to his senior management team and reported back. Among the improvements required and made were:

- scheduling of weddings for the convenience of the happy couple (the customers) rather than caterers, the registrar and photographers;
- ensuring that the wedding champagne remained cold and the wedding canapés fresh;
- extending the range of bridal and bridegroom wear to cater for all shapes and sizes;
- providing a more secluded area for weddings to take place;
- providing proper computer links for those working at the resort so that they could be in constant touch with colleagues in other locations and with head office;
- providing iced water for all brides and bridegrooms and their guests;
- providing umbrellas in case of sudden showers of rain (a locational hazard);
- in-building delays caused by thunderstorms (another locational hazard) into the total offering.

This was further reinforced by a commitment to ensure that all senior managers spent at least one week in the frontline upon appointment. Everything was driven by the commitment to the quality of the service provided to customers and clients. Summing up, Mr Garley stated that, while no lasting damage had been done to the product and service on offer before his return to the frontline, it was apparent that there were the beginnings of complacency.

Source: *'Back to the Floor'*, BBC Television (2000).

More generally, a lot of firsthand knowledge, understanding and experience are gained very quickly. As it is firsthand, there is no denying or diluting the experience. If senior managers and others with real influence are placed in the position, then they have the power and authority to propose and implement substantial change very quickly when they return from the frontline.

Frontline organisation development

Frontline organisation development occurs where production and service staff are given the responsibility and the task of identifying, ordering and proposing changes in their own domain. These are then reported back to the organisation and its senior managers. The process involves requiring individuals or groups to analyse and evaluate every aspect of their part of the working environment and making specific proposals for improvement. Carried out effectively, it develops skills, knowledge and understanding in all those involved, as well as reinforcing collective attitudes and values. The benefits are:

- the requirement to crystallise issues into genuine improvements and advances rather than making general gripes and moans;
- the requirement to look anew at the particular working environment and to establish reasons why things work (or fail) as they do;
- the requirement to structure, order, prioritise and cost proposals;
- the requirement to structure and order presentations to senior and functional managers in order to gain their support.

In all this, there is inherently willingness and commitment of the frontline staff to their own domain and to the organisation as a whole. So long as there is full organisational support and a fundamental willingness either to accept and implement proposals, or to explain clearly and unambiguously why they cannot be implemented, the approach is a major contribution to organisation and staff development (see Summary Box 7.7).

SUMMARY BOX 7.7   Sid's Heroes: Stena Cross-Channel Ferries

Sid Joynson, the Management Consultant, developed organisations from the frontline. Staff were seconded away from their jobs for short periods of time and in groups. They then attacked every aspect of the frontline product, service and customer provision from their own point of view, before producing a presentation to organisation senior management.

One of these seminars was filmed by BBC television on board the Dover to Calais cross-channel ferry *Stena Invicta*. With the full support of the company, he indicated what the group (all catering, customer service and sailing crew) were supposed to do, and how to approach customers and clients.

The secondment was short, for a period of two days only. At the end of the period, the group devised and structured a presentation to the company senior management. The proposals made included:

- attention to the absolute basics, including putting up more signs and arrows directing the ship's passengers to particular facilities;
- handling customer complaints and proposing a range of remedies to be applied at the crew's discretion rather than following reference to more senior management;
- establishment of real, rather than perceived, customer views including complaints by going out and asking them their opinions about food, bar, restaurant and other facilities;
- asking for regular visits by company senior managers to the ships to see the issues for themselves;
- addressing complaints and grievances about working patterns.

The proposals were structured into a presentation. Everything was fully costed and benefits demonstrated. The report was accepted in general by the company. However, it foundered on the implementation of specific actions. There existed a prevailing divided company culture between the senior management based on-shore, and operations based on the ships. Consequently, nothing was ever fully supported or implemented in practice. The company subsequently failed and in 1998 was merged with P&O, the largest operator on the route.

Source: 'Sid's Heroes: Stena Cross-Channel Ferries', BBC Television (1996).

Brainstorming groups

These occur where people are pulled away from their jobs for short periods of time (no more than a week, and sometimes other pressures dictate that this must be carried over a weekend or away from the normal work pattern) to give undivided attention and maximum energy and priority to something that has suddenly become an issue or which now needs resolving.

Initially, brainstorming activities are carried out in familiar ways and the results evaluated. When final proposals are arrived at however, they are then immediately implemented rather than merely being presented to others for them to take up. This has the benefits of:

- requiring the job to be completed by the end of the short prescribed period;
- total undivided attention and support of all those involved;
- maintaining the creative brainstorming burst of energy beyond proposals and recommendations and through to implementation;
- the avoidance of institutionalisation of the issues. Even if the answers, products or services produced are not perfect there is at least a tangible, useful and valuable result and demonstrable progress (see Summary Box 7.8).

SUMMARY BOX 7.8   The Institute of Management open management programme

The first Institute of Management open management programme was devised by management teaching staff at Mid Kent College over one long weekend in 1990. The group produced everything – syllabus structure, outline, substance, delivery modes, workbooks, support materials, and required library and other resources.

The process was started on the Thursday evening, and the final result, consisting of a structure, rational and ten workbooks, was delivered to the Institute of Management on the following Monday evening, typed, printed, bound and in a uniform format.

This initiative was a major project and development, and arose as the result of a short group secondment. It took the college into new fields and markets, and staff into new areas of expertise, and fresh ways of developing their existing expertise.

The initiative fell down because there was no full institutional support from the college. The project and secondment leader left the group shortly afterwards. It subsequently became expected that staff would solve trivial and operational problems in this way in their own time.

Self-interest and self-starting

Projects based on self-interest normally come about because the organisation cannot, or will not, support them. Everything then descends upon the individuals concerned (these are very rarely group ventures) who have then to commit their own resources, energy and time to ensure that the particular issue is brought to fruition. The great benefit of this is that nothing is going to get done unless the individual is totally committed. However, problems always arise when:

- individuals come up with something of real value off their own back, and the organisation then takes (or tries to take) the result;
- individuals are not adequately rewarded, compensated or recognised for their efforts or someone else steals the credit;
- individuals try to commercialise or further develop their work away from the organisation, leading to friction, conflict of interest, professional, occupational and personality clashes.

While recognising that no organisation can, or should be, responsible for allowing individuals to pursue every idea that occurs to them, it is important that a certain amount of latitude and flexibility are present so that ideas can be evaluated on their own merits, and so that they can be supported where it is accepted that there are genuine prospects of development, advancement and success. More generally, this also reinforces the need to attend to the requirement for personal as well as professional, occupational and organisation development.

Costs and benefits

The costs and benefits of projects and secondments are summarised in Table 7.1.

Conclusions

Overtly, project work and secondments concentrate heavily on the development of skills, knowledge and expertise; and this may be further reinforced where there is a technological element or where it is concerned with the implementation of new technology and associated working practices.

Table 7.1   Costs and benefits

Costs	Benefits
• Fixed – giving staff time over to this work; supervising it • Variable – essential additional resources (often minimal)	• Collective and individual confidence, identity, commitment and loyalty • Product and service development • New opportunities become apparent • Enhanced capability and expertise • Enhanced and positive individual and collective attitudes

There are also extremely valuable spin-offs in the development of behaviour and attitudes. It is impossible for new and pioneering work, and reappraising existing and overtly well known situations, not to influence behaviour; and this is much greater when the outcome of the project or secondment is new technology, new approaches or a change of job and work priorities. Also, any organisation that supports and underpins this sort of institutional and employee development is certain to create and enhance general attitudes of flexibility, dynamism, responsiveness and an overall positive, creative and willing approach to anything that may have to be faced. All this is then compounded where organisations and their senior managers implement the results and recommendations of project work and secondments, and give credit in public where it is due.

It is finally essential to recognise that no project or secondment is ever an end in itself. The work is certain to open up new ideas, product and service possibilities for organisations, groups and individuals. Where such work may lead, and where it is required to lead, must always be a concern of monitoring, review and evaluation processes.

QUESTIONS

1 Produce a project brief for a junior manager required to research and establish the feasibility of a website update for your organisation. Which parts can be prescribed and which parts have to be left more open, and why?

2 An 18-year old is about to start her first job in the headquarters of a large organisation. She is to have four secondments of three months each in the first two years of employment, in marketing, human resources, finance and office services. What should she be getting out of each and why? How would you ensure that this did occur?

3 How should action learning and *Back to the floor* be integrated into management and organisation development programmes?

4 What advice would you give to a junior member of staff having to make a presentation to senior management for the first time?

5 You work for a company that produces high-value, branded, bottled water. There is a pollution scare at the bottling plant. A project approach to address and resolve the issue is decided upon. Which approach would you recommend and why? How long would you need to identify, tackle and resolve any issues brought to light?

■ ⊻ 8 Monitoring, review and evaluation

'We asked ourselves what we did wrong and we couldn't think of anything.'
The Lockheed senior management team, after a string of commercial failures brought the company to the brink of bankruptcy, 1982

Introduction

In common with all organisational activities, training and development must be subject to rigorous scrutiny, monitoring, review and evaluation. Whatever the training and development taking place, and whether group or individual, organisations and their senior managers need to know the following:

- Whatever is being commissioned, supported, provided and resourced is successful in whatever terms that is measured.
- Where there are the shortfalls and concerns, these are raised and evaluated with the trainee, their superior and the training provider (if any).
- Where organisation and employee development approaches to problems and issues are proposed, successful and effective processes and outcomes are achieved.
- Where new programmes, ventures and initiatives are being developed, these are reviewed and evaluated for initial success, positive results and teething troubles, as well as into the longer-term future. Where longer-term existing and familiar programmes continue to operate, these continue to be reviewed and evaluated for currency and continued effectiveness.
- Where something is no longer doing its job effectively, it is dropped or replaced.
- Where qualified technical and professional staff are being employed, the organisation continues to meet its statutory and moral obligations to them in terms of continuous professional and occupational development and also ensures that it benefits from this.

Basis

The basis for the effective monitoring, review and evaluation of all organisational and employee development activities is to establish what is being addressed, by whom, when, where and why.

What

All programmes, activities and events should be assessed for quality, effectiveness and durability; and quantity if appropriate (e.g. how many staff attended a particular course; how many are currently on different forms of development). All programmes should also be addressed against the following:

- **Need:** whether the need identified was met; if so, why?; if not, why not?; other benefits and drawbacks that accrued, with reasons.
- **Timescale:** whether what was required was delivered when required; if so, was this appropriate in fact?; if not, why not?; any consequences of this and what must now happen; the effect of this on other activities both operational and developmental.
- **Beneficiaries:** the extent to which those on the event benefited, with reasons; derived beneficiaries and reasons (e.g. the organisation, department, division, function, customers, suppliers); who else might benefit from attending or participating in future such events, with reasons.
- **Content:** currency and appropriateness of content; pace, emphasis and priority in attention to content; relevance, usefulness and value of content; relationship between content, workplace application, and professional and occupational enhancement and development.
- **Delivery:** quality, value and expertise of trainer/facilitator/supervisor/mentor in their field and in delivering the particular event; substance and presentation balance; immediate and enduring value.
- **Aims and objectives:** what were they?; were they appropriate?; were these met?; if so, why?; if not, why not?; was it possible to meet them?; if so, why?; if not, why not?; was it valuable anyway?; if so, why?; if not, why not?; if attending an event put on by outsiders, e.g. residential or college course, were the aims and objectives set by the provider compatible with the requirements of the attendee and the organisation?; if so, how and why?; if not, why not?

These matters should then each be addressed by a variety of people in different sets of circumstances.

Who

Everyone involved should ideally take an active, individual and collective part in monitoring, reviewing and evaluating all training and development activities as follows:

- **Trainee:** against the aims and objectives of the event; capability before and after; against their own required and desired aims and objectives; for quality, value and currency of content; for contextual factors (see Summary Box 8.1).

  Trainees are also likely to reflect on events some time after their completion to understand and evaluate the extent to which what they learn has been put into practice, any discrepancy between what they learned and how it is now being applied, and what further opportunities and requirements are now apparent. Trainees are also certain to form a general view of the extent to which it was beneficial or not, and whether it has had the additional benefit of providing real or perceived achievements; personal, professional, occupational added value; and increased general employability.

- **The trainees' manager:** against the aims and objectives of the event, whether these were met, and if so, why; and if not, why not. Trainees' managers also need to be able to assess the relative contribution of each activity to all employee and organisation development. They need to be aware of what trainees were expected to get out of the event, as well as general and derived benefits to the department. It is also essential to be able to assess trainee attitudes, behaviour and performance before and after the event. Questions of value for money, value for opportunity costs and other resource usage have also to be addressed. Managers and supervisors of trainees attending events should also be considering these effects during performance appraisal; and considering the broad range of benefits of the particular event. They need to be looking for attitude and behaviour development as well as pure performance; and they need to be looking at what potential is becoming apparent as the result of sending or placing staff on particular events. Above all, they need to be assessing increases in enhancement, development, quality and consistency of performance, and the development of positive attitudes, values and commitment.
- **The managers' manager:** against the aims and objectives of the event; its relationship and contribution to all employee and organisation development; costs and charges, value accrued and other benefits; the specific contribution to functional development and effectiveness. More senior managers are required to take a broader view of strategic employee and organisation development so that they have a full understanding of what they envisage

when they feed training and development plans into strategic planning; and so that they have a clear understanding of what they are going to get as the result of sending people on particular events. More senior managers should be looking for overall increases in collective as well as individual effectiveness of performance, attitudes and behaviour and relating these to the training and development effort. They need to understand the relationship between employee and organisation development and changes in behaviour and performance in their own domain.

- **Trainers, event leaders and facilitators:** this is the output of their professional practice and therefore the subject of continuous reflection and evaluation. This is required from the following points of view.
  - **Their own:** the extent to which they have faith in their material, subject or expertise, and the ways in which they deliver this; constraints placed by trainees and their managers and client organisations; harmonising their own aims and objectives, and priorities, with those of their trainees; constantly reviewing for currency of material and delivery; recognising and developing preferred learning styles. Both during, and also at the end of, each event in which they are involved, they need constant and substantial feedback as part of the development of the provision. At the end of each event, there should always be a brief formal evaluation. This should either be a structured open discussion with attendees or a structured feedback sheet that concentrates on aims and objectives, quality of substance, delivery and material, the learning environment, and domestic issues (see Summary Box 8.2).

SUMMARY BOX 8.2   Happy sheets

Happy sheets are superficial and insubstantial ways of reviewing learning events. They come in the following forms:

- Concentration on quality of the training environment where this is good.
- Concentration on output rather than content where this is what is required (e.g. for courses where there is an exam at the end, waiting until the results are known before evaluating).
- Skewing the feedback sheet to cast the best possible light on the event.
- Concentrating on any other real or perceived strength of the event at the expense of the total (e.g. location, where this is understood or believed to be desirable; mix of exercises and materials rather than substance; over-structuring questionnaires so that broad comments and concerns cannot be addressed).

The training manager at an oil company always received consistently excellent feedback. He explained this as follows. 'I always run my courses in Paris at four-star hotels. On the last night of every course, we provide a slap-up meal and a free bar. The following morning we start early. We always give trainees something practical that looks substantial, and is demonstrably achievable by all. Then we have a buffet brunch at twelve, after which I get them to evaluate me. It never fails.'

At the core of this review should be: the quality and currency of materials; external pressures and how these were accommodated (e.g. syllabus constraints); mix and cohesion of groups (if this applies); individual and collective motivation and morale; and the space and capability to accommodate 'alsos' (see Summary Box 8.3).

SUMMARY BOX 8.3   'Alsos'

'Alsos' apply mostly to off-the-job training courses, projects and secondments. Those undertaking these events as trainees often have things that they would **also** like to get out of them. For example:

- 'My secondment to marketing is not just to broaden my knowledge and understanding but also because I would like to get into marketing.'
- 'I am attending professional studies to get the qualification and also to get a better job at a bigger firm.'
- 'I am attending this residential weekend on IR skills, and could you (the tutor) also have a look at my project draft.'

and more insidiously:

- 'I am attending this class in Paris/Hong Kong/Wolverhampton because of the opportunities of sightseeing/social/other activities.'

The trainer or event organiser will arrive at a wholesome, consistent and acceptable view of which 'alsos' they are prepared to accommodate, and which to refuse.

- **The trainees':** however good or strong the quality of the event in the professional opinion of the trainer, this is diluted when, for whatever reason:
  - the group does not gel or mix effectively;
  - the right material is delivered in the wrong way or context;
  - there is no discernible cohesion or progression in the eyes of the trainees;
  - there are personal, professional or occupational clashes;
  - the event comes to be dominated by one or two powerful or influential personalities;
  - there are problems with the learning environment (e.g. noise, heat/cold, quality of food and facilities.

    Much of this may be largely outside the control of the trainer. However, when they do occur, they need full review and evaluation so that approaches to dealing with them in the future can be drawn up (see Summary Box 8.4).

When

Each of the parties indicated above needs to be aware of when they should monitor, review and evaluate. It is usual to indicate the following:

- In advance, to assess the likely outcome and results of particular events.
- Immediately at the end of events to reflect on the quality, substance, context, delivery and relevance while everything is still fresh in everyone's mind (the good and the bad).
- After a period of time of between 1 and 3 months so that a broader and more considered evaluation is achieved and so that long-term effects are beginning to become apparent.
- At the next performance review or appraisal so that the specific event is seen in the broader context of the total development of employees.
- If it is being applied, regular evaluation of what has been learned is likely to come up in the course of daily routines.

This can all be fed into organisation and employee development strategic reviews, and should include the informed opinions of everyone involved.

Where, how and why

The ideal is an open and positive exchange of views between all concerned. This is then summarised in writing and agreed by those involved.

This sounds onerous and bureaucratic. It need not be. It simply ensures that the key points are retained for future reference. It enables any misperceptions and misunderstandings between what was required or anticipated, and what was actually delivered, to be recognised and addressed. It enables the balance of interest – personal, professional, occupational and organisational – to be assessed and maintained, and where necessary, put right. It enables the question of standards and intensity to be assessed by all concerned – whether the content was too easy, too hard, too intense or too superficial for particular attendees (see Summary Box 8.5).

SUMMARY BOX 8.5   Standards and intensity

This approach is more straightforward for some events than others. It is relatively easy to review both in-house and off-site courses in this way.

It still needs to be considered for such things as computer-based training, projects and secondments. For example:

- things that go wrong with computer-based training and other virtual packages overwhelmingly include technological glitches and superficial responses as people work their way through them;
- things that go wrong with projects and secondments include overwhelmingly a lack of substance, purpose or direction. This especially applies to secondments. Their effectiveness and value are often damaged or destroyed through a lack of substance in the programme supporting it. This leads to frustration on the part of the trainee and to stress in the department where the secondment is taking place.

This also enables any serious problems and issues to be brought out into the open. Where the trainer has patently not delivered what was promised or indicated there must be further detailed investigation to establish the reasons for this. Where the trainee has either not attended, not attended fully or not participated, this too must be fully investigated.

It is important to recognise that where bad or inadequate performance is proven or strongly indicated, this may lead to disciplinary action. Where external training providers are involved, this may lead to litigation to recover course fees under trades' description legislation. Where an employee is concerned, not to be seen to follow this up may lead to others following suit, and a dilution of the overall employee development effort. Where an outside training organisation is concerned, in practice the word soon gets around that, for whatever reason, it is currently 'off the boil'.

This also enables a broader view to be taken. However good the training and development might be, there may be no discernible improvement in organisation, departmental, divisional or functional performance or culture. Or it may be that once employees have followed a particular programme or project, they leave because what they can now do is more highly valued or gives better opportunities elsewhere. This can then be reviewed from both a strategic and operational point of view. Either remedial action can then be taken, or at least the organisation understands that it can normally only hold on to particular employees for a certain length of time, and it can then concentrate on getting more out of them over this limited period.

Other factors

Pre-evaluation

This is implicit, if not always stated, in matching or reconciling what is on offer with what is required. Some trainers formalise this by carrying out pre-testing and pre-evaluation tests and questionnaires in order to:

- have a better idea and understanding of the current capabilities of those coming to them;
- help assess whether or not the standard of material is going to be suitable for the proposed trainee;
- help build a foundation of background knowledge so that delivery and exercises can be more tailored to suit where this is appropriate.

More generally, some employers send summaries of pre-identified needs, and also job and work descriptions, to reinforce this. This clearly works best when it is related to rigorous, organisation-based, training needs assessments and performance appraisals.

This process can also be extended to request that employees carry out, and bring with them, some sort of pre-preparation or pre-event exercise. This is clearly only going to be fully effective if either there is some format for accepting or rejecting the attendee on the basis of the pre-preparation, or if it is to be used more generally as pre-evaluation by the event leader to tailor the context according to the quality of pre-preparation overall (see Summary Box 8.6).

SUMMARY BOX 8.6   Pre-preparation

Extensive pre-preparation is only feasible when what is to be delivered is known, believed or perceived to be of high added value. Whatever is done must also be of direct benefit to the event and its attendees, and to be seen as such – either fully integrated with the event's substance, or else that the event is conducted on the basis that the pre-preparation has been done by everybody. Asking people to carry out extensive work which is then ignored simply ensures that everyone gets off on the wrong footing. On the other hand, high-quality, relevant pre-preparation raises expectations and gives a tangible basis for full review and evaluation before, during and after the event.

Post-testing

This is carried out at appropriate, prescribed and predetermined times after the event. In general, the purpose is to assess how far the trainee's behaviour, attitudes, skills, knowledge, expertise and technological competence have moved during the event and, by implication, as the result of it.

It may also be demanded on a formal or informal basis. The formal is where there is an examination or assignment at the end of the programme or event, or where what has been learned is now to be put into practice. The informal is where there is some clearly understood end piece (e.g. an oral presentation to senior management) but which does not carry any formality.

This is clearly a useful and valuable part of monitoring, review and evaluation. It also imposes certain disciplines. If an examination or test is to be taken, then a part of delivery has to be concerned with examination or test techniques, because that is what attendees will expect. Where the primary purpose of attending is to pass a test or exam, it must be recognised that everything else is secondary in the eyes of attendees. Further, the event will receive favourable or unfavourable responses based on passing or failing whatever the intrinsic or substantive qualities of the event or leader may have been.

Producing reports

Some organisations ask trainers on external courses, and those supervising project work and secondments, to produce formal reports on the particular trainees (the reverse also sometimes applies). On longer and more substantial events, they may also ask for interim reports. This is most effective where the whole process is open and transparent and when the trainee has a clear indication of how well they are doing and what is to be said about them. It is important to be clear on what is being reported and why.

This is clearly diluted when the process is closed or where it is known, believed or perceived to be used for other reasons (see Summary Box 8.7).

SUMMARY BOX 8.7   Reporting back

For 15 years, a merchant bank had been sending its junior management staff to an outward-bound centre in the west country. The staff members had all been identified as potential high fliers by the bank.

The centre held (and holds) an excellent reputation in this form of management development and its clients come from industry, commerce and public services.

The merchant bank staff were always sent in groups of six. They were put through a week-long intensive programme of skills development that identified and brought out leadership qualities, tenacity, courage, creativity and endurance. The centre then reported back on each to the bank.

This long-term and overtly mutually beneficial relationship came to a sudden end. A trainee on whom the centre had reported favourably was given immediate promotion upon his return; and then three months later was arrested and charged with fraud (and subsequently convicted).

The bank wrote to the centre cancelling all future work. In its letter it stated that: 'Any centre such as yours that can recommend such an individual for a senior position is clearly not competent at anything.'

The centre replied that it had never recommended anyone for anything. It always only ever commented on the performance of individuals on its courses.

Costs and benefits

The costs and benefits of effective monitoring, review and evaluation are summarised in Table 8.1.

It is clear from this that the main requirement is an attitude shift rather than expenditure of fresh resources. Once monitoring, review and evaluation are given priority, and that this is acceptable to all, the actual cost is very small.

Conclusions

This part of the employee and organisation development process is as important as any other. Yet it is the part that is most frequently ignored or under-valued. To

Table 8.1   Costs and benefits

Costs	Benefits
• Work involved in devising and implementing acceptable formats and procedures • Opportunity costs • Staff time (fixed costs) • Development of perceptions and reality of understanding value and contribution of effective monitoring, review and evaluation • Administrative costs (again, likely to be fixed rather than variable)	• Understanding where, why and how effective development has taken place • Understanding where, why and how things have gone wrong • Providing information to be used as a basis for effective remedial action

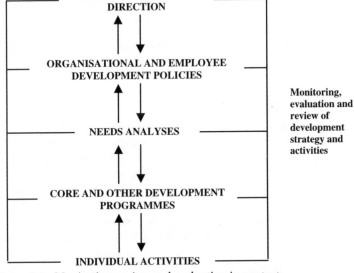

Figure 8.1   Monitoring, review and evaluation in context

make it effective requires the ability to think in the ways indicated, and this can be achieved and implemented at very little cost.

Organisations need to know why and how collective behaviour, attitudes, skills, knowledge and expertise are being developed, the extent to which they are contributing to effective and profitable performance, and where gaps and shortfalls are occurring. Monitoring, review and evaluation is therefore part of the total process and needs to be engaged at each stage as follows (see Figure 8.1).

It is important to be able to relate the 'narrow contribution' of each activity to the whole range of organisation and employee development being undertaken and to be able to understand and evaluate the full impact and contribution made to total profitability and effectiveness.

Organisations also need to be able to assess the effectiveness of specific activities. At present, this especially refers to management development, and specific expertise and technological skills and aptitude. In the case of management development, the contribution of particular events and activities to overall effectiveness needs to be evaluated in terms of functional drives, priorities and achievements as well as collective attitudes, values and behaviour. Developing specific expertise concentrates on skills and technological proficiency; and again, it is only possible to know just how effective or otherwise this is if it is rigorously assessed.

Effective procedures and mechanisms for strategic and operational monitoring, review and evaluation are essential in organisational development and change programmes. They must always be present in bespoke, off-the-shelf and consultant-led business process re-engineering, total quality management and empowerment programmes, so that everyone knows how much progress is being made, why and where the shortfalls and problem areas are.

Finally, all training and development programmes, activities and events must have in-built their own assessment processes. No event or programme is ever fully effective, nor is its design complete, unless these are present.

QUESTIONS

1 How would you evaluate an MBA programme for success/failure from the following points of view:
- the student?
- the university?
- the sponsoring organisation?

2 What measures should be used to monitor the effectiveness of a core organisation programme such as a fire drill or induction programme?

3 Identify and cost out the factors involved in getting everyone in an organisation to monitor, review and evaluate all in-house employee development activities.

4 You have been seconded to your Chief Executive's department. What costs and benefits are involved? How should this secondment be measured for success/failure? When, where, and by whom?

5 Consider Summary Box 8.7. On the basis of what you are told – what went wrong and why? How could this have been avoided?

■ ⋎ 9 Designing training programmes

'If you want $10 million for new plant, provided the figures stack up, it is yours for the asking. If you want $250,000 for training, people look at you as if you are mad'.

Tom Peters, '*The World Turned Upside Down*', Channel 4 (1986)

Introduction

All training and development programmes and events should be based on needs and wants, analyses and appraisal, and the ability to respond to demands, and to fill the gaps identified with these activities. The variety of means and methods available is applied using understanding of preferred learning styles, together with opportunities available at work and on-the-job, and also off-the-job and away from the organisation.

This is the broad context in which organisational, professional, occupational, group and individual training programmes are put together effectively. In this context, programmes consist of:

- delivering the core and key programmes and demands (see Chapter 3 above);
- responding to specific behavioural, attitudinal, skill, knowledge, expertise and technological demands, wants and needs;
- responding to general demands, wants and needs;
- responding to other issues such as continuous professional and occupational development;
- responding to the needs, wants and demands of sponsors of training and development activities;
- attention to specific issues, for example those arising because of job enrichment or enlargement; the introduction of flexible working practices; those requiring training as a result of a poor performance review.

All programmes require specific aims and objectives, learning and development outcomes, and a means of monitoring, review and evaluation.

Aims and objectives

These need to be quite specific. Generalities should be written as a preamble, introduction or notes elsewhere on the programme. Aims and objectives should be precise and clear (see Summary Box 9.1).

It is usual to write these as follows:

'The purpose of this programme is to . . .', followed by specific objectives, outcomes and outline coverage. It is usual also to give an 'attendee summary' – this is sometimes written as: 'Who should attend'. People are then in as little doubt as possible. For example, the aims and objectives for an in-house emergency procedures programme might look like this:

In-house emergency procedures and fire drill

The purpose of this programme is to ensure that everybody knows what to do in the case of an emergency, and the fire alarm sounding.

Attendees will learn what to do in the case of an emergency and how to leave the building.

By the end of the programme, attendees will be able to:

- find the quickest way out of the building from wherever they happen to be when the alarm sounds;
- reach the assembly point;
- understand what to shut down, and why, before leaving.

Who should attend

- Anyone who has not been on this event before.
- All new starters.
- Anyone who is unsure of the procedures or any part of them.

Outline coverage

- Statutory duties.
- Access to emergency exits.
- Location of assembly point.

This is short, simple and direct, and clearly indicates the coverage and target population. It is an essential discipline for those designing training events because it requires them to think in precise terms about what they are doing, why and for whom. It also enables trainees, and potential attendees, to assess what they are going to get out of such an event should they attend it. Monitoring, review and evaluation also starts most effectively with precise aims and objectives, and outcomes.

They should also reflect what is being offered, why and to whom, so that everyone is clear at the outset. It gives everyone a clearly understood point of reference for subsequent review and evaluation. If aims and objectives are written in precise terms, then success and failure, and the reasons for this, become much easier to assess. This precision is required regardless of the target audience, or whether what is being designed is a single and simple event (as in Summary Box 9.1 above), or an extended programme covering many events, or a syllabus taught college or university programme.

Process consultation

Process consultation needs to involve the following:

- Sponsors of particular training events: they are, after all, paying for what is to happen. They therefore have a legitimate interest in what is to be delivered, how, when, where and why, and the precise outcomes intended (see Summary Box 9.2).

SUMMARY BOX 9.2   Sponsors' responsibilities

There is a commercial and public service advantage in having highly trained staff. Those who sponsor training and development need to understand, however, that these activities are only of value if the learning can subsequently be put into practice, and that other rewards are forthcoming. Training and development without opportunities to put into practice what has been learned quickly lead to frustration. Good staff then leave to take up positions where their expertise can be used, and where levels of both intrinsic and extrinsic reward are forthcoming. All sponsors therefore have this direct interest, though this is very often not fully understood.

- Supervisors and (where applicable) mentors of employees: where training needs analysis and performance appraisal work well, supervisors and mentors will already have had a substantial input. Problems arise when this is neglected or skimped. It becomes operationally inconvenient to release staff for training. Staff can also become more difficult to manage if they are either being over-trained for their current role, or if they find that proposed training activities are constantly being cancelled.
- Facilitators and tutors: to ensure that aims, objectives, content and delivery are suitable and adequate for the trainees, in terms of their present capability, and time and resource constraints. Especial attention is required to the extent of employee participation and involvement in particular events, as well as the ability to practise what is to be learned.
- Trainees: at its most effective, much of the trainee's contribution to the process is at the needs analysis and appraisal stage. Employees interested in their own future normally have a good understanding in advance of the nature of activities that interest them. They understand the likely demands placed by day-release study, residential short courses, and other input.

  Where project work and secondments are to take place, employees normally establish the exact nature of their remit with sponsors, supervisors and mentors. This is so that they understand at the outset where the process is likely to take them in terms of their own future prospects, as well as producing the required valuable work.

Target audience

There are specific rules depending on who is being targeted.

Directors and senior managers

These groups always need the financial implications of what is being delivered, especially how much something is going to cost, and how much it is to make for the particular organisation. This therefore should always be addressed and made clear. It is normally necessary to concentrate on strategic rather than operational or technological issues. Presenters must be recognisably expert or else senior staff will not attend. For external events, it is also necessary to set a level of charge higher than for more junior staff, and use a good-quality venue, otherwise a perception of lack of value is given (see Summary Box 9.3).

SUMMARY BOX 9.3   Events for directors and senior managers: examples

- **Internal briefing on implications of computer-based training:** use boardroom; coverage to include costs and charges, programme demonstration, likely frequency and density of usage, benefits, other implications. Use expert and give brief CV if he/she is not a household name – and pay him/her well (economic rent). Duration – maximum half day, two hours is more likely.
- **Externally provided one-day seminar on risk management:** use perceived high-quality venue; good coffee and refreshments; extended networking and discussion opportunities; use experts and possibly a keynote speaker; offer opt-in and opt-out sessions; core coverage of costs and benefits, what organisations now need to do, demonstrable immediate returns as well as continuing benefits; case histories; high charges/high perceived value. Duration – maximum one day; half day is more likely.

In general, it is usual to have concise and substantial notes available in support of what is said and discussed to be given as reinforcement, and available to those who suddenly cannot make it, or who have to rush off at short notice.

Other technological experts and managerial staff

These groups balance substance, presentation, facilities and application (see Summary Box 9.4).

These categories of staff also expect to know how attendance is going to
enhance their expertise, employability, performance and profile. Aims and objectives may make this clear. Other event notes and delivery must overtly cover
this. The only exceptions are:

- MBA programmes where there is a more or less universal belief and perception that gaining this qualification does enhance employability and profile;
- in-house recognition for professional qualifications, certificates and
  diplomas, reinforced by organisation-based beliefs and perceptions that
  opportunities do, and will, open up.

On anything longer than half-day, there normally needs to be a mix of lectures,
exercises, case studies, assignments, individual, group and project work. It is also
vital that sufficient time is given for debrief and discussion of everything that
attendees are given to do. All things being equal they will have worked hard and
enthusiastically. They expect:

- feedback on their efforts and opinions;
- the opportunity to debate matters arising and points of contention;
- understanding of what they have done well and why, and what they have not
  done so well and why;
- what they are supposed to have learned and how this will benefit them and
  their organisation.

It is also essential for these groups and individuals that materials and exercises
used are up-to-date. The proliferation of managerial, professional, occupational
and expert journals and courses means that these categories of staff are
increasingly more widely read and generally aware. Training events are always
seriously damaged when the material is clearly out-of-date or insubstantial.

Supervisors and junior staff

These groups balance substance with speed of delivery and presentation; ensure
that application is demonstrated at every stage; and pay equal attention to

facilities. The key issue is to ensure that everyone takes at least one lesson away from each session or event that they can understand and apply, or see how it could/should/might be useful. Where it is necessary to deal with theoretical or esoteric material, the reasons for this must be made clear, otherwise it will be rejected.

Use of time

Ideally, sessions should last between 30 and 90 minutes depending on the nature of the event and the material being covered. In general, no session should be longer than two hours, and there should be stated breaks at these intervals at least. The only exception to this is where attendees are doing group or project work and can arrange their own breaks.

Where events consist of more than one session, there should ideally be a mix of activities and delivery modes. This engages different skills and aptitudes, different preferred teaching and learning styles. It also ensures that there is active rather than passive development of behaviour and attitudes as well as skills and knowledge. Many universities and colleges of higher and further education are very bad at this, and there is a responsibility on course leaders, tutors and lecturers in these institutions to ensure that presentation, as well as substance, is varied (see Summary Box 9.5).

SUMMARY BOX 9.5   Time factors applied (1)

Some specifics to be aware of include the following:

- **The graveyard shift:** the session immediately after lunch. This should always be used for group or practical work unless there is an overriding reason not to do so. If a lecture or film is put into this slot, then response from attendees is invariably reduced.
- **The end of the day:** the last session of the day needs two or three substantial points, supported by case study or video material, and followed by a summary. This is because people will be looking forward to going home (or if on a residential course, going to have a bath). They are also likely to be getting tired.
- **Evening classes:** those who run any session in the evening – classes, practicals or workshop sessions on residential courses – need to ensure that there is plenty of time to get everything done 'at a walk'. In these sessions, unless there is a very good reason, the knowledge, belief or perception of being pressurised or stressed normally leads to rejection of the material and the event.

Structuring of events around shorter sessions gives plenty of scope for a variety of teaching and learning methods to be applied. It gives a clear message of recognising different preferred learning styles. It develops greater all round capability and understanding. Long sessions delivered in the same way (whether lecture or practical) invariably lead to boredom and frustration. This demonstrates an interest in the well-being of attendees, and recognises their need to receive, learn and use the material or expertise, as well as that of the trainer or tutor to give it out.

Keeping sessions short also requires trainers and tutors to prioritise what they are going to do. A session lasting an hour limits the material that can be covered effectively, and means that the tutor has to think about what can best be delivered, how and why.

A session that lasts three hours is, in many ways, less of a discipline unless it is then subdivided and different teaching and learning methods, and activities, engaged. Where a specific skill or aptitude is being taught, short and subdivided sessions mean that steps along the way have to be identified and in-built. Where knowledge is being imparted, the bones and basis can be dealt with, and then its application demonstrated subsequently through other means. It is essential to give adequate time for exercises, group work, practicals and feedback. Structuring sessions into precise time spans gives an indication that:

- the tutor has thought everything through fully;
- attendees have a perception of the energy and depth of work required (see Summary Box 9.6);
- there is a clear indication of the quality and substance of the event overall.

SUMMARY BOX 9.6   Time factors applied (2)

Once they are finalised, programmes should always be followed. Allowing sessions to overrun gives an impression of lack of forethought or discipline on the part of the trainer or tutor. The following should be especially noted:

- Feedback, discussion and plenary sessions must be adequate in length. Following an example or case study, these should be at least 30 minutes. Less than this gives an impression of superficiality and a lack of value to the work. If there is a large number of groups or individuals involved and from whom to hear, these should be subdivided so that everyone gets their say, and also remains fully involved.
- Skills demonstration sessions must be long enough to present the opportunity to have a go, and to have minor or teething problems put right. There must also be sufficient technology and equipment available so that those being trained and assessed do not spend ages hanging around waiting for their turn.
- Evening sessions on residential courses must have a distinctive substance if they are to have any value. Films, discussions and case studies must at least illustrate the substance of what has been taught and learned earlier, or as a precursor to what is to happen the following day. Group and individual case work and assignments must be followed up, assessed, debated and debriefed immediately the following morning.

Otherwise, everything should begin and end on time. Variations in timings and extensions to sessions or work, should always be agreed and formalised between trainer/tutor and attendees.

Extended time periods

These have to be considered for project work, secondments, continuous professional and occupational development, and those on professional studies and syllabus courses at universities and colleges of higher and further education. In general, the employee development elements are integrated with job, work and occupational activities. Ideally, opportunities should be provided along the way for professional and occupational experience related to the project secondment or course.

Because of their real or perceived longer-term investment in staff when using these activities, some organisations engage in learning and development contracts. These may require that the employee undertakes to remain with the organisation for a predetermined period of time after successful completion or that promotion, advancement or further opportunities are conditional upon satisfactory completion.

Long-term timescales must be sufficiently long for effective learning and development to take place, and sufficiently short to retain enthusiasm, interest and drive. For example, there used to be a very serious motivational problem for CIPD tutors keeping students interested on courses of study that were wholly assessed by unseen examination after a period of two years' study. To be effective:

- Syllabus-based taught courses and continuous professional and occupational development programmes require regular assignment work and monitoring, review and evaluation. This should be supported in-house even if primarily conducted by the particular college, occupational or professional body.
- Secondments require pre-planned and integrated assignment and project work, whether supervised and assessed in-house or by an outside agency.
- Projects require an agreed schedule as outlined above (Chapter 7, Summary Box 7.2).
- Continuous professional and occupational development requirements need to be scheduled into individual jobs and occupations so that the value of having qualified and expert staff is recognised and enhanced. Staff in those occupations are normally extremely employable. If therefore professional development is not scheduled by one employer, this becomes a reason for finding another.

Group size and mixes

Size

Training and learning events are designed for people and the resultant group size is a function of the following:

- **The numbers wanting the event which influences how the material is to be delivered.** For example, the basic coverage of a Michael Porter business strategy seminar may be very similar but its delivery is greatly varied according to whether he is:

- speaking to a group of 500 senior managers at the Grosvenor House Hotel;
- speaking to a group of four, as he did with Richard Branson, Tessa Blackstone, Julian Metcalfe and David Sainsbury on the *World Turned Upside Down* television series;
- producing a 30-minute video version for use in business schools;
- consulting one-to-one with commercial or public service clients.

- **Expectations.** For example, it is *expected* that driving lessons take place on a one-to-one basis. Similarly, it is *expected* that large groups will mostly be required to sit and listen rather than actively participate; and *expected* by those in smaller groups that they will have the opportunity to participate and be involved.

- **The institution producing the event.** Organisations running events in-house can influence this absolutely. For example, if they want groups with no more than six, they simply repeat the event four times if 24 persons require it. Conversely, many university taught courses pack large numbers into lectures and support these with smaller or individual seminar and tutorial sessions.

- **The person or institution delivering the event.** People will put up with inconvenience or cramped conditions for short periods of time in order to catch a talk or lecture by a famous or expert person (e.g. Tom Peters (management); Robert Winston (medicine); Michael Wood (history)). They will also do this for introductory sessions at least from professional and occupational bodies (e.g. RICS, RTPI, INLP). In each case however, the material has to be worthwhile, and where follow-up is envisaged, facilities have to be at least adequate.

- **The material to be taught.** While this is influenced to an extent by the members demanding the event, there are some absolutes:
  - Skills, development and demonstration courses should never have more than six – it is unreasonable to expect individuals on these events to sit through more than five demonstrations, tests and debriefs before having a go themselves.
  - Courses involving group presentations should never be greater than four groups. Again, more than that means that there is too much uninvolved time.
  - Events requiring access to technology, machinery or equipment should never have more attendees than technological provision. Computer, secretarial, machine usage and other courses should always have enough equipment for each attendee. Nobody on such an event should be required to wait around for equipment to become available.
  - The material must be tailored to the core or primary group of attendees. It may also be necessary to give consideration to secondary or peripheral groups if these make substantial numbers.

Mixes

With size comes mix. Group diversity and mix may be considered through: age; gender; experience; background/occupation/profession; pre-qualifications;

location; national, cultural and ethnic origin; primary and understood language; disability; financial status; employing organisations. It may also be considered through a known, believed or perceived mutuality of interest in the material or development on offer.

It is important to realise that while events are designed with a known collective expectation in mind, that individuals also come with additional complimentary, and sometimes conflicting, demands (see Summary Box 8.3 above). There has to be sufficient scope to accommodate this as far as possible. Event leaders, trainers and tutors have to be prepared and willing to deal with whatever attendees may ask or produce – and this includes behaviour and attitudes, as well as skills, knowledge, expertise and technological factors (see Summary Box 9.7).

SUMMARY BOX 9.7   Designing for the peripherals

The best way to make this as effective as possible is to ensure that the event leader is the first to arrive and the last to leave. Anything not dealt with during the event can then be cleared up during breaks or at the end.

It is also necessary for event leaders to be aware of, and to be able to manage:

- prominent or disruptive personalities;
- those who chatter to fill a silence;
- those who say nothing at all and do not contribute;
- negative attitudes expressed either through silence or sullenness; or through constant interruptions of: 'This does not apply to us', or 'Our industry/organisation/sector is unique';
- overt personal, secondary and hidden agenda.

In each case, the only design element required is to understand that each of these is potentially present in all situations. Such personalities and attitudes are only tolerated until the next break. At this point, the event leader must have a discussion aimed at getting the substance of the event back on track. Where these attitudes come out in projects and secondments, whoever is responsible for their supervision will take exactly the same action.

Where there is a collection of strong, dynamic, assertive and expert characters, the best event leaders always make this work in their favour. These characters are invariably easier to enthuse and commit to whatever is in hand. They are also the first to see – and say – when material is poor or insubstantial. Where individuals and groups are less assertive, a part of the function of all event leaders is to get them to begin to express themselves as a by-product of the event.

Costs and benefits

The costs and benefits of designing effective training programmes are as follows (see Table 9.1).

Table 9.1 Costs and benefits	
Costs	**Benefits**
• Overwhelmingly, fixed costs. There is very little, other than materials usage, that has to be paid for in addition	• Effective, targeted, accurate and understood training and development • Knowledge and understanding of what is possible in certain circumstances and under particular constraints • Producing events to an outline formula which is professional, substantial and easy to understand

Conclusions

So long as the principles of programme and event design are known and understood, there is very little to go wrong. While this approach to structuring and organising the material may appear straightforward, if the work is done in this way, this means that every aspect of purpose, structure, context, content, delivery and mix is fully considered before being finalised.

Programmes are required for all aspects of behaviour, attitudes, skills, knowledge, expertise and technological development at all levels. The principles outlined in this chapter apply whichever is being attended to; and attitudes especially, are reinforced where it is known and understood that events have been properly structured and designed.

The cohesion of programmes, together with the quality of materials and expertise in the delivery, are what gives all programmes and events their basic value. However, this value is only optimised and maximised if what is learned enhances expertise and employability, and can be put into practice. Approaching the structure and design of events from the point of view of:

• establishing aims and objectives;
• knowing and understanding the target audience, and its likely and possible demands;
• using the time available in a structured and varied manner;
• understanding the opportunities and constraints of different group sizes and mix;

means that there is always a sound basis on which to build, whatever the event and whoever it is for. It also makes straightforward the choice and use of materials and equipment on particular events.

QUESTIONS

1 What alternative methods are available to cover effectively health and safety training for office staff? What is likely to enhance and dilute the effectiveness of such a course and why?
2 Design a short programme for senior managers on:

(a) 'Your organisations' implications for joining the euro'. What are you going to include, how long is the programme to last, and what are the learning outcomes? Suggest alternative approaches to each session.

(b) 'Leadership and aptitude development training for frontline, junior and first-line supervisory staff'. What are you going to include, and why? Identify learning outcomes; and be as precise as possible with these.

3 Design a secondment training and development programme for yourself on the basis that you are to be seconded for three months to the Parmalat dairy corporation at Parma, Italy.

4 You have been called to give a talk at a business studies course at your local college. The students are all professional people on the first year of a Diploma in Management course. Suddenly one of the students, a woman in her early twenties, gets out of her chair and lies down on the floor in front of you. How might you handle this situation?

5 Design a one-week programme for management trainees to be undertaken immediately after they have left university/college. This is to be a residential event at a hotel. Each day is to be broken down into five sessions. There are 20 attendees. State aims and objectives for each day. State why you have included what you have included, and what everybody is expected to gain from this.

■ ☑ 10 Training and development equipment and resources

'If you didn't overpay for premises, technology, staff and equipment, you were unfashionable.'

Gerald Ratner (1990)

'I never had training or practice equipment. I always trained and practised in the gear that I was going to use for games.'

R.C. (Jack) Russell, England wicket-keeper (1996)

Introduction

All equipment and resources are only as good as the people using them. The purpose of this chapter is to review the uses, misuses and abuses of the different resources available, and to understand the opportunities and pitfalls that go with them.

Some events have absolute resource and equipment requirements. As stated in the previous chapter, the teaching of technological, computer and secretarial skills requires one workstation per student, and where there is a greater demand than this, classes must be divided or potential trainees turned away.

Others have expectational absolutes. In Western cultures, where workbooks and handouts are to be issued, there must be enough to go round. If one-to-one tuition, support or attention is provided for an individual, this should be made available to everyone else who demands it. If the opportunity to practise on a simulator or in a laboratory is made available to one, again it should be offered and open to all.

Others still have perceptual absolutes. There is an increasing perception that textbooks and other printed material should be supported by website and/or CD-ROM, tutorials, case examples and tutor's materials.

There are also presentational absolutes. The expertise and delivery of persons such as Robert Winston (medicine), Tony Robinson (archaeology) and Roslay Klein (physics) demonstrate that anything can be brought to life and made interesting.

Precise technological skills are expected to be taught and learned in terms of context and application, as well as to absolute standards.

All of this requires the use of equipment and resources in support of the particular development, teaching and learning in question.

Equipment and resources

The following equipment and resources are more or less universally available. Their mix and value clearly varies between organisations, professions, occupations and activities, as does use, misuse and abuse.

Overhead projector, blackboard, wipe-board, flipchart

These are used most effectively for guiding trainees through a talk or lecture, or summarising points of a discussion or case study. Used least effectively for more then 20–30 minutes without a break or change, or as the substance of the talk or lecture, rather than in its support or illustration.

Slide shows (including Power-Point)

Slide transparencies are best used to illustrate specific aspects of technical subjects such as architecture, archaeology, mechanics, construction, engineering and catering. They are less effective when either there are too many slides, or again when they dominate, rather than illustrate, the material in the intended learning.

Power-Point has a transient intrinsic value as a mark of technological excellence. Photographs, diagrams and charts can be delivered through Power-Points. It is again less effective when allowed to dominate rather than support proceedings. It is useless when it provides the entire substance for a talk or session.

Simulators and laboratories

These are best used to test hypotheses, skills and knowledge in a safe environment (e.g. flight, driving, surgical skills). So long as the laboratory or simulator is a full replica of reality, absolute standards of skills and expertise can be achieved to a greater extent before the individual is placed in a real situation under supervision. They have great value in demonstrating the advantages and consequences of particular courses of action, and environmental pressures and constraints.

The main weakness is the safe environment itself. Eventually, those learning in this way have to come out into reality (see Summary Box 10.1).

SUMMARY BOX 10.1   Simulators and reality

After finishing his international rugby career, Tony Underwood was taken on by easyJet as a trainee airline pilot. His progress was recorded by television cameras as part of the Carlton TV series *Airline*. Underwood stated that he was nervous about entering the programme and also about the simulator training. However, the quality was so high that when he finally sat in the co-pilot's seat in a real airliner, that part was covered. What was not covered was the full realisation of responsibility – for the well-being of the airliner and passengers; for taking off and landing on time; for the reputation of the company; and for following procedures and instructions during take-off and landing.

They also have to learn the full context in which this expertise is to be delivered, e.g. the culture of the airline, or the constraints of specific hospital theatres. Simulators are effective when integrated with on-the-job activities so that expertise and context are learned together.

Organisational, professional and occupational libraries

All organisations should develop a general reading resource based on their industry and sector, its professions and occupations, requirements for continuous professional and occupational development, and general awareness and interest. It reinforces general identity, as well as providing intrinsic and extrinsic interest and value. These resources should be open to all employees. They should be kept fully up-to-date including the provision of corporate subscriptions to periodicals (see Summary Box 10.2).

SUMMARY BOX 10.2   John Jarvis

John Jarvis is a medium-sized building company operating in south-east England. The company has a normal annual turnover of between £60 million and £70 million per annum. At the turn of the 21st Century, the company went through an organisation development and change programme as part of its response to competitive pressures and incursions into its markets from larger national organisations. A small part of this involved the company taking out subscriptions to the journals of its client groups. In particular, it began subscribing to local government and health service periodicals.

On a flash of inspiration, the general manager placed a quarter-page advert in both local government and health service journals for an initial period of six months. This was unusual for the construction industry in that companies tend to advertise in their own trade press rather than that of clients.

The result was immediate. Enquiries led to invitations to tender from both sectors. This, in turn, resulted in the company being awarded additional contracts to the value of £12 million. This was as the result of a tiny and peripheral organisation development activity.

These resources lose value if they are not kept up-to-date or if subscriptions and materials acquired no longer serve the interests of the organisation and its staff.

Videos

When used effectively, video presentations are extremely successful illustrations and core examples of how things work (e.g. the human body), how particular principles may be applied (e.g. engineering), and how to deal with certain situations and people (e.g. business and management). The following approaches are available:

- using off-the-shelf, high-profile branded material such as that produced by video arts for business and management training and education;
- using programmes produced for mainstream television to support the particular lessons being delivered; such material is produced by the BBC and independent television education organisations, as well as certain *fly on the wall* documentaries;
- using short clips to illustrate the effectiveness or otherwise of advertising and presentational skills (see Summary Box 10.3).

SUMMARY BOX 10.3   Other factors in video usage

- **Branded material:** this becomes of lesser value if it dominates, rather than supports, the core lesson or learning. For example, excellent film though it is, *'Meetings, Bloody Meetings'* is always remembered for the antics of John Cleese rather than the core lessons. This material is normally quite expensive, and value needs to be assessed in advance of purchase or hire. It also loses its currency when everyone has seen it.
- **Leadership training:** much effective leadership training is supported with filmed illustrations from fact-based war films (e.g. *'12 O'Clock High'*, *'A Bridge Too Far'*). Problems again arise if the film dominates, rather than supports, the learning. This can be compounded if trainees want to see the whole film (*'A Bridge Too Far'* lasts over three hours).
- **Television programmes:** again the problems are length and dominance. The ideal length of video film or clip for training purposes is approximately 20 minutes; and should never be longer then half an hour. Any longer than this and the programme takes over, and trainees watch the film rather than learn the lessons.

So long as this is recognised, a great range of documentary, real life, *fly on the wall* and factual material is available for use, as well as open university and overtly educational productions.

Video can also be used by organisations and trainers to:

- Film trainees in particular learning and operational situations for the purpose of illustration of activities, and the broader context of the organisation. The weakness of this is that it is expensive to produce and can pass out-of-date very quickly.
- Filming employees in particular training and development situations for the purposes of illustration, discussion, debate and debrief. The great benefit of this is to enable trainees to see themselves as others see them, and to note the strengths and weaknesses of performance and behaviour. To be fully effective however, it is extremely time consuming. Debriefs especially, must be capable of accommodation within any time constraints that may exist (see Summary Box 10.4).

Computer equipment and the internet

This clearly presents a great opportunity for training, learning and development. It is cheap and more or less universally available. It suffers at present from being viewed as a substitute for many other forms of learning, especially attendance at courses. Many computer-based programs are excellent; others are superficial and insubstantial. They can be used for: business simulations; personality and characteristics assessment; aptitude testing; and project prototype and pilot testing; as well as more general demonstrations and 'What if?' scenario approaches to projects, technological developments, organisational problems, and other issues as part of more general development and advancement (see Summary Box 10.5).

University, colleges of higher and further education, and commercial training organisations, can also put their own materials, course and event structures, case studies and exercises on to the internet. These can then be downloaded at the convenience of those who need or want them.

Again, it is necessary for active and physical support. Some organisations provide tutored or facilitated chat-rooms; others, teleconferencing or video conferencing. Others, still, provide physical face-to-face support.

Above all, the cultural and behavioural need for real and perceived substantive support and feedback must be acknowledged and met. The Open University has had to increase the quality and visibility of the tutorial and seminar support that it provides over the years, and this is a lesson to all those who seek to provide effective, virtual and internet-based events (see Summary Box 10.6).

SUMMARY BOX 10.6   The convenience of computer-based training and the internet

The perception of convenience and easy access has to be reinforced by engaging active interest. Because something is perceived to be convenient does not make it intrinsically useful, valuable or worthwhile. It has to be actively and positively presented as such. The following points must be understood as a precursor to assessing the likely value of on-line provision to users:

- It must actively engage one or more of the criteria of personal, occupational, organisational or professional interest.
- It must provide both convenience and benefits; and the benefits must transcend those present in other provisions (e.g. an actual benefit of going off-the-job to events is the ability to reflect on practice away from work pressures).
- It must not be perceived to be a cheap alternative. Nobody likes 'cheap' things (though they do like 'good value').
- It must be easily accessible. In June 2001, the web@WORK survey found that 41 per cent of all British workers spent three hours or more per week surfing the net while at work – and that much of this was taken up with dealing with glitches or failing to get into the required site or part of sites. This quickly becomes a nuisance, and applies to training and development sites exactly the same as others.
- It must be a support mechanism rather than the driving force. Culturally, people expect detailed physical briefing and feedback delivered by an expert in response to precise issues on anything more substantial than general awareness programs and information.
- It must be current. Expectations here are much higher. It is generally acknowledged that books and periodicals can, and do, become out-of-date; web material should never be so. Indeed, many textbook and educational publishers now view one of the most valuable aspects of the web as the ability to update printed and published material on a regular basis.
- It must have demonstrable positive learning and development outcomes. Failure to include or incorporate this into web-based teaching and learning materials reduces it to a one-way or general communication.

Source: 'Office Angels', web@WORK Survey (2001).

The key to effectiveness is to use the equipment, and the opportunities afforded, to develop and enhance material and exercises so that the whole basis on which learning takes place, and on which courses and events can be structured, is enhanced rather than diluted and replaced.

The internet is also an excellent source of general material. However, there is not at present any guide to quality, depth or breadth of coverage; nor to be fair, do most websites make any claims in this direction. It is important to recognise, therefore, that the best use of articles and features on particular websites is likely to be to broaden, illustrate and enlarge what is already known, rather than as a substantive body of knowledge or expertise. It is an excellent source of general reading, and case studies and examples for discussions on taught courses. It is an excellent source of data when what is required is a quick, rather than deep, body of knowledge for research projects, pilot schemes and feasibility assessments. It is not a substitute for teaching and development, nor is it of any value as a learning resource unless the active tutorial support is present.

Case studies

Case studies can come from anywhere, as follows:

- company and organisation histories and development;
- examples produced by universities, colleges and other training providers drawn either from fact, or else anonymised or 'factionalised' for reasons of security or currency;
- examples drawn from newspapers, journals and websites;
- excellent and faulty products and services drawn from the workplace for study and evaluation;
- examples drawn from competitors so that what they have done may be assessed and evaluated;
- extreme cases, triumphs and disasters.

Case studies drawn from any source are only effective as long as there are direct and precise lessons to be learned, or as illustrations and discussion points around certain principles. The following must always be remembered:

- Real life, pre-produced case studies (such as those available from case clearing houses) are always out-of-date by the time that they are studied. They are therefore normally best used to learn lessons from the past or to demonstrate principles.
- Studies of current workplace practice and present and recent products and services are best used as the basis for assessing what succeeded and failed, and why; rather than to try and produce recipes and blueprints for future success.
- Studies of competitors and real or perceived excellent companies, organisations, products and services must concentrate on principles rather than trying to replicate what others have done.
- Triumphs must be studied in the context in which they took place so that the principles on which they occurred are clearly identified.

- Disasters are best assessed in terms of human costs, the processes that cause them, and the consequences arising as the result.
- Products and service case histories should concentrate on quality, value, durability and customer demand (and the absence or lack of these where the product or service has failed).
- Problem-solving cases must look at broader issues, processes and ranges of solutions rather than asking those using them to guess at possible outcomes.

All cases should be approached from the point of view of debating and discussing matters arising, analysis and evaluation of lessons, consideration of the full range of issues and *possible* solutions where problems are involved. They must *never* be used as blueprints for others to follow. In this way, lessons can be learned from past successes, failures, drives and initiatives. These greatly help to inform the present and future. However, it must always be remembered that they never predict the future.

Role plays

Role plays are used to bring out and illustrate the behavioural factors inherent in particular situations. They are especially useful in illustrating the relationship between behaviour and performance (i.e. what is done and how it is done), and the advantages and limitations of adopting particular attitudes and approaches to certain situations. They are of value in:

- sales training to illustrate the possibilities, limitations and consequences of taking certain approaches to customers and clients;
- industrial relations training to illustrate the behavioural aspects of negotiating, discipline, grievance and disciplinary handling (see Summary Box 10.7);

SUMMARY BOX 10.7   Industrial relations training and role playing

The experience of running negotiating skills role plays has emphasised to many teachers, tutors and lecturers the absolutely critical nature of debriefing fully at the end. Individuals on these events have been found to slip so easily into traditional roles and adversarial positions that, unless handled carefully, prevailing and above all adversarial attitudes are likely to be reinforced rather than broken down. These activities need further reinforcement of how and why people are likely to behave when placed in these positions if this form of attitudinal structuring and development is to be understood.

Source: D. Walton and J. McKersie, 'A Behavioural Theory of Labour Relations', McGraw-Hill (1957); UNISON, 'Human Resource Management', core programme (2000).

- supervisory and junior management skills to illustrate the advantages, benefits and consequences of adopting particular approaches to operational problems and issues;
- presentation skills in which attendees are asked to act as advocates for a particular organisation, individual point of view or cause in making their presentation (see Summary Box 10.8);

SUMMARY BOX 10.8   Presentation skills and role playing

- Attendees on a presentation skills course were asked to put £1 into a kitty. They were then asked to produce a short presentation (five minutes maximum) on behalf of the charity or cause of their choice. The money was to be donated to the winning presentation.
- Attendees on a supervisory studies course were asked to act as advocate for a brilliant new invention produced by a new member of their department. They also had to produce the product costs and benefits in no more than five minutes.

In each case, the rest of the group acted as the presentation evaluator. They were not allowed to vote for themselves. A full debrief as to why each presentation scored well, or not so well, was then engaged.

These are simple exercises and often do no more than make people think, act – and talk.

- interpersonal, inter-professional and inter-occupational attitudes and behaviour in which attendees are asked to adopt the roles of different occupational groups. This is to illustrate how barriers exist between groups and individuals. This should then lead to a discussion around the opportunities and consequences of this, and how and why these might be broken down if required.

Quality of training and learning environment

Any discussion of training methods, equipment and resources must consider the physical and behavioural aspects of the broader learning environment.

Physical

The physical quality of the training and development environment is a major reflection of its integrity and value. Paying attention to this takes the form of:

- a full assessment of the physical environment, its strengths, weaknesses and shortcomings;

- a full assessment of the expectations placed on those attending particular events, and what is expected of them;
- prioritising those areas that require attention and upgrading;
- assessing what can be done immediately and organising people to do it;
- lobbying for additional resources and activities where required.

If none of this is possible, then those responsible need to recognise that they will have to deal with problems of lack of value, under-performance, and declining effectiveness.

A good-quality training and development environment is based on functional comfort. This involves the provision of the correct equipment, resources and support. It requires attention to the needs of individuals and groups, whatever the course or event on which they are engaged. Basic human needs also need to be addressed. Everything should be delivered in conditions of fundamental quality. In particular, problems occur where:

- some staff are known, believed or perceived to be accommodated in better conditions than others – and this is compounded when this is known, believed or perceived to be on the basis of seniority or influence;
- different standards are applied to those undertaking different events – for example, those on project work or secondments are provided with full backing and resources, while those on off the job courses are not;
- the overall training and development environment is fundamentally unacceptable – where for example, there are constant interruptions, distractions due to noise, heat or cold, and where the general standard of furnishing is poor or inadequate.

Behavioural

The behavioural aspects of the learning environment are established and reinforced by the physical qualities. Particular attention is required in the following:

- In-house facilities including on-the-job provision, where cleanliness, equipment décor and other resources must be known, believed and perceived to be at least the quality of the organisation's general quality of working life.
- Off-site facilities and resources, especially so that there is no perception or belief that some categories of staff are being dumped in a poor-quality learning environment; and so that there is no perception or belief that different staff groups receive different quality of provision and learning environment according to grade, status or seniority.

Behavioural aspects are reinforced by the volume and currency of other materials available and the extent to which these are exclusive to some groups, or made available to all staff regardless of occupation. They are also reinforced – positively and negatively – by the quality, comfort and suitability of rooms and furnishings (see Summary Box 10.9).

SUMMARY BOX 10.9   Organisation culture and quality of the
learning environment

Organisations give strong impressions of their underlying attitudes, values and priorities
through attention to the overall quality of the working environment. Organisations
in operating difficulties invariably cancel subscriptions to trade, professional and other
press; remove flowers and plants from reception areas; and remove subsidies from staff
refreshment and canteens.

The same perceptual approach is also evident when assessing the quality of the
training and learning environment. Old and outdated induction videos and slide
presentations; minimal subscriptions to trade, professional and occupational journals;
uncomfortable, unsuitable and tatty furniture, and inadequate equipment – all are
symptomatic of a lack of fundamental value for training and development. Organisation
and employee development are both likely to have had budget cuts and priorities
downgraded, and equipment replacement and refurbishment postponed or cancelled,
where the organisation has got into operational difficulties.

In neither case do the cuts make any positive contribution to alleviating operational
difficulties. They are symptomatic of an easy, unconsidered and wrong response to
other issues. The error is compounded because of strong perceptual and behavioural
messages that are given out.

Source: T. Peters and R. Waterman, 'In Search of Excellence', Macmillan (now Palgrave) (1982).

Costs and benefits

The costs and benefits of ensuring an up-to-date, valuable and effective training
and development environment, materials, methods and resources are as
summarised in Table 10.1.

Table 10.1   Costs and benefits

Costs	Benefits
• Some variable costs especially subscriptions, books and software • Fixed-cost commitment that allows staff to review and evaluate different materials as a part of their working life • Planned refurbishment and maintenance costs • The equipment and facilities charges and costs	• Attitudes, behaviour and values reinforcement (positive if investment is made; negative if not) • Collective and individual confidence in organisation and employee development • Groundwork for effective development activities • Opportunities to gain full potential of particular activities (e.g. video, computer-based training, case work and role play) • Support for on-the-job training, projects and secondments

Conclusions

The extent, quality, pressure and usage of each of the methods and resources indicated, together with the nature of the broader environment, clearly indicate the value placed on training and development, and reflect the organisation priority accorded.

Each of the methods and resources is only as valuable as the expertise with which it is used, and this also reflects the priority and commitment accorded to activities. All equipment, methods and resources are only used effectively in support of programmes and events delivered by experts. Used properly, they enhance the intrinsic quality and value of what is done. Used in conjunction with each other, they give variety, pace and interest to events, as well as addressing and developing different learning styles. They support, illustrate and make memorable the basic lessons required. They never create a quality event in isolation from this.

Used effectively, resources, methods and equipment introduce, develop and reinforce individual and collective behaviour and attitudes, because they reflect high levels of respect and value for skills, knowledge and expertise. They provide the environment and groundwork that is essential for the initial and continued development of skills, knowledge, expertise and technological proficiency. Corporate attitudes to maintenance and development of these training resources, methods and equipment reflect (positively or negatively) the relative value and priority. They also clearly indicate the quality of the level of additional support required – mentoring, coaching and counselling.

QUESTIONS

1 Consider the following short case.
The *Post-It* pad was invented by an employee of the 3M company in the USA. He sang in his local church choir and he wanted markers for his hymnbook that would not fall out of the book when it was lifted up. The pads were first popularised within the company through the enthusiasm of employees and the constant use of them for the myriad of purposes to which we now all put them.
   (a) How could this short case be used as training material, for what reasons, when, where and by whom?
   (b) How would you develop it to make it relevant to human resource management, marketing, strategy development, and organisational change?
2 Your company has decided to make its annual report available on computer to all staff. What development activities are now necessary so that maximum coverage and understanding are achieved?
3 Your organisation is thinking of putting its induction and initial job training programme on to the company website. Carry out a full assessment of costs and benefits. What other actions are required to ensure that this is successful?
4 How would you brief people who are to be recorded on video for the first time?
5 Role play a confrontation between a customer and your organisation, using telephone extensions in which the individuals concerned are physically removed from each other. Then repeat the exercise for the same scenario face-to-face across

a table. What conclusions can you draw from the different patterns of behaviour? What are the main lessons to be learned for:

(a) those who use the telephone?

(b) those responsible for customer care training?

6 Outline the requirements necessary for a presentation to senior management by a junior member of staff. How are you going to measure this for success/failure? When, where and why?

M 11 Mentoring, coaching and counselling

Adam Faith: 'I have brought you up from nothing. I have nursemaided you every step of the way. I have kept everyone away from you – police, photographers, sharks, conmen – the lot. I have made you.'

David Essex: 'You made me what I am. You didn't make me.'

Source: '*Stardust*', United Artists (1972)

Introduction

Mentoring, coaching and counselling are three similar approaches to the issue of providing support, direction, guidance and influence in the pursuit of long-term and sustained organisation and employee development:

- Mentors provide advice, trust and support over a sustained period of time, for the duration of a project or secondment, university or college course; and for those on planned development paths. They also act as sounding board, reflector, inquisitor, devil's advocate, analyst and evaluator.
- Coaches may also be involved in long-term enduring relationships, but their role is more essentially concerned with specific skills, knowledge, expertise and technological proficiency.
- Counsellors also offer advice and guidance, but their role is broad in scope and may additionally involve mediation, advocacy, arbitration, conciliation and cheerleading when required.

These roles clearly overlap. However, they are not always fully interchangeable. There is a distinctive set of attributes for each in addition to the areas of overlap as follows (see Figure 11.1).

Context

From the trainee's point of view, the most critical role is that of mentor for long-term sustained development and improvement. Coaches are more likely to be involved in specific skills and expertise development, and counsellors in the resolution of problems and impasses (see Summary Box 11.1).

From the point of view of the mentor, coach or counsellor, the relationship has to be based on mutuality of interest, trust and confidence. The mentor, coach or

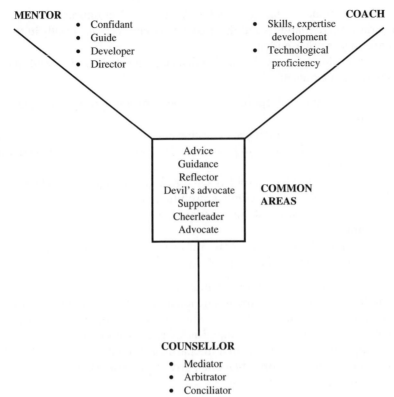

Figure 11.1 The relationship between mentoring, coaching and counselling

SUMMARY BOX 11.1   Professional tennis coaches

All of the world's top tennis players have their own coaches. These are chosen on the basis that they are able to develop the player's game, build on strengths, and work on weaknesses.

The relationship appears to work best when it is confined to on court activity and the skills and expertise of being a top tennis player. The relationship appears to become compromised when the coach is drawn into other roles or feels bound to do this. This happens for example, when the coach feels that the player is making excuses for poor performance rather than addressing deficiencies, or that the player has come to the conclusion that he/she can or cannot play on particular surfaces. The coach then gets drawn into mentoring and counselling, and this appears to affront the players in some circumstances.

In the working environment, it is therefore vital that the precise role is established as clearly and as accurately as possible if these kinds of problems are to be avoided.

Source: 'Henman ditches coach Felgate', *Daily Telegraph*, 3rd May 2001.

counsellor has to be capable and willing to make the commitment for as long as the relationship demands – and this may have to be seen, especially in the case of mentoring, as open-ended.

The relationship is certain to be beneficial only if clearly understood rules are established at the outset:

- complete openness of approach, frankness and directness of language and presentation;
- complete integrity, mutual respect, value and trust;
- willingness of both parties to listen to, acknowledge and respect each other's point of view;
- commitment to resolving problems, issues and blockages; and in some cases, this is likely to extend into conflict resolution;
- commitment to personal, occupational, organisational and professional development;
- identification of specific, general and overall results and benefits required from the relationship on the part of each.

In general, this means a complete mutuality of interest. The consequence of this is to recognise that when there is no longer this mutuality, it is time to break the relationship and move on. This is certain to happen with coaching (when the particular attribute has been developed as far as it can go at present or within the relationship) and counselling (when the particular situation has been resolved). It also happens with mentors when one party or the other changes personal and professional direction and priority.

Qualities

The qualities that each must bring to the relationship are enthusiasm, commitment, dynamism and (as stated above) integrity. If someone chooses or tries to attach themselves to another for reasons of expediency, then the relationship is immediately corrupted. This can happen from both points of view. For example:

- Senior managers or experts may take on the role of mentor, coach or counsellor to those identified as high fliers so that they can develop the next wave of talent in such a way as to ensure that this never becomes a threat (see Summary Box 11.2).
- Some junior staff seek out mentors in positions of known, believed or perceived authority and influence because they believe that this will be good for their careers or a shortcut up the organisation ladder.

From both points of view, there is a potential for choosing a scapegoat or somebody to blame if things go wrong. Junior members of staff given a high profile and demanding project or secondment may make sure that everyone knows who is guiding them through it, and if it then does go wrong, the finger can be pointed at the mentor. Senior managers may overtly mentor junior staff through projects, secondments and initial professional, technical and occupational developments knowing that they will get the credit for successes, and that they will have someone to blame if things do go wrong (see Summary Box 11.3).

Outputs

The outputs of these relationships must include the following:

- a steady stream of capable, willing and dynamic employees making known and noticeable contributions to overall organisational performance whatever their occupation or profession;
- positive, noticeable and sustainable organisational, occupational and professional development and advancement;

- positive attitudes and behaviour;
- the next wave of mentors, coaches and counsellors.

If any of these are not apparent, then the process requires some form of strategic review. This process is overtly time and resource consuming in organisational, professional, occupational and personal terms; and returns are required on this investment. Organisations must therefore be aware of what they want from these relationships as much as those directly involved (see Summary Box 11.4).

SUMMARY BOX 11.4   City Communications

City Communications was founded in 1996 by Andrew Marchant. He started the company because he saw a niche in which complete corporate communications, packages and equipment would be valuable to organisations that did not want to spend expensive administrative time, energy and resources dealing with a whole range of providers. For a fee therefore, City Communications would provide telephone, fax, telex, e-mail, internet, land-line and satellite fixed and mobile communications and equipment, and would also handle the billing side on behalf of clients.

The venture was extremely successful. Marchant acted as mentor and coach to sales and back-up teams and met with them every morning between 8.00 am and 9.00 am. The mentoring role was primarily for guidance, support and problem-solving.

During the period 1996–2001, no salesperson or member of the back-up staff left and the team grew from three to twenty. However, the meetings still took place every morning without fail.

In 2001, the company was bought by a major international telecommunications company for £18 million, at a price of £5 per share. Three months later, the share price was down to 26p.

The new owners had cancelled the meeting arrangement, and the mentoring and coaching, as an unnecessary cost and waste of time. Marchant himself had left at the time of the buy-out and was not replaced. The result was that cohesion was lost, and for the first time sales dropped. Later, clients started not to renew contracts and instead looked elsewhere. The sales team also started to drift off and find other jobs with competitors.

So a full, positive and managed understanding of these relationships is essential in the context of business policy and performance. Outputs must also be actively managed whether the relations are professionally demanded, in-built into policy and direction, or allowed to emerge *ad hoc*. This is especially important to note because these outputs are required whether:

- the relationship was ordained or commanded;
- mentors, coaches, counsellors and trainees were assigned to each other;
- the relationship was structured or in-built;
- trainees with a particular qualification, occupation or profession automatically are assigned to a particular member of more senior staff;

- the relationship was chosen by one party or both;
- either the trainee approached the senior who agreed, or vice versa;
- the relationship was *ad hoc*, and arose as the result of the trainee needing support for a particular project, assignment or piece of work, and so found someone who knew something about it, and in whom they would have confidence;
- the relationship was developed by the senior, often through asking a junior to carry out a piece of work as the result of which a mentoring, coaching or counselling relationship began and developed.

The quality and basis of the relationship also allows for the outputs to be agreed and developed much more thoroughly. These include the following:

- the precise remit, whether this is something specific, or support through the initial period of work;
- derived outputs, recognising and pursuing opportunities and initiatives that become apparent as the primary purpose develops;
- attitude and behaviour development alongside skills, knowledge, expertise and technological proficiency;
- the identification of potential, primarily the potential of the trainee. Opportunities and possibilities are also certain to become apparent to the mentor, and also for the particular organisation, departments, division or function.

It is also likely that the work output and relationship will have to be limited or prioritised in some way. Especially if initially successful and overtly very productive, positive and harmonious, it can start to dominate the working lives of those concerned, and other areas of output then start to suffer.

Nature of relationship

Tannenbaum and Schmidt (1958) produced the leadership and decision-making model shown in Figure 11.2.

This may be adapted to the relationship between mentor, coach, counsellor and trainee, as shown in Figure 11.3.

The more prescriptive approach is likely to be concerned with coaching in particular skills, expertise and technology where there are clearly known and understood right and wrong ways of doing things (see Summary Box 11.5).

SUMMARY BOX 11.5   Brian Clough

'I would be coaching, showing the players how I wanted something done. Occasionally – very occasionally – one of them would disagree with me. We would talk it through for 20 minutes or so. He would put his point of view and I would put mine. Then we would agree that I was right.'

Source: *'Football Stories'*, Channel 4 Television (2001).

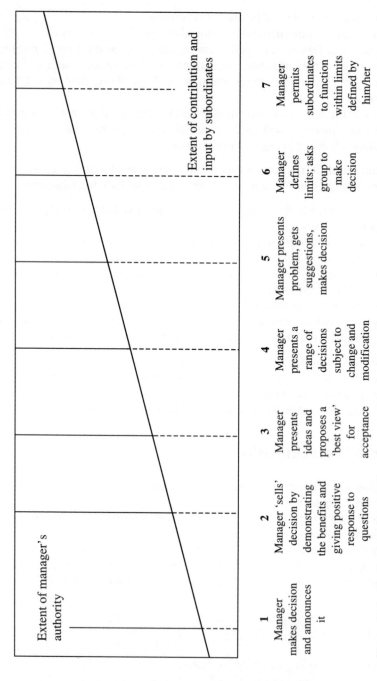

Extent of manager's authority

Extent of contribution and input by subordinates

1	2	3	4	5	6	7
Manager makes decision and announces it	Manager 'sells' decision by demonstrating the benefits and giving positive response to questions	Manager presents ideas and proposes a 'best view' for acceptance	Manager presents a range of decisions subject to change and modification	Manager presents problem, gets suggestions, makes decision	Manager defines limits; asks group to make decision	Manager permits subordinates to function within limits defined by him/her

Figure 11.2 The leadership grid. The purpose of the grid is to illustrate the autocratic–participative range that is available in organisational and managerial decision-making. It also provides a sound basis for forethought. Certain types of decision will be better understood, and accepted, if they are delivered in particular ways. [*Source:* Tannenbaum and Schmidt (1958).]

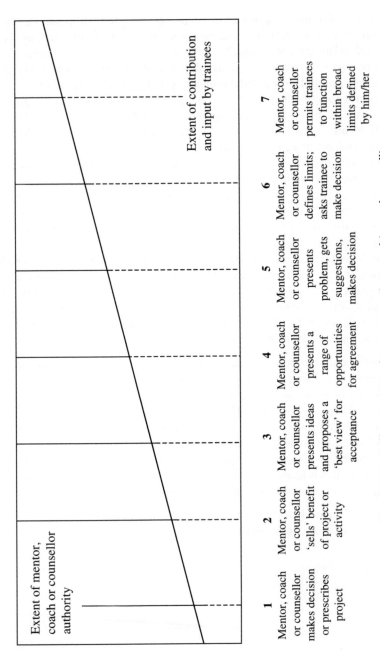

Extent of mentor, coach or counsellor authority

Extent of contribution and input by trainees

1
Mentor, coach or counsellor makes decision or prescribes project

2
Mentor, coach or counsellor 'sells' benefit of project or activity

3
Mentor, coach or counsellor presents ideas and proposes a 'best view' for acceptance

4
Mentor, coach or counsellor presents a range of opportunities for agreement

5
Mentor, coach or counsellor presents problem, gets suggestions, makes decision

6
Mentor, coach or counsellor defines limits; asks trainee to make decision

7
Mentor, coach or counsellor permits trainees to function within broad limits defined by him/her

Figure 11.3 Different approaches to mentoring, coaching and counselling

The more prescriptive approach may also be required when something has been fully discussed, debated and analysed, but a clear way forward is not apparent. It is then the responsibility of those involved to agree something. The mentor, coach or counsellor takes overall responsibility, and so may prescribe or direct from a point of view of total honesty, integrity and involvement.

Participative approaches are best used overall. Even where there is no doubt about what has to be done, full agreement is necessary on how, when and why. There are certain to be questions of reconciling this work with other organisational, occupational and operational pressures.

It also involves recognising what is actually to be gained from the work, the situation and the relationship. Again, a leadership model may be adapted in terms of 'the managerial grid' developed by Blake and Mouton (1986). The managerial grid is a configuration of management styles based on the matching of two dimensions of managerial concern – those of 'concern for people' and 'concern for production/output'. Each of these dimensions is plotted on a 9-point graph scale and an assessment made of the managerial style according to where they come out on each (see Figure 11.4). Thus, a low score (1:1) on each axis reflects poverty in managerial style; a high score (9:9) on each reflects a high degree of balance, concern and commitment in each area. The implication from this is that an adequate, effective and successful managerial style is in place.

Other styles that Blake and Mouton identified are:

- **9:1** – the country club – production is incidental; concern for the staff and people is everything; the group exists largely to support itself.
- **1:9** – task orientation – production is everything; concern for the staff is subordinated to production and effectiveness. Staff management mainly takes the form of planning and control activities in support of production and output. Organisational activity and priority is concerned only with output.
- **5:5** – balance – a medium degree of expertise, commitment and concern in both areas; this is likely to produce adequate or satisfactory performance from groups that are reasonably well satisfied with working relations.

The grid of Figure 11.4 can be adapted as shown in Figure 11.5. This makes it clear what can be expected:

Figure 11.4   The managerial grid. [*Source:* Blake and Mouton (1986).]

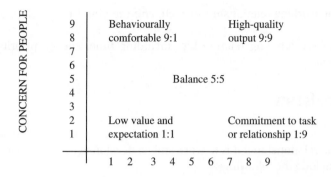

CONCERN FOR TASK, PRODUCTION AND OUTPUT

Figure 11.5   A leadership model

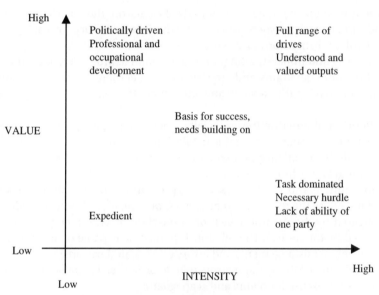

Figure 11.6   Quality of the working relationship

- **1:1** – low-value, low-quality, unrespected work – which is normally therefore badly carried out and delivered.
- **9:1** – country club, insubstantial work, and based on a mutually cosy, comforting – and insubstantial – working relationship.
- **1:9** – the work or task is everything; and the work and the relationship can only be sustained in the long-term so long as the work has overwhelming known, believed or perceived mutual value and reward when completed.

From this, a clear indication may be gained of the following (see Figure 11.6):

- quality of the working relationship along the dimensions of personal, professional, occupation, task and output;

- value of the working relationship to each, and the premises on which this is based;
- intensity of the working relationship, including time, energy, priority and commitment.

Characteristics

From this, it becomes evident that a number of traits and characteristics are required in the relationship if it is to work and be developed over long periods of time. These include the following:

- **Influence:** recognising the nature and extent of the influence of the mentor, coach, counsellor and trainee; understanding the legitimacy of each; agreeing never to pull rank or expertise in the interests of defence of a point of view.
- **Empathy:** understanding the demands of each from the other's point of view; and understanding when, where and why it is necessary for each to adopt particular positions on some issues.
- **Sympathy and understanding:** for organisational, professional, occupational and operational strains and stresses that are certain to occur from time to time, and having the capacity and willingness to seek alternative approaches when required.
- **Patience and equanimity:** especially when things go wrong or it becomes apparent that something is going to take longer or more resources to complete successfully. If patience and equanimity are not present, it normally means that the relationship is not strong.
- **Non-punitive and non-adversarial approach:** the relationship is destroyed instantly if, as the result of something happening, disciplinary procedures are instigated by the mentor, coach or counsellor, or grievance procedures are invoked by the trainee. The relationship must be capable of accommodating all mistakes, misjudgements and errors other than those arising from deliberate negligence. Mistakes and errors that do occur need to be put right, and not used as the excuse for blame and scapegoating.
- **Responsibility:** in these relationships, responsibility is mutual and shared. If (as invariably is the case) the mentor, coach or counsellor is more senior, then there is an additional responsibility to ensure that this position is used as a resource to advance the relationship and the work, and not as an undue or tainted influence (see Summary Box 11.6).
- **Authority and accountability:** these are shared. If there are failures, the mentor, coach or counsellor is accountable in public (whatever may subsequently be said in private). Mentors, coaches and counsellors are also accountable for resources consumption, lobbying and gaining credence and acceptance for the work. Trainees are accountable to the mentor, coach or counsellor for the quality, value, volume and delivery of the work as agreed. They are also responsible and accountable for raising problems, issues, opportunities and anything else that may become present or apparent along the way (see Summary Box 11.7).

SUMMARY BOX 11.6   Tainted characteristics

Each of the characteristics indicated may be tainted as follows:

- **Influence:** influence is tainted and corrupted when the mentor, coach or counsellor ensures that the trainee does something in certain ways in order to get the results that the former, for whatever reason, requires. Influence is also tainted when mentors, coaches and counsellors use their position to build up a retinue and following based on patronage. Influence is tainted when trainees use their position on the project, assignment or secondment to undermine the position of the mentor, coach or counsellor.
- **Empathy:** empathy is tainted when either party takes an expedient action or produces a piece of work in such a way that they know how the other will react given the circumstances. Understanding the other's position therefore becomes a means of manipulation rather than an aid to the working relationship.
- **Blame and scapegoating:** these are present when patience and responsibility are not, and when a punitive and adversarial approach is adopted. In these cases, the professional and personal aspects of the relationship are destroyed. The relationship will only continue if there is some overriding residual value in the work, otherwise the whole is certain to be lost.

SUMMARY BOX 11.7   The nursing course that failed

The project development manager of a new university agreed to act as mentor for a graduate management trainee. This person was to be groomed and fast-tracked into university general management.

One of the first projects given to the trainee was to calculate the hours requirements for nursing students. The division and figures required were for college tuition, and practice placements. The figures were agreed and delivered to the university's nursing department.

The figures were wrong, and this meant that the course had to be restructured. For those already on the programme, this required extra attendance at university, longer shifts on placement, and increased private study. The students sent a deputation to the programme development manager to ask the university authorities to reconsider and to look at other alternatives.

The programme development manager refused to consider anything. Over the following three months, half the students left the course. The trainee was promoted away from the situation. Once he had left, he was blamed for everything. The programme development manager is still in post.

Table 11.1 Costs and benefits	

Costs	**Benefits**
• High usage of fixed-cost elements especially staff time on one-to-one and/or group mentoring, coaching and counselling activities	• High and sustained behaviour, attitudes, skills, knowledge, expertise and technology development and maximisation
• High priority required for effectiveness, and therefore high opportunity costs	• High staff loyalty and commitment
• High resources usage where there are extensive projects	• Next generation of mentors, coaches and counsellors
• May include variable costs where travel and secondments are concerned	• The practice becomes institutionalised
• Initial training and development of expertise in mentoring, coaching and counselling	• Contributes to culture, attitude and values change and development

Costs and benefits

The costs and benefits of having effective mentoring, coaching and counselling activities in place are as summarised in Table 11.1.

Conclusions

It is apparent that, conducted properly with full institutional support, and full collective and individual awareness and understanding, mentoring, coaching and counselling are:

- excellent long-term and sustainable means of organisation and employee development;
- expensive in terms of resources and expertise, time and consumption.

The approach has therefore to be viewed as an investment in organisation and employee development on which there are tangible, understood, accepted and anticipated returns. It is not to be a cosy relationship between superiors and subordinates, nor the means of getting substantial bodies of work carried out on the cheap in the name of training and development.

Critics of mentoring, coaching and counselling point to the difficulties in measuring returns and relating them to such initiatives. Where returns and other requirements are not clearly articulated, it is essential that further work is done to make these as precise as possible if the approach is to be fully effective. It is certain to be successful only if it is:

- recognised as having value;
- known what that value is;
- fully integrated into organisation and employee development strategies.

QUESTIONS

1 What are the pros and cons of trainees choosing their own mentor for support during a particular project or secondment? What should trainees be looking for and why?

2 Outline a two-day briefing session for junior and middle-ranking managerial, professional and technical staff entitled 'Mentoring the next generation'. What are you going to include in it, and why? Structure the programme according to the lessons learned in Chapter 3.

3 Helen Copeland, a management trainee with an internet bookseller, has just finished a project entitled 'Selling magazines and periodicals on the internet'. She has been mentored through this by Ian Woods, the information services manager. The project has been accepted by the company as being very good but *ahead of its time*. Two months later, the company announces on its website that it is to start selling magazines and periodicals. The accompanying press release gives full credit to Ian, and Helen is not mentioned.

   On the basis of what you are told, evaluate the relationship between Helen and Ian. What now needs to happen?

4 Consider Summary Box 11.4. What should the company that took over City Communications have done, and why?

5 When should productive and effective mentoring, coaching and counselling relationships come to an end, and why?

6 Discuss the view that mentoring, coaching and counselling are nothing more than the mollycoddling of trainees who should be learning to stand on their own two feet.

■ Ⅳ 12 Organisation and employee development strategies

'*In order to be a top ten player, all I had to do was to get out of bed. Everything else that I did – the hours of practice, the fitness training, the diet, the lifestyle – was to keep me at the top. It was all to do with the difference between being number ten and number one.*'

Martina Navratilova

Introduction

The enduring effectiveness of all organisation and employee development depends on the collective and individual approaches adopted. As with all other organisational and managerial activities, a strategic approach is essential so that:

- everyone understands what is available and expected;
- resources and priorities are clearly allocated;
- outputs, requirements and measures of success and failure are clearly indicated.

Within this broad framework, individuals and groups can then be fitted into particular on-the-job and off-the-job training, projects and other activities in an orderly, structured and predetermined way (see Summary Box 12.1).

SUMMARY BOX 12.1   Police training (1999)

At its conference in February 2000, the Society of Chief Police Officers addressed the question of the quality, costs and benefits of the training given by the UK police forces to their staff. This was because a report produced by the Police Federation at the end of 1999, concerned also with the quality and value of police training, had concluded that £100 million per year was spent by the service on untargeted and unquantifiable training and development.

The Society of Chief Police Officers found that there was no strategic, ordered or prioritised approach. Results and outputs were not analysed, monitored, reviewed or evaluated. It was impossible to place any genuine value on much of the work and to measure improvements and advances in collective and individual effectiveness in any area.

Source: *People Management*, 'News Digest', February 2000.

Progress can then be measured on a collective and individual basis, against the activities in which they participate, what they are supposed to be learning and have learned, and their own effectiveness and motivation. Organisations can then measure this in terms of their improvements in effectiveness, productivity, product and service outputs, and recruitment and retention of staff.

A strategic approach

Porter (1980) identifies the following generic strategic positions, one of which must be chosen by all organisations if they are to be fully effective in the pursuit of their activities:

- **Cost leadership:** the drive to be the lowest-cost operator in the field. This enables the absolute ability to compete on price, long-term, where necessary. To be a cost leader, investment is required in up-to-date production and service technology and high-quality staff. Cost leadership organisations are lean form with small hierarchies, large spans of control, operative autonomy, simple procedures, and excellent salaries and terms and conditions of employment; and each of these brings its own organisational and employee development needs.
- **Focus:** concentrating on a niche and taking steps to be indispensable, and to satisfy as many of the customers in, and demands of, that niche. Investment is necessary in product, technology and staff expertise, understanding the nature of the market, and how this is expected to develop. Again, each of these has strategic, organisational and employee development needs.
- **Differentiation:** offering homogeneous products and services on the basis of creating a strong image or identity. Investment is required in marketing, advertising, brand development, distribution and customer and client service. Again, there are clear development needs indicated.

From a strategic, organisation and employee development perspective, the following specific requirements are apparent:

- **Cost leadership:** investment in skills, knowledge, expertise and technological development in order to maximise and optimise staff and equipment output over sustained periods of time. Maintaining cost leadership in any sector is dependent on long-term maximised return on investment on all resources, and this includes continuous high levels of investment in human resource development. In the long-term, it is normally necessary to attend to full multi-skilling and flexibility of work and working patterns.
- **Focus:** investment in fully flexible working, multi-skilling and attitude and behaviour development so that technology, specialism and output can be geared to any potential customer or client in the sector.
- **Differentiation:** investment in customer and client service and care. Organisation development concentrates on streamlining processes and practices, and maximising resource usage at the frontline.

This may also be viewed as follows from the point of view of groups and individuals within the organisation:

- **Cost advantage:** concentrating on maximising production and output means developing individual skills and knowledge, and reinforcing attitudes and behaviour. This enhances the employee's employability. It develops broader knowledge and understanding of the particular organisation and its sector. It is also likely to identify potential and opportunities for the future.
- **Focus:** on specific individual and group skills. This, in turn, creates greater involvement and participation, and often leads to staff-led business and organisation development initiatives. A high degree of loyalty, commitment and motivation is generated where this is fully effective.
- **Differentiation:** employees differentiate themselves through activities undertaken, and experience and qualifications gained and held. This also reinforces employee, customer and client perceptions, and understanding of expertise, commitment and confidence. Everyone prefers to deal with those who are demonstrably capable and qualified. This, in turn, develops and reinforces positive collective attitudes and behaviour.

  Organisations that differentiate themselves through concentrating on employee development also gain reputations for being 'good employers'. Staff are attracted because of the training and development on offer, and the opportunities for variety, enhancement and interest that this is understood to bring.

However, the broader context has still to be right. This, above all, means the opportunity to put into practice what has been learned, and to develop the new skills, knowledge and technological proficiency into expertise. Organisations fall down on this when:

- employees are developed in particular skills and knowledge, and then have to wait to put this into practice, which causes frustration;
- employees are put through particular qualifications without the required professional or occupational support (this is an enduring problem at present with the public professions of medicine, nursing, teaching and social work);
- employees are offered opportunities which are then not delivered. This is an enduring problem in such occupations as civil engineering, construction management, and architecture where individuals arrive at work with university and college qualifications only to be told that they now have to serve extended periods of time before being given measures of independence and autonomy.

Each of these can be overcome provided that the organisation and employee development approach is structured to harmonise the needs of individuals with those of the organisation.

Raising expectations

There is nothing overtly wrong with raising peoples' expectations. Most prefer to work in an environment where they are to be well rewarded in return for high levels of expertise and quality of work and output. However, problems always arise when unreal and unachievable expectations are raised. Many organisations do this – misguidedly – with the best will in the world. They give clear perceptions in job advertisements and recruitment literature of excellent training opportunities just to make themselves attractive to well qualified potential staff. This must then be delivered. If it is not, it becomes known and believed to be purely expedient and those caught in this way quickly move on (see Summary Box 12.2).

SUMMARY BOX 12.2   Graham Richards

Graham Richards graduated with a first class degree from one of the UK's top universities. His degree was in construction management, and he was made a variety of job offers. He chose to work for a small regional building company in south-eastern England. This was because he was promised:

- a good starting salary;
- excellent continuing professional training and development;
- early autonomy and responsibility.

He met the owners and directors of the company who were very pleased with what he had to offer. He accordingly started work during the summer after he graduated.

He spent the first three months of his employment learning the business and becoming familiar with all of the company's sites and contracts.

However, after that, as Christmas approached, nothing much else happened. He went to see the company Chairman, Dennis Edwards. Edwards had founded the company in 1960, and had built it up from being a 'jobbing building' firm into a £30 million enterprise. Now in his seventies, he was looking to find the next generation of managers to ensure the company's long-term survival. He told Graham: *'We were very pleased to take you on. The truth is, however, we were not sure what to do with you once you had been taken on. None of us were quite sure what a "graduate trainee" was, or could do. The thing is, you clearly know the industry. However, it is clear that you need much more training and development if you are to be successful. So we do rather think that it would be better if you found yourself another job'.*

Graham pointed out that the company had gone to a lot of trouble to attract his attention and then recruit him. He also pointed out that training and development was supposedly on offer. Edwards replied: *'Yes, but everyone has to say that don't they? The truth is, if we hadn't have said that, you would never have come to work for us in the first place.'*

Graham left the company, and the industry, and went into financial services.

The training and development environment

Whatever the strategic position of the organisation, the training and development environment must be of good quality so that:

- What is planned is fully supported. This means ensuring that the right equipment, facilities and resources are present and kept up-to-date, and that both in-house and external expertise can be made available when required. This is easily achievable if planned for and budgeted; less so if it is *ad hoc* or at the mercy of the whims of directors, seniors and general managers.
- What is planned can be delivered. This means ensuring that induction, initial job training and other core activities are an absolute priority when required and that those on scheduled off-the-job programmes, projects and secondments have the time and resources allocated. Again, this is most effective if recognised and planned for in advance.
- What is delivered can be measured and assessed. Organisation and employee development strategies are broken down into over-arching goals and more precise aims and objectives and sub-aims and objectives. If this part of the process is designed effectively then the value of any activity undertaken can be assessed accurately.
- What is delivered is of intrinsic value and supports and reinforces dominant attitudes and values. This happens anyway. Where the training and learning environment is poor, those attending events feel unvalued and demotivated. Where the environment is good, there are no obstacles to success except the quality of the event itself, and the motivation and commitment of those on it.

The following requirements are also essential:

- What is planned is known, believed and perceived to be of enduring and demonstrable value. A primary demonstration of this is that people go willingly on all events; the only thing that prevents them attending is a genuine work crisis or emergency (not general pressures of work).
- The value delivered over a long period of time satisfies personal, occupational, organisational and professional demands, and is known, believed and perceived to enhance and develop behaviour, attitudes, skills, knowledge, expertise and technological proficiency.
- A positive organisational, departmental, divisional, functional and group culture is developed and enhanced. Everything that is planned and implemented should always develop harmony, cooperation and openness rather than conflict and group, occupational and professional exclusivity. Where professional and occupational groups do develop a siege mentality, it is always detrimental to overall organisational cohesion (see Summary Box 12.3).

So long as this is understood, strategy and policy decisions can then be taken in the following areas:

- What equipment, facilities and expertise to own and retain, and what to buy in when needed.

A key problem facing the NHS at present (quite apart from funding shortages) is the prevalence of behavioural and attitudinal barriers around each of the key professions and occupations:

- Managers are taught budgeting, political priorities and facilities management;
- doctors are taught medical skills, interventions and an exclusive body of knowledge, skills and expertise;
- nurses are taught patient care, some procedures, and ward and patient management.

The only one of these groups that is also taught about cohesion and multidisciplinary teamworking is nursing. Additionally, this is in the knowledge that it remains an ideal, not a reality. All the rest of healthcare training and development concentrates on the exclusivity of each group rather than the harmony required.

- What events to offer on- and off-the-job, to whom, when, where and why.
- How present and future needs are going to be identified and analysed.
- How to gain a cohesive and unified organisational approach to all aspects.
- How to offer fundamental equality of opportunity in each area to everyone.
- Having a collective and corporate view of the priorities in behaviour, attitudes, skills, knowledge, expertise and technological proficiency development, and in ensuring the professional, occupational, organisational and personal mix for all (see Summary Box 12.4).

Tait's Greetings Cards Ltd produces cards for all occasions – birthdays, Christmas, celebrations, births, marriages and deaths. It also produces high-quality stationery and postcards under licence to branded providers. The company employs 60 people in a small village. Of these, 30 are production staff, 20 work in sales, and there are 10 management and administration staff.

Alistair Tait is the company's Chairman and Chief Executive. On organisation and employee development he states:

'We have no training policy or strategy. All that we insist on is that staff do 30 days' training per annum. As long as at least one event is directly work-related, they can do whatever they like with the rest. We chose 30 days because that is about the usual commitment of a day-release college course which staff can do if they want. We wanted to give everyone the same opportunity.

'If people want to do this during the day, that's fine by us. If they want to go to evening classes, that's fine by us too. We give them work time off in lieu. So if the evening class is two hours, then they get two hours off on one day.   (continued)

> 'In my 17 years in charge, we have had no complaints. The whole approach costs us about 3 per cent of payroll. The only slight intake of breath I ever had was about 9 years ago, when my secretary suddenly announced that she wanted to do a HGV driving course. I let her go, and she left us shortly afterwards to work as a lorry driver. However, she rejoined us three years ago and is now our transport manager. And she still makes at least one run per week.'

Source: London Chamber of Commerce and Industry (2001).

Strategic approaches to training needs analysis and appraisal

The problems that have to be addressed and overcome include the following:

- Perceptions of fairness and equality of approach, and the ability to have needs and wants recognised and addressed regardless of occupation, location, hours worked or length of service (as well as, in practice, regardless of age, gender, ethnic origin, disability, marital status or domestic lifestyle).
- Perceptions that whatever is identified will be tackled in fact through training and development, rather than disciplinary and poor performance procedures.
- The application of performance appraisal to everyone regardless of occupation, location, hours worked or length of service.

The best organisation and employee development training needs analysis and appraisal strategies ensure that everything required is in-built into regular supervisory and managerial practice, and punctuated with formal reviews every 3–4 months. This is then supported by open, agreed, concise paperwork systems (ideally of no more than one sheet) jointly completed and signed.

Expressed in this way, it appears very simple. It is simple provided that it is structured, implemented and acted upon as a matter of corporate policy. It becomes complicated and corrupted when the paperwork becomes unwieldy and over long, when it is not jointly or openly completed, and when the formal review dates are too far apart (see Summary Box 12.5).

SUMMARY BOX 12.5   Telecommunications

A large UK telecommunications company runs an extremely complex performance appraisal process. The company requires both managers and subordinates to fill in a four-page document on the performance of each member of staff every three months. These are then discussed and agreed at formal reviews conducted at the end of each three-month period.

In practice, the process works sketchily. The paperwork is seldom fully completed, but at least it concentrates on priorities. Formal reviews tend to concentrate on future needs rather than past analyses because of other time and work pressures. The implementation of development needs tends to arise as the result of lobbying by the employee because managers and supervisors do not have enough time to carry out needs analyses fully.

At its best, the system clearly works to an extent. At its worst, it is largely unvalued, a chore that causes stress and pressure especially during busy periods.

However, the collective view is that it is better to have this than nothing because it is a useful support for those employees who want to get on and progress. It is supported in principle by the company's six recognised trade unions.

The company has recently had a number of business and trading difficulties. As a consequence, the Chief Executive left and was replaced. The new Chief Executive expressed the view: 'Get rid of the appraisal system. And get rid of all the staff who are no good. We don't need all this to tell us that.'

Source: Anthony Nile, production engineer, June 2001.

360 degree appraisal

This is the term used to describe appraisal of senior and managerial staff by their subordinates. It is culturally contentious in the United Kingdom, European Union and North America because it goes against the norm of seniors appraising juniors and telling them what to do to improve.

The approach is most effective when subordinates are given a precise set of criteria against which to rate the performance of their superior. Again, this should be undertaken as a continuous process and punctuated by regular formal reviews carried out in open plenary session (see Summary Box 12.6).

SUMMARY BOX 12.6   360 degree appraisal at Unilever

Unilever piloted a 360 degree performance appraisal strategy in 1998 and 1999. They used a group of production and service managers on whom to test the approach.

The staff were given a simple form and ratings scale on which they were asked to grade their manager on such things as fairness, evenness, accessibility, problem-solving and departmental organisation.

At the pilot stage, two contrasting opinions emerged:

- 'It was the most nerve-racking experience of my life. I never knew my staff thought of me like this. I guess I've learned a lot though' – Tony Pond, product development manager, after his first formal review session with his staff.
- 'I don't know what he's worried about. He always used to write stuff about us, often without having seen us for weeks. This is up-front, open and supported' – Johan Sachs, product development technologist, after the first session with Tony Pond.

The company never fully evaluated the results. Implementation was, and remains, piecemeal with the choice of whether to continue with it or not left up to individual Vice Presidents, divisional and departmental Heads.

Source: 'Trouble at the Top', BBC2 (2001).

Problems arise when seniors take the criticism personally and use the appraisal process to victimise those who criticised them. It is certainly true that complete mutual confidence is required to ensure that the process works effectively. Seniors must be receptive to criticism and prepared to act on it. Juniors must be prepared to be constructive and use the opportunity to advance their point of view for enhancing departmental performance, as well as that of the particular manager or supervisor.

Other approaches

Other strategic approaches are:

- **Peer review:** in which individuals or groups assess and appraise the performance of their colleagues and equals. The main problem here to overcome is unwillingness to be fully open where it is clear that there is malpractice of some kind.
- **Collective review:** in which groups assess the performance of their own department, domain, division or function. The main problem here is collective unwillingness to acknowledge the fact when things are evidently going wrong (see quote at the top of Chapter 7, and also Summary Box 12.7).

SUMMARY BOX 12.7   Problems with other approaches

- **Rodney Ledward:** Rodney Ledward was a gynaecologist practising in south-eastern England over the last part of the 20th Century. He was struck off for malpractice in 1998. He was first assessed by his peers in 1986 for conducting procedures that were self-evidently wrong; they also drew attention to his lack of precision in carrying out operations. He was widely known to be incompetent by all those who worked with, and near, him; and this included both the surgeons and other medical staff. However, this peer and collective review was never formalised, and he was able to practise for a further 15 years before the process was formalised.
- **'Lessons will be learned':** this is the phrase always used in education, social services and health service reports when a tragedy has occurred as the result of collective failures to assess situations and act on evidence. In these reports, collective appraisal is deliberately avoided in the interests of ensuring that there is no need to apportion, accept and shoulder responsibility.

For both the specific and the general case, the result was, and is, that attitudes, behaviour and performance development needs were never properly identified or implemented. Neither was a strategic or managerial overview taken of what was wrong, what should be done as the result, and how improvements were to be noted and measured.

- **Inspections:** carried out internally or externally in the interests of gaining snapshots of individual, collective, departmental, divisional, functional and overall corporate performance. Organisations may be required to have inspections because of:
  - statutory obligation (e.g. health and safety at work);
  - function and activities (e.g. schools);
  - nature of activities (e.g. chemicals, oil, defence equipment, airlines);
  - occupational mix (e.g. the employment with those whose profession or occupation requires regular inspection of initial and continuous professional development).

If any organisation either requires, or chooses, to have inspections for any purpose, then it must be prepared to accept the findings, conclusions and recommendations, evaluate them, and where necessary, these must be implemented. Not to do so negates the value of inspection, dilutes the potential for organisation development, and devalues the efforts of staff in ensuring that the particular activities are as successful and worthwhile as possible.

Training and learning contracts and agreements

Many professions and technological occupations and expertise require contracted or agreed arrangements between the organisation, the individual and the training provider (e.g. college, university) and statutory body (e.g. NJCEIC, trade unions, ENB).

Some organisations produce training and learning agreements for all staff attending any event. This is so that everyone is clear what is to be gained from attendance and participation, and why this particular event is appropriate.

Some organisations produce no agreements at all. They write a full employee development commitment into general terms and conditions of employment (as with Tait's Greetings Cards, Summary Box 12.4). The Body Shop requires its staff to work one day per month on a community project or other social activity, and this is again written into terms and conditions of employment.

Whether formalised or not, all training agreements need to make clear:

- the purpose, aims and objectives of attending the event;
- costs and benefits of attending the event;
- where the event stands in the organisation and employee development process;
- any specific demands that the event may make;
- how the learning and development is to be implemented.

This may be written up by all concerned. It should be written up by the organisation. It **must** be written up by the employee and superior. After the event, it should then be signed off as part of the monitoring, review and evaluation process; and at this point, any opportunities or shortfalls and misperceptions can be written in.

Continuous professional and occupational development demands

Continuous professional and occupational development demands are also in effect a contracted responsibility for organisations employing staff whose professional or occupational body demands minimum periods of this form of training and learning. The numbers of professions, occupations and their representative bodies requiring this is greatly increasing, and this is being reinforced constantly by EU Directives. In practice also, this extends to many other occupations in the interests of keeping those who practise in them current and up-to-date, and therefore fully effective.

Whatever the sources, the interests of everyone are best served by having 'the agreement to train and develop' institutionalised and harmonised with organisation purpose and direction; human resource and staff management policies and priorities; and operations, jobs and work patterns. Both collectively and individually, everyone then knows where they stand.

Costs and benefits

The costs and benefits of a strategic approach to organisation and employee development are as summarised in Table 12.1.

Conclusions

The main purpose of a strategic approach to organisation and employee development is to ensure that everybody is clear about:

- what is on offer, to whom, when, where and why;
- the extent to which this is institutionalised and prioritised;
- the analytical and evaluative basis on which needs are assessed;
- the contribution of other factors such as peer review and inspections.

Table 12.1   Costs and benefits

Costs	Benefits
• Fixed costs incurred in strategy and policy inception and delivery • The proportion of fixed costs given over to organisation and employee development, and therefore not available for other activities • Variable costs incurred in some provisions, but these are at least known and understood in advance	• Structure and order are apparent • Clarity and mutuality of purpose and understanding • Clear statements of responsibilities and obligations • Prior knowledge of what can, and cannot, be delivered • Clear, formalised and open basis for needs assessment, implementation, monitoring, review and evaluation

A genuine strategic approach to this means that both resources and priority are allocated to ensure that whatever is delivered and implemented is effective. If this is then tied in with business policy and priorities, the organisation requirement for developing and improving staff is satisfied. If the other factors – professional, occupational and personal – are also acknowledged, then there is a sound basis for effective all-round organisation and employee development, and highly motivated and committed staff. There is also a clear basis for the identification and development of specific needs in each of the areas of behaviour, attitudes, skills, knowledge, expertise and technological proficiency.

QUESTIONS

1 What customer care training is required for those coming into:
   (a) retail;
   (b) telesales;
   (c) internet sales
   for the first time? How should a strategic approach to these be drawn up?
2 Consider Summary Box 12.4. What are the strengths and weaknesses of this approach?
3 How would you seek to improve the appraisal scheme outlined in Summary Box 12.5?
4 Construct a simple strategic approach for the inspection of the public service disaster or tragedy of your choice. What are you aiming to assess and why? What implications would your approach have for those working in the service? What is the approach that you should take to writing recommendations for employee development needs?
5 Construct a training agreement for the following:
   (a) a junior member of staff on a part-time MBA course for two years;
   (b) an apprentice electrician;
   (c) a newly qualified journalist going into their first job on a regional newspaper.
   Who have you involved, and why? What are the general and specific responsibilities placed on each and why? What are the benefits and drawbacks of this approach in each of these cases?

■ ⋎ 13 Organisational training functions

'Those who can, do. Those who cannot, teach.'

Anon

'Those who can, teach.'

Slogan produced to attract graduates
into the school-teaching profession, Department for Education (2001)

Introduction

Before its merger with the Chartered Institute of Personnel and Development, the Institute of Training and Development identified seven clear roles and functions which those involved ought to be able to perform. Given the acronym PADIMAC these were:

- **Practitioner:** the ability to deliver programmes, especially organisation-based core programmes, as and when required.
- **Adviser:** a resource available to other departments, divisions and functions to provide high-quality and accurate advice and guidance on devising and implementing programmes for other staff, and proposing and implementing development solutions to problems.
- **Designer:** of courses, programmes and events, including providing precise aims and objectives, learning outcomes and structures for projects and secondments.
- **Information:** holding and developing a bank or database of events to be disseminated around the rest of the organisation ideally targeted at those most likely to benefit. The best organisations ensure that training and development functions hold information on training needs analyses and the results of performance appraisals. The best organisations also ensure that they are aware of government schemes and support from public finance for particular initiatives.
- **Manager:** of the training budget and resources, including acting as advocate, cheerleader and lobbyist on behalf of the value of training and development, and the expertise held in the particular function.
- **Administrator:** handling the paperwork aspects, matching events with provision, contribution to management and financial accounts. Some training

functions carry out this work on behalf of all departments placing staff on events; others devolve the activity.

- **Consultant:** providing input into strategic and operational approaches and initiatives as and when required (see Summary Box 13.1).

SUMMARY BOX 13.1   Dilution of the training function

The overwhelming problem suffered by training and development functions in many organisations is lack of influence. Everything invariably has to be seen in this context, and it can be found across all sectors. In those organisations where a high value and priority is placed, organisation and employee development activities are fully integrated with business policy and operational development, and this is clearly the primary purpose and aim of all functions. More specifically, the problems arise from:

- institutional and managerial unwillingness to see training and development as anything but a cost, a drain on resources; together with a lack of ability to make the connection between structural, strategic, organisational and employee development and improvement in performance and activities;
- collective and cultural inability to agree who is, and should be, responsible for employee development activities – government, individuals, professional bodies, organisations;
- collective and individual inability and unwillingness to agree the overall remit and responsibilities of what should constitute a standard or blueprint for employee development functions;
- lack of prescribed, statutory and clearly understood and acceptable responsibilities and obligations placed on organisations.

The problems are compounded when senior managers, shareholders' representatives and public service governors and trustees seek short-term cost-cutting measures for some reason. Cancelling or diluting the training budget is easy and has no discernible short-term negative effect. This reinforces collective perceptions that training and development are costs rather than an investment – and so the problems continue.

Initial conclusions may therefore be drawn:

- there is a high level of complex expertise inherent in organising, structuring and providing enduring effective training and development;
- there is a wide variety of levels of influence in the function.

This may be illustrated as shown in Figure 13.1.

This indicates the likely output and enduring value of organisational and employee development, and the particular point of view from which this can be evaluated and assessed.

Strategic position

To be effective, strategic organisation and employee development requirements must reflect the actual balance of expertise and influence. If requirements and

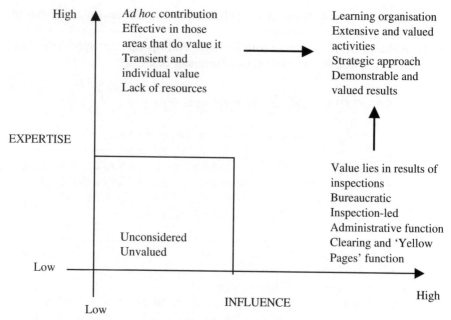

High

Ad hoc contribution
Effective in those
areas that do value it
Transient and
individual value
Lack of resources

Learning organisation
Extensive and valued
activities
Strategic approach
Demonstrable and
valued results

EXPERTISE

Value lies in results of
inspections
Bureaucratic
Inspection-led
Administrative function
Clearing and 'Yellow
Pages' function

Unconsidered
Unvalued

Low

Low   INFLUENCE   High

Figure 13.1   The balance of expertise and influence in organisation training functions

the present strategic position are out of balance, one or the other has to be remedied. The key features are as follows.

Learning organisation

If the strategy requires a learning organisation and all that is present is a sound bureaucratic structure, then investment is required in design and delivery experience. In the short-term this normally means hiring consultants, universities and colleges of further and higher education and expertise on off-the-job training. In the medium to long-term, investment is required in developing expertise and resources in-house. This may be as a specialist strategic function, contributing to business policy and priorities; or it may be in developing training, capability and activities in all staff whatever their occupation. It may also be a combination of the two. Where a learning organisation is required, this is invariably the case (see Summary Box 13.2).

SUMMARY BOX 13.2   Financial services

Financial services have been traditionally delivered by merchant banks and specialist institutions. In order to develop and enhance their own position, a collective strategic view was taken by a high street bank that their counter staff could, and should, be offering and making available financial products such as pensions, mortgages and high growth savings plans to customers over the counter.

With varying degrees of commitment (and therefore success), the high street banks now require their staff to do this. The most successful have been those that have supported staff with continuous input, including product awareness, customer relations and continuous service training.

The least successful have concentrated on centre-based cold-calling and telesales. This is symptomatic of an administrative and bureaucracy-led employee development function, requiring expertise in which it is not prepared to invest or support, either at the frontline or through a specialist function.

Source: Alliance and Leicester Plc (2000); Abbey National Plc (2001).

To be fully effective, learning organisation strategies require continuous investment and priority in both the expertise and administrative aspects of their training function so that delivery and support remain of the highest possible quality.

It is also necessary to ensure that everything that is carried out clearly contributes to organisational, business, product and service performance. The administrative side must ensure that procedures, the clearing function, appraisal, training needs analysis, monitoring, review and evaluation remain current and effective, and contribute to the targeting, development and enhancement of expertise.

Expertise must remain current. There is no value in continuing to employ experts if their capability does not remain current, or if wider business development takes the organisation away from this resource. Genuine priority in this area is likely to mean hiring expertise on a retained, consultancy or short-term contract basis. Those who are employed full-time have a professional priority in ensuring that their expertise remains current and of value in its application, and in developing it in line with operational demands (see Summary Box 13.3).

SUMMARY BOX 13.3   Yesterday's people

One of the strongest arguments in favour of developing training expertise as a distinctive profession or occupation is that it remains current provided that:

- it is known to make a clear contribution to organisation effectiveness and success;
- the expert is fully inducted into the strategic, operational, behavioural and cultural aspects of the organisation at the outset of employment.

Problems arise when those who have had extensive occupational experience then move into training and development, but do not remain familiar with present and projected behaviour and performance requirements. Training and development then gets delivered on the basis of 'what used to happen' rather than what is required currently.

To be effective, star operational performers must ensure that they have the same strategic, operational, behavioural and cultural awareness that would be required of anyone coming into the organisation or situation for the first time.

Source: 'Trouble at the Top: IBM', BBC2 (1999).

Expertise

Where there exists a high level of expertise with little influence, effectiveness is limited as follows:

- those who value the expertise are prepared to use it on a piecemeal or *ad hoc* basis;
- those who turn to it in times of crises or emergency;
- those who suddenly see an opportunity (see Summary Box 13.4).

SUMMARY BOX 13.4   The blinding flash of light

'For the life of me I couldn't see what we were doing wrong. We let people work from home, from the car, hours to suit – the lot. We paid well, expenses were good also. We gave our people laptop computers with internet connections. But still they left us after a few months.

'I had been to business school and in desperation rang my old tutor. He said: "Get them in once a month. Three line whip, it's compulsory. Bring them into the office for the whole day. Then when they arrive, give them two substantial organisation and staff training sessions. After that, they should have plenty of opportunity to mix, socialise, go around the building and meet their friends and colleagues. Feed them and water them, and if they want, put them up at a hotel overnight."

'At first, I couldn't see the value. But after six to nine months, it was apparent that complaints had fallen, and that output and commitment were beginning to rise. It took nearly two years to note any discernible improvement in turnover. However, those who came in to work under this regime tended to stay. Probably those who left over this period would have done so anyway – they had thought themselves into this position and nothing was going to shift them.'

Source: Simon Cullen, Ernst & Young business development manager (2001), summarising the effects of a programme introduced on 31 December 1999.

Problems where this exists are therefore:

- it is an expensive, under-used and unstructured resource in any case;
- it is likely that the resource itself is spending time producing proposals in order to try and drum up business (at which it is self-evidently unsuccessful, or else its influence would be greater) rather than playing to its expertise and strengths across the board;
- it is viewed as a luxury and is therefore vulnerable to cuts or abolition when immediate cost savings are required (thus reducing the overall training and development effort and effectiveness still further).

Increasing the influence of the function is therefore an operational priority. To do this, it is essential to engage in:

- internal public relations activities;
- the production of a continuous flow of achievements presented in positive and concise terms;

- the production of training and development proposals in ways that are known and perceived to be of value to departments, divisions, functions and individuals;
- attending management meetings at all levels and contributing from the point of view of the training and development function (see Summary Box 13.5).

SUMMARY BOX 13.5   Realpolitik

More insidiously, it is often necessary to engage in organisational, informal and political systems to improve the effectiveness and value of the public relations and lobbying approach.

Community awareness training at the Royal Ulster Constabulary (RUC)

Because of the strong social, cultural and religious divides in Northern Ireland, this was a strategic priority for many years. In practice, however, it was stated and carried out but never reinforced. All police officers went through a stated programme as a part of initial training, and there were regular updates throughout their period of service.

Though widely carried out, the content of the programme was never fully believed in or valued. The Catholic community especially continued to believe that it was not well served by the RUC. This was brought into sharp focus by the political Good Friday Agreement of 1999 and subsequent recommendations for continued development of the police force. Active participation and increases in recruitment levels from the Catholic community were only achieved through the widespread leaking of recommendations of the Patten Report; and this was given further political significance and media coverage through the proposal to change its name to the Northern Ireland Police Force.

Source: C. Patten, 'The Future of Policing in Northern Ireland', HMSO (1999).

Administration

Administration-based organisational training and development functions are effective so long as everyone understands that this is their contribution. Effective outputs of this kind of function are:

- speedy, effective and targeted dissemination of information on courses and events;
- speedy and effective booking, payment, invoicing and expenses procedures;
- centralised analysis and evaluation of needs, appraisals and the effectiveness of events, together with the provision of effective data to those to whom it applies;
- generating the monitoring, reviewing and evaluating of the effectiveness of inspections;
- generating and promulgating databases of opportunities and events, and presenting these to people to whom they apply;
- budget management and reporting.

This is a bureaucratic approach to the direction, management and contribution of organisation and employee development. As with all functions, bureaucracy is excellent and effective so long as processes and procedures are supportive of the main effort, rather than becoming the driving force. They also require constant review and evaluation so that they can be abolished, replaced and updated where necessary and desirable.

Problems occur where procedures are not updated and when they, rather than the outputs, become the driving force. Further difficulties arise when:

- bureaucracy goes into areas outside its remit or expertise and this is a problem whether it encroaches of its own volition or is told to do so by senior managers (see Summary Box 13.2 above);
- existing procedures remain in place following organisational change, restructuring, technological refurbishment, merger or takeover;
- new procedures are put in place without the abolition of the old;
- procedures are unvalued, misunderstood and therefore, not followed (see Summary Box 13.6).

SUMMARY BOX 13.6   Procedures

Procedures exist to ensure that everything is done in orderly, understood and accepted ways in support of organisation, professional and occupational activities. Reasons for their existence must be known and understood, and capable of support and acceptance by all. Problems arise when some or all of this is missing. For example:

A prestigious department at one of the country's top universities suffered for years from declining status and standards of quality, value and output. Resources were being misused, facilities and expertise were out-of-date. Staff and students felt unvalued, and numbers fell away.

The Head of Department took early retirement. He was replaced by a City analyst who convened a project team composed of teaching and research staff. Working over two weeks of the summer holidays, the team reviewed and updated teaching provision, assignment programmes and course content. This was then presented to the university on the 6th of August for approval with a view to implementation in September at the start of the new academic year.

By the end of August nothing had happened. Impatiently, the new Head of Department rang the university Vice Chancellor. He was told that unfortunately none of this would be possible for at least two years because university procedures demanded that the proposals were scrutinised by teaching and academic committees, and these would not now be meeting until November; and that by that time, it would be impossible to get the new courses into the university central clearing system in time for publication to the next wave of students.

The new Head of Department resigned and left having achieved nothing except frustration and further demoralisation all round. He was replaced by an acting Head of Department, a senior lecturer with many years' experience. He calmly introduced all of the proposed changes within the existing framework.

Unconsidered and unvalued employee development functions

Taking this approach to employee development is overtly sound provided that it is explicitly stated and understood. Where this is the case, everyone then clearly knows and understands that responsibility for training and development rests in their own hands.

In practice, very few organisations that actively take this view are prepared to be explicit and honest. Symptoms of an unvalued function in most situations are:

- under-funding and under-resourcing;
- applying financial management and budget cuts to training and development;
- cutting training and development provision because of other work pressures and operational demands rather than harmonising these;
- cutting back on core programmes and offerings and seeking cheaper alternatives (e.g. web-based);
- cutting back on support, appraisal, mentoring and guidance (see Summary Box 13.7).

SUMMARY BOX 13.7   The student nurse

A student nurse, a woman in her mid thirties was coming to the end of her final hospital ward placement before qualification.

The whole course had been extremely hard. There was little support either on- or off-the-job. However, the woman had worked in social care and had other qualifications. She was also very highly motivated so she had done well in spite of everything, and had achieved consistently good results in the college work and on the different hospital and community placements.

One evening at 10.00 pm the student nurse was asked to contact the relatives of a dying patient to get them into the hospital as quickly as possible. Because of the lateness of the hour and a mistranscription of the family name, this took longer than anticipated. The student then went to the toilet.

The charge nurse, also a woman in her thirties, followed her into the toilet, spat at her and was physically and verbally abusive for 'taking so long over a few phone calls'.

The student complained about her treatment to her college tutor, hospital man-agement and union (Royal College of Nursing) representative. Each replied as follows:

- the college tutor berated the student for working nights when college policy explicitly stated that this should not happen;
- the hospital management representative stated that the charge nurse was under a lot of pressure and to discipline her would only make matters worse;
- the Royal College of Nursing representative stated that handling difficult situations was all part of a nurse's training.

Accordingly, the student gritted her teeth and completed the qualification. She then went to work as a supermarket cashier and shelf filler for wages similar to those she would have received had she stayed in the health service.

Source: Nene College, Northampton (2001).

The total approach is therefore dishonest. This is compounded when organisations and managers know the problems but refuse to address them, especially when resources are available or could be made so.

The other main symptom is where organisations blame market forces, competitive pressures, high residential costs – anything but their own commitment to the quality of working life and development of their people. Employees working for these organisations know and understand this from their own experience. Again, problems are compounded where employees and their representatives propose solutions based on organisation and employee development as well as policy changes that are then rejected without discussion or explanation.

Relating organisation strategy and the training function

It is essential therefore to be clear and honest about where the employee development function lies in relation to these issues. This can then be related directly to strategic purpose and direction (see Chapter 12) in order that its contribution is known and understood, and opportunities and consequences for other activities be assessed and evaluated. The main conclusions that need to be understood are as follows.

Cost leadership/unvalued function

Organisations that genuinely seek cost leadership but do not value (or indeed have) a development function of their own, commit themselves to buying in this expertise whenever they acquire new technology or markets, new ways of working, and when they require problem-solving and other specific skills. In practice, it is much more the case that cost leadership organisations have highly developed training functions with these activities fully integrated into everything else.

In general, an unvalued function detracts from full effectiveness of all activities unless there is this commitment to buy in expertise, whatever the generic strategic position.

Focus/*ad hoc* contribution

This is the most positive case for maximising high expertise/low influence resources. In this case, the function has no strategic input, but is proactively called on when business and operational factors demand, and in response to specific requests from other parts of the organisation. The approach needs careful management if it is not to become effectively a support function for those that choose to use it on a regular basis. To be as effective as possible, it still has to be able to respond to specific requests from occasional users.

Otherwise the *ad hoc* contribution is likely to be as the result of an unstructured and therefore undervalued strategic approach. It is, in turn, much more likely that the *ad hoc* approach requires attention and a precise remit applied (see Summary Box 13.8).

SUMMARY BOX 13.8 'What do we want from our training and development function?'

The answers to this question lie at the core of the effectiveness, or otherwise, of the remit. Many organisations still take the following approaches:

- to be an effective provider of training and development;
- to integrate this with organisation and business priorities;
- to offer development to all staff;

– without then going on and saying precisely what they mean. This is very often because senior managers, directors, shareholders' representatives and public service governors have no clear idea themselves about what they require, what is possible, or achievable. Many are also unwilling or unprepared to take advice from elsewhere. The problem may be made worse by shareholder or governor perceptions that known or perceived increases in staff costs may adversely affect the share prices or the attitudes of public service funders.

It is therefore essential that the question is addressed precisely. There is no problem in doing this with production and service delivery functions, and the same approach is required for employee development.

Differentiation/bureaucratic contribution

This is effective when the training and development function works as outlined above (see page 155). Organisations that pursue strategies of differentiation require high-quality, highly motivated and fully trained staff, and whether the training and development function is bureaucratic or learning organisation, this must be the priority. Its effectiveness is measured in terms of the success, value and profitability of product and service outputs, customer and client satisfaction, and management, professional and occupational development.

Bureaucratic functions dilute differentiation strategies when they add cost rather than value. A key part of differentiation is concerned with delivering enduring customer and client satisfaction (some would say delight), and generating their loyalty, and this is entirely dependent on the operational staff with whom they deal (see Summary Box 13.9).

The key contribution made by a bureaucratic training function is therefore to ensure that all frontline needs are prioritised and met. This includes evaluating analyses and appraisals, and lifting requirements out and addressing these first. Other professional, occupational and personal demands and wants are then met

Boo.Com was established in 1997 as an online footwear retailer. Founded at the height of the first (and very glamorous) wave of internet investments, it established itself as an excellent employer and wonderful place to work. Projecting itself as a learning organisation, all staff were able to book and attend any training and development event that they wished.

However, this brought problems of its own in this case and there are lessons for all organisations.

The approach was unstructured and untargeted. The result was that while many professional, occupational and personal requirements were met, those of the organisation were not.

There was no clear direction or remit. Requirements for customer and client service were never identified or addressed. The company had no customer hotline or means of dealing with complaints or wrong deliveries until shortly before it closed in 2000. The company attracted up to half a million hits on its website per week. However, sometimes as few as 700 of these per week would be translated into orders – and no attention was paid to this either.

Boo.Com was overtly pursuing a strategy of differentiation – a perceived attractive alternative to retailer shoe shops. In practice, this key element of strategy was misdirected and therefore ineffective. Especially at the foundation stage, any organisation must concentrate its training and development priority on customer and client service if it wishes to compete in this way. Professional, occupational and personal demands can then follow later.

later. Pragmatically, if there are to be budget or resource cuts, organisational priority is last to suffer rather than first. It is also much more likely that personal and professional demands will be accommodated by individuals concerned in the short-term at least, especially if they know and understand the reasons why.

Roles, functions and resources

The combination of PADIMAC elements, preferred strategy and direction, and functional remit, forms the basis on which individual employee development departments are structured. This, in turn, provides a key for defining the following:

- Department structure, roles and responsibilities. Training controllers and directors, officers and advisers, and administrators, all have very different responsibilities, remits, job descriptions and work coverage across sectors, and at different organisations within the same sector. To be fully effective, this must reflect the basis on which the whole function is built; and if this is not clear, then specific roles, functions, responsibilities and authority will not be either.

- Reporting relations. Again, the effectiveness of these is based on clarity of role, function, remit and priority. Where the value of the employee development function (or indeed any other) is not clear, then others within the organisation are uncertain as to how or why to deal with them, and what may be expected from them. This invariably causes a reduction in respect and value.
- Derived roles and responsibilities in employee development in other functions. This reflects the extent to which functional, operational and expert (and high quality and status) staff have direct responsibility and authority for their own development activities. This may again be plotted on a continuum (see Figure 13.2).
- Agreement on the circumstances under which staff will (and will not) be recommended for training and development activities, or placed on projects and secondments. The key issues are clarity and equity. It is damaging to collective and individual morale where these are known, believed or perceived not to exist, and that some staff get better opportunities dependent on who they work for, where they work and in what job.
- What expertise to employ and what to buy in under what circumstances, the precise remit, and required output.
- The location of expertise – especially where this is based at the head office of a large organisation with diversified and extensive regional activities; or conversely, where there is high quality expertise in the field but no clear direction or coordination from head office.

Costs and benefits

The costs and benefits of an ordered, structured training and development function are as summarised in Table 13.1.

Conclusions

The enduring problem with creating and delivering effective organisation training functions is that of contribution. This is often very difficult to measure and so organisations and senior managers do not do so – and so the function becomes institutionally undervalued. This is compounded where expert advice and guidance are clearly and readily available.

Table 13.1 Costs and benefits

Costs	Benefits
<ul><li>Fixed costs – staffing, accommodation and equipment</li><li>Capital costs – also including accommodation and equipment</li><li>Economic rent on specific expertise (and this applies to administrative as well as operational and delivery)</li></ul>	<ul><li>Clarity and purpose of function</li><li>Strategic input</li><li>Precise and understood contribution</li><li>Capability to measure training and development effectiveness and performance against a wide range of criteria including financial</li></ul>

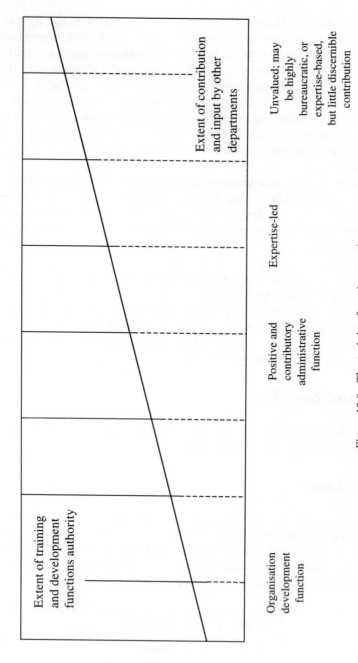

Figure 13.2   The training function continuum

Powerful organisations adopt the pragmatic – some would say expedient – view of actively and strategically downgrading their development effort and function, and buying in required expertise when needed. These organisations also tend to be prepared to pay premium rates of salary and other terms and conditions of employment for functional expertise when required rather than developing their own.

So long as this is clearly stated and adopted as a strategic approach, it is capable of being sustained in many sectors. However, the absence of an employee development function means that those presently in post have to take responsibility for their own advancement. The expert and highly motivated then become marketable and employable commodities in their own right. In times of skills, knowledge and expertise shortage this then contributes to auctions for these qualities.

When they are fully effective, employee development functions are the key foundation stone for:

- effective personal, organisational, occupational and professional development;
- attending to the key skills, knowledge, expertise and technological development required;
- reinforcing and developing behaviour, attitudes and values on which the best and most enduringly successful organisations are founded.

QUESTIONS

1 What actions should be taken by training and development professionals in order to enhance the profile of what they do, and the respect and value in which they are held by others?

2 You overhear a senior manager of your organisation saying 'I do not know why we have a training and development function. They make no contribution to the organisation.' You arrange to see the senior manager afterwards. What are you going to say to him/her and why?

3 Outline the advantages and disadvantages of placing all organisational and employee development in the hands of specialist consultants and outside providers.

4 What qualities are necessary in an employee development function for the effective delivery of:
   (a) core training programmes?
   (b) effective occupational and professional training provision?
   How might this be structured into a functional/departmental format?

5 Produce a structured approach for an employee development function/department, the purpose of which is to raise its own profile within the rest of the organisation. What actions are necessary: immediately; and in the medium to long-term? How would you measure this for success/failure?

■ ⋈ 14 Organisation development

> *'I was always conscious that I was making people come to work when they did not want to. They would rather be doing other things. So we created the conditions whereby people not only had to come to work in order to earn a living – they also wanted to come to work.'*
>
> Ricardo Semler, *'The Maverick Solution'*, BBC2 (1999)

Introduction

Organisation development (OD) is the generic term given to strategic approaches and initiatives for improving organisational effectiveness through emphases on the capabilities, capacities, qualities and motivation of those who carry out the work. These are supported through harmonising and integrating individual and collective training and development within all departmental, divisional and functional operations and activities.

OD depends on the development of staff and management for commercial, industrial and public service success and effectiveness. It follows from this that there are roles for change mechanisms, change agents, change catalysts and key appointments with key qualities, as well as training and development expertise and activity in order to take the organisation in the preferred directions.

The OD process is aimed at changing, forming and developing culture, values, attitudes and beliefs in positive and constructive ways, as well as paying specific attention to the enhancement of skills, knowledge and technological proficiency.

The precise nature of OD varies between organisations that adopt the approach. In general, the key values and qualities reflect:

- a measure of conformity and the willingness of the staff to go down the paths indicated;
- obsession with product and service quality;
- strong customer, client and supplier orientation;
- universal identity with the organisation at large on the part of all staff;
- setting a moral or value-led example and taking an active pride in the organisation and its work on the part of all concerned;
- designing, implementing and supporting the required management and supervisory style;
- higher output per member of staff;
- accuracy in prioritising those activities that contribute directly to organisation profitability and effectiveness;

- the capacity to develop fully flexible skills, knowledge, attitudes and behaviour;
- a much more open and cohesive culture and *esprit de corps*;
- the institutionalisation of both collective and individual development.

The OD process requires expertise and commitment in all of the component parts of collective and individual development – performance assessment, management and appraisal; problem raising and acknowledgement; access to information; resourcing and implementing individual and collective development activities, including project work and secondments; integrating monitoring, review and evaluation as strategic, as well as operational, commitment.

The key outputs of OD include the following:

- the development of positive and collective culture, attitudes, values, beliefs and ethics;
- the generation of commitment to the organisation on the part of everybody concerned;
- coping with change and uncertainty in products, services, technology, markets and the environment;
- the management of conflict.

In summary, a working environment and organisation culture are created whereby each of these issues is positively addressed. Problems are recognised early. Because of the fundamental openness of the approach, everyone's interest is engaged in resolving them.

The development of positive culture, attitudes, values and beliefs

Organisation culture is an amalgam and summary of the ways in which activities are conducted and the standards and values adopted. It encompasses the general atmosphere within the organisation, prevailing attitudes, standards, morale, and individual and collective identity. It is an essential feature of effective organisation creation and performance. It has its roots in the following:

- **History and tradition:** the origins of the organisation; aims and objectives of founders, first owners and managers; traditional philosophy and values; the respect and value with which these are currently held; the ways in which they have developed.
- **Nature of activities:** historical and traditional, and also current and envisaged; the general state of success and effectiveness; technology and expertise; and management style.
- **Technology:** the relationship between technology and work structure; attitudes of the workforce to technology; pay, status and reward levels in relation to technological proficiency; alienation factors and steps taken to address these; levels of technological stability and change; levels of expertise, stability and change.
- **Past, present and future:** myths and legends; the relationship of the past with

the present and future; special pressures (especially struggles and glories) of the past; the extent to which the organisation is living in the past, present or future.

- **The purposes, priorities and attention:** in relation to performance, staff, customers, suppliers, the community and environment.
- **Size:** the relationship between size and structure; the extent of proliferation of divisions, supervisory structures, management and reporting relationships, rules, processes and procedures; the relationship between occupations and professions.
- **Location:** geographical location; social and ethical norms, values and pressures; the ways in which these are harmonised with the organisation.
- **Management style:** the extent of its basis of integrity, value, respect, mutuality and trust; the nature of that style – autocratic, participative, involving, democratic (none of which need be wrong, all of which need to be understood and accepted); the nature of superior/subordinate relations.

Organisation approaches to developing culture requires attention to each of the following points. At its best, it is reinforced and developed through induction and initial job training stages, and every other development activity that takes place; it is reinforced through prescribed standards, attitudes and values, and patterns of behaviour, and the ways in which work is ordered, structured, supervised and carried out.

Culture is:

- learned – rather than inherent or instinctive;
- shared – by all those present; consequently, acquired attitudes and values have to be capable of acceptance and internalisation by all involved;
- continuous – cumulative in its development as it is passed on from one generation to the next;
- symbolic – an outward representation of collective and individual feelings;
- integrated – so that organisational behaviour (how things are done) is integrated with what is done and why;
- adaptive – based on human qualities of adaptability, creativity, innovation, imagination and the need to progress and develop;
- regular – setting standards of behaviour, rights and rituals, with which everybody can be comfortable;
- norms – establishing distinctive standards of behaviour;
- dominant values – advocated by the organisation and required by those who work there;
- rules – underpinning the required attitudes and values, and providing development and, where necessary, sanction when these are not adhered to;
- climate – conveyed by the environment, the physical layout, working relationships in order to form a collective general, behavioural and perceptual set of feelings among those who work.

The development effort therefore is to ensure that everyone indeed understands 'how things are done' as well as what is done and why. The process must result in collective attitudes and values that are:

- designed and defined by the organisation's top managers, rather than allowed to emerge as the result of a collective inertia;
- positive, not negative, so that the fundamental approach is to what can be achieved rather than to the barriers to achievement (see Summary Box 14.1);

SUMMARY BOX 14.1   'The enemy is out there'

'A friend once told the story of a boy that he coached to play baseball who, after dropping three catches, marched into the dug-out. "No-one can catch a ball out there," he said.

There is in each of us a propensity to find someone or something outside ourselves to blame when things go wrong. Some organisations elevate this propensity to a commandment: "Thou shalt always find someone else to blame." Marketing blames manufacturing, manufacturing blames engineering, engineering blames marketing. For many companies, "the enemy" has become Far Eastern competition, trade unions, government regulation, or customers who have taken their requirements elsewhere. "The enemy is out there" however is almost always an incomplete story. "Out there" and "in here" are usually part of a single system. The remedy lies in the organisation's own hands.'

Source: P. Senge, 'The Fifth Discipline', Century Business (1992).

- strong not weak, so that everyone has full confidence that how, when, why and where they do something is fully integrated with the organisation's position, attitudes and values;
- positively acceptable and capable of compliance rather than nebulous and incapable of rejection (see Summary Box 14.2).

SUMMARY BOX 14.2   Acceptance and rejection

Strong positive cultures are not all things to all people and this means that some will reject them. For example:

- **Nursing:** the micro-culture on some NHS hospital wards is so all-pervasive that the staff effectively develop their own total lifestyle based around patterns of work. In particular, social events are organised so that they work together and can rest and play together. Dominated by the siege mentality existing across the NHS at present, and reflected in individual hospitals and wards, the problem facing individuals is whether to adopt the total lifestyle or seek work elsewhere.
- **Japanese manufacturing:** the macro-culture of many Japanese car and electrical goods organisations operating in the West demands that staff attend out-of-hours functions as part of the work commitment. Again, the pressure to comply is very strong and not always acceptable.

In both cases, there is a cultural discord between how things are done at work, and personal priorities in the rest of life. They are not always easily capable of reconciliation.

Collective and individual employee development therefore concentrates on:

- instilling the required and desired attitudes and values, and generating understanding of the reasons for these in relation to essential business and service performance;
- underpinning these with the corporate approach to induction, initial and continuous job training, and the delivery of the core programme;
- supporting everything through a clearly understood, accepted, positive and open staff management style (again, whether autocratic, participative or democratic).

No stated or overt culture development survives an adversarial or dishonest management style or general organisation ethos where what is stated is unsupported or gone against in practice and delivery.

Generation of commitment

Generating collective and individual commitment to the approach requires:

- the integration of organisational goals with personal expectations – this means a long-term and enduring commitment to professional, occupational and personal development, as well as organisation priorities;
- creating a structure of reporting relationships that provides space and encouragement for collective and individual development, rather than restrictions and restraints;
- open, participative and involving functioning of the organisation with full access to information;
- fundamental equality of opportunity, normally based on a single set of rules and regulations (rather than those that vary according to status, occupation or expertise);
- mutual openness, respect, value, trust, consideration and support among different levels and occupations;
- the open recognition and discussion of conflict with the emphasis on identifying and resolving issues rather than institutionalising them;
- managerial behaviour and styles of leadership and supervision based on visibility, openness, honesty and integrity;
- recognising individual, as well as collective, needs and expectations; and recognising and valuing every individual contribution;
- implementing systems of pay and reward that are known, believed and perceived to be based on fairness and equality rather than status and influence;
- investing in the quality of the general working and learning environment;
- providing opportunities for personal, occupational and professional variety, enhancement and career progression, as well as organisation success, profitability and effectiveness;
- generating a positive *esprit de corps* – a team spirit – that gives high levels of

feelings of pride, identity and acceptance by the organisation, and feelings of loyalty, mutuality, trust and security.

A key feature of OD is therefore the level of attention paid to the general environment in which work is carried out. If this is effective, then the required basis for the development of the other activities is assured.

Coping with change and uncertainty

The OD approach to change and uncertainty takes the view that both are inevitable and that they are best overcome by instilling attitudes, values, standards and expertise capable of accommodating and responding to this. This is in contrast to those organisations that go through business process re-engineering and other restructuring and re-sizing programmes as a response to profits warnings, budget cuts, stockmarket, media and governor pressures (see Summary Box 14.3).

SUMMARY BOX 14.3   Body Shop

Body Shop, the organic cosmetics company, was founded by Gordon and Anita Roddick in 1976. At the outset, both the concept – using organic produce to make cosmetics, and also the distinctive ethical approach – paying Western prices for third world crops – were either ignored altogether or dismissed as unworkable commercially.

However, the company grew steadily over periods of recession and high unemployment, at exactly the same time that people were having to look hard at non-essential expenditure.

The collective overriding ethic was, and remains, to 'do right by everybody – staff, suppliers, customers, communities and shareholders'. This collective ethic came to be widely understood early in the development of the company. The result of this was to ensure a steady stream of potentially high quality and committed staff. The company has had a staff waiting list since 1978.

The other main problem to be faced was managing media and stockmarket expectations. The company consistently produced lower net margins than the rest of the cosmetics and department store sector. However, by making clear the long-term strategy and its foundations in OD, sectoral confidence and support were assured at times when more traditional organisations suffered from profits warnings and loss of confidence.

In the management of change, OD concentrates on the following.

Primary beneficiaries

So long as these remain customers and clients, the development effort is directed at their service and levels of satisfaction and quality that are as certain as possible to retain them and generate the capability to offer further products and services in the future.

In pursuit of this staff training has to concentrate on the following:

- speed, flexibility and quality of response together with the development of attitudes of responsibility and autonomy;
- technological proficiency and capability so that equipment in use at present is maximised and optimised, and that future innovations and consequent changes in expertise are accepted and implemented quickly when required;
- the ability to solve problems and address complaints whenever they arise (see Summary Box 14.4).

SUMMARY BOX 14.4   Staff as primary beneficiary

Organisations that adopt this approach have to place genuine intrinsic and extrinsic value on their staff. This may be summarised as a commitment to 'high quality work and high levels of commitment and motivation in return for high and enduring levels of reward'. Thus, for example:

- Body Shop do not pay more than many retail organisations. However, they do offer greater professional and occupational development opportunities, as well as work away from the organisation in the community.
- Sanyo UK pay approximately 130 per cent of what is on offer at Philips, Ferguson and Bush, and other indigenous electrical goods manufacturers. This is in return for full flexibility of working and requirements to develop. The company also points proudly to a staff absenteeism rate of 0.5 per cent (the equivalent of every member of staff taking an average of one day's sick leave only per annum).

Other beneficiaries

This refers especially to shareholders, suppliers and communities.

Potential problems with shareholders' representatives arise when the benefits of OD do not become immediately apparent, and those responsible come under pressure to drop it, dilute it or reduce the desired levels of investment. Certainly shareholders, and their representatives, need educating in the costs and benefits of the approach because the financial aim is to optimise long-term security, and therefore owner value, and not short-term attractiveness.

Suppliers may also need to be convinced of the approach especially if they are used to dealing in orderly and familiar ways with bureaucratic and traditional functionaries. Emphasis is therefore required on the long-term potential for the relationship, and the value and importance of enduring quality, service and mutuality of interest as well as billing arrangements.

A spin-off of successful and enduring OD is the value of 'corporate citizenship'. All communities prefer to have known, believed and perceived good employers in their area (see Summary Box 14.5).

When Eurotunnel, the Channel Tunnel operating company, first established itself, it took on an OD approach to all of its non-construction activities. It paid particular emphasis to supplier, staffing and community aspects.

Suppliers were drawn from the local business community wherever possible. This was underpinned with an open invitation to those in the locality to tender for the supply of any product or service whatsoever. However, only contracts already awarded to those from outside the area would be considered.

Staff were also drawn from the local community wherever possible. An open organisation and management style was adopted from the outset. This was underpinned with full personal, occupational and professional opportunities made available to all staff from the inception of their employment. Promotion, variety, enhancement and project opportunities were, and are, always offered in-house before expertise is sought from elsewhere.

The community relations initiative was reflected in each of the above. It was underpinned additionally with an information archive, education and exhibition centre available to all. The company provided materials for schools and colleges, guest speakers, clubs and societies, and sponsorship of local and social events.

For all the political controversy surrounding the Channel Tunnel, the organisation itself was accepted from a very early stage. Great loyalty was generated among the staff, as well as the community. The approach became a key feature of the immediate generation and sustenance of an operating profit (as distinct from the servicing of the capital debt) founded on high and enduring levels of staff capability and commitment.

Barriers to change

Beyond this, OD requires specific efforts in identifying and surmounting the physical and psychological barriers to change. These include the following:

- **Location:** this is a barrier when, for whatever reason, it becomes impossible for the organisation to continue to operate in its current premises.
- **Tradition:** this is a problem where there has been a long history of successful work in specific, well understood and widely accepted ways.
- **Success (real and perceived):** if the organisation is known, believed or perceived to be successful in its current activities, then there is a resistance based on: 'why change something that works?' This is reinforced if there is a long history of overt stability and prosperity, and patterns of occupation based on enduring technology and expertise.
- **Failure:** this is a barrier to change where a given state of affairs has been allowed to persist for some time, leading to the view that this is simply 'one of those things'. Resistance occurs when someone determines to do something about it, upsetting an overtly comfortable and orderly status quo, whatever the state of the organisation.

- **Technology:** this is a problem and barrier where specific patterns of work and activity have existed for long periods of time. Technological change disrupts patterns of work and causes requirements to retrain, and this leads to real and perceived undervaluing and loss of collective and individual self-respect in terms of what was done in the past. Technological change has also disrupted social as well as work and occupational groups.
- **Vested interests:** needs for organisational change are resisted by those who are, or perceive themselves to be, at risk or threat from the change. Vested interests are found in all areas. They include senior managers; operational staff; people in support functions; and those on promotional and career paths for whom the current order represents a perceived, clear and guaranteed passage to promotion and influence.
- **Managerial:** managers and supervisors also become familiar and comfortable with accepted and understood ways of working, and are likely to resist when these are to be disrupted.
- **Bureaucracy:** the bureaucratic barrier occurs where patterns of order and control, supported by procedures and processes, have grown up over long periods; the problem is worse where the bureaucracy is large and complex and a significant part of the total range of activities, and carries considerable influence.
- **Redundancy and redeployment:** people expect their jobs to be threatened because of technological and occupational change, and this is based on current and recent histories of high levels of unemployment.
- **Political drives in public services:** these have come to be widely perceived as expedient and self-serving to the interests of politicians rather than those who work in the services, or their customers and clients. It is also widely understood and perceived that political drives cause additional stress and strain on those working at the frontline of the particular service.
- **Fear and anxiety:** these are human responses to concepts and situations that are unknown and uncertain, and are the initial response to any change that is proposed. If allowed to get out of hand, fear and anxiety can become an exercise in the devising and promulgation of hypothetical scenarios that could, in certain circumstances, become problems on the changing landscape. Not only does this constitute a waste of organisational resources, but interactions such as these among those involved feed on themselves, generating negativity and unnecessary internal turbulence.
- **Perfection:** at the point at which change is proposed suddenly everything concerning the status quo becomes 'perfect'. Anything that is proposed as an alternative has to address the barrier that, because it is unknown, it is therefore imperfect.
- **'It cannot be done' and 'there is no alternative':** these are barriers to confidence and understanding based on a lack of true, full and accurate information, especially concerning how things are to be implemented. They become collective and individual entrenchments, especially when being asked to defend a contentious or controversial position. Conducted in isolation, each of these attitudes simply becomes a challenge for others to think of alternatives. Each of these attitudes also underpin the absolute requirement

for those responsible for driving and implementing change to explain themselves fully, together with the opportunities and consequences arising (see Summary Box 14.6).

SUMMARY BOX 14.6 'Do not fix what is not broken'

This is received wisdom in a variety of human situations. It does not apply to OD employee development or the management of change.

In industrial, commercial and public sector organisations, it is a very short step from this attitude to complacency, insularity and perceptions of immortality and infallibility. Any organisation loses reputation very quickly if it does not maintain *and develop* its absolute standards of skills, knowledge and expertise, investment in product and service technology, and attention to the needs of customers and clients.

Neither is it enough purely to spend money on organisation and employee development. Consider the following example.

Ford UK

Over the period 1975–2000, Ford UK consistently spent approximately 5 per cent of payroll costs on staff training and development. However, because it did not address organisational priorities and was not strategically targeted, monitored, reviewed or evaluated, output at the factories rose very slowly (to a maximum 60 cars per member of staff, per annum in 2000, compared to Nissan UK's 115 cars per annum, per member of staff also in 2000). Structural and organisational problems were never addressed. Institutional problems of racism, cultural and social barriers tended to be enhanced by the individual attention given to training rather than the collective attitudes and values that were more likely to emerge if an overall collective, orderly and strategic approach had been taken.

Source: 'The problems at Ford UK', *People Management* (May 2000).

Conflict

The other main area with which OD is concerned is the management of conflict. Conflict is inherent in all human situations, and this includes places of work. Conflict takes the following forms:

- Argument and debate, including the requirement to resolve personal and professional disputes and differences; and to reconcile strongly held points of view – often from the highest possible moral and professional standpoint.
- Competition – including competition for jobs and work, between departments, divisions and functions, and for resources and support.
- Warfare – in which individuals, departments, divisions, functions and organisations engage in open, adversarial and aggressive interrelationships.

The culture and climate should be created that enables positive resolution to argument and debate. There may, under certain circumstances, be positive outcomes from competition. However, warfare is always bad – for morale, motivation, output, product and service quality. It is expensive in terms of resource consumption, management staff and time, and lost customers, clients and orders (see Summary Box 14.7).

The sources and causes of conflict that OD must address are as follows:

- Competition for resources and the basis on which this is conducted.
- Lack of absolute standards of openness, honesty, trustworthiness and integrity.
- Lack of shared values, commitment, enthusiasm and motivation.
- Unfairness, unevenness and inequality of personal and professional treatment, often linked to perceptions of favouritism and scapegoating.
- Physical and psychological barriers based on status, expertise and department, divisional and functional activity.
- Inability to meet expectations and fulfil promises; often compounded by the use of complex and bureaucratic language in communication.
- Expediency and short-term attention to problems and issues.
- The presence and influence of vested interest groups and lobbies, and the basis on which these were founded.
- Divergence between corporate, group and individual aims and objectives.
- Inter-departmental and inter-group wrangles concerned with territory, prestige, influence and activities.

- Individual and collective personality, group and occupational clashes where these are not resolved. These are compounded when there is a lack of clarity of activities, or where certain individual and collective roles overlap. This may be compounded further where there is no clarity over reporting relationships, or where an individual or group has to report to two superiors.
- Hidden, secondary and parallel, agenda; where it is known, believed and perceived that what is being stated is dishonest for some reason, or not telling the full story.

To this may be added the following factors:

- The parties to the conflict, and the extent of their known, believed and perceived occupational and organisational influence.
- The issues in dispute, and strength of feeling that the parties involved have concerning them.
- The sources of energy of the conflict, and the length of time that it is allowed to run.
- Needs for behavioural symbols such as the necessity to be known to win or to have a triumph; the consequences of placing a group or individual in the position of defeat.

OD approaches to the management of conflict include the following:

- Staff management and supervisory development programmes paying attention to absolute standards of honesty, integrity, respect and value; standards and quality of communication and visibility; presentation skills, information giving and understanding.
- Concentration on the outputs of needs analyses and performance appraisal, performance measurement and the remedial action required; this is only effective if based on empathy and mutual identity and commitment.
- Attention to systems, procedures and practices, and the attitude with which organisational bureaucracy is delivered, and the priority accorded; developing rules, procedures and precedents to minimise the emergence of conflict.
- Reconciliation of sources of potential conflict by commissioning group, project and product and service development work.
- The development of a climate in which face-to-face confrontation is used to address and resolve serious problems.
- Where necessary, training and development in the use and purpose of consultation, participation, negotiation and problem-solving activities.

The recognition and management of conflict so that the positive attitudes and values are preserved is a major contribution of OD. Moreover, if this part is not successful, then it is likely that other efforts will be diluted.

Costs and benefits

The costs and benefits of organisational development are as summarised in Table 14.1.

Table 14.1 Costs and benefits

Costs	Benefits
• High, long-term and fixed • Loss of short-term shareholder and backer confidence • Derived variable costs – to pay for courses, events, consultants, expertise, projects and secondments • Derived fixed costs as a proportion of staff time • High levels of wages and rewards	• High and enduring levels of professional, occupational and organisation capability, motivation and morale • High and enduring steady-state levels of performance • Few genuine crises and emergencies • Mutual confidence and respect • Positive approaches to all aspects of work • Reduced need to attend to hygiene factors or institutionalised problem-solving – leading to reduced need for HRM, IR and financial management departments, divisions and functions

It is also essential that absolute strategic and moral commitment does not cause feelings of infallibility of introversion. OD must be targeted at long-term survival, effectiveness and profitability as well as respect and value.

Conclusions

The keys to effective OD are long-term investment and harmonising and integrating all development activities into mainstream operations and functions. It is based on equality of treatment, mutuality of interest, and collective positive identity. Effective OD is dependent also on positive collective attitudes, open and continuous communication and participation, and universal access to all aspects of organisation information. If one or more of these elements is missing or diluted, then the whole tends to fall.

Adopting OD approaches to both strategy and operations on the part of more traditional organisations requires a fundamental shift of collective attitudes as well as investment priorities. This often means a change of directors and other senior staff, and the appointment of what is effectively a project manager or OD champion, whose remit is then to drive the whole process through, and to ensure that the commitment of all staff and backers is engaged. This also requires extensive management development efforts if it is to be fully realised.

QUESTIONS

1 How can divergence of interest between organisations, their shareholders and backers, shareholders' representatives and public service governors be best addressed and reconciled?
2 Identify the steps necessary, and investment needs arising as a consequence, to change formalised bureaucratic institutions into those primarily concerned with customer and client service.

3 Identify the elements required, and assess the costs necessary as the result, for a staff development programme, the aim of which is complete openness and honesty in communications.
4 What elements are required in induction and other core training programmes to ensure that a positive culture and active commitment are instilled in new staff from an early stage? What expertise is required on the part of those delivering these programmes as the result? What organisational support is also required?
5 What attitudes of professional and occupational responsibility are required of all staff working in organisations pursuing OD strategies?

■ ☑ 15 Management development

'Every work organisation is concerned with being effective. Upon the attainment of its aims and objectives rests the success and ultimate survival of the organisation. The quality of management is central to organisation development and improved performance.'

L.J. Mullins, *'Management and Organisational Behaviour'*, F.T. Pitman (1999)

Introduction

Management development is concerned with three distinctive activities:

- the development of managers and supervisors;
- the development of all staff through the activities of managers and supervisors;
- the development of overall organisational capability (see previous chapter).

Any discussion of management development has to start from the premise that the skills, qualities and expertise required of good and effective managers can be taught, learned and applied. The vast range of management courses, activities, expertise and qualifications would tend to support this view at least to an extent (see Summary Box 15.1).

SUMMARY BOX 15.1   Rosabeth Moss Kanter and common sense

The alternative view offered most often is that management is 'common sense' and that therefore anyone can do it. The evidence is to the contrary.

Promotion paths

The traditional approach in much of the Western world was to promote the best professional or operative into the position of manager. Thus, the best teacher became head teacher; the best plumber, plumbing manager; the best footballer, football manager.

This last illustrates the point most graphically. Very few of the world's top football players have enjoyed long-term managerial success once they have stopped playing.

Those who have gained real managerial success are those who learned the trade, partly as the result of not being able to achieve maximum excellence on the field of play.

Figureheads

Others point to the success of individuals such as Richard Branson and the Roddicks. In practice, both of these explicitly acknowledge their own shortcomings; and went to a lot of trouble to surround themselves with the highest quality available expertise to compensate for this.

Rosabeth Moss Kanter when interviewed by Tom Mangold on this point was asked explicitly: 'Is this not just common sense?'

To which she replied: 'Sense, yes. The evidence supports it. Common? Not if you consider all the failures, problems and sheer waste that occurs as the result of bad management decisions.'

Source: Rosabeth Moss Kanter, 'Business Matters', BBC (1998).

In practice, management development concentrates on:

- organisation development and managing change;
- behaviour, attitudes, skills, knowledge, expertise and technological proficiency development;
- product, service and operational advancement and improvement;
- delivering this expertise in its environment;
- integrating managerial expertise with organisation and environmental pressures, opportunities and constraints;
- increasingly, managing across cultures and in transforming occupations, professions, industries and sectors (see Summary Box 15.2).

SUMMARY BOX 15.2   Right or wrong?

A further problem becomes apparent when looked at from the point of view of change, environment and cultural pressures. For example, when an organisation changes name, attitudes, priority or status (e.g. as the result of merger or takeover, privatisation or technological change) then it is *assumed* that present management expertise and qualities must be wrong. Those involved are therefore removed. Something has then to be put in its place. So long as this is different this is *assumed* to be right.

Given that only 13 per cent of mergers, takeovers, privatisations and technologically-driven changes are wholly or mostly successful, there is an overwhelming need for attention in these areas and a managerial requirement to question these assumptions in the first place.

Source: Industrial Society, 'Managing Mergers and Takeovers' (1999); Institute of Management (1999); 'The Long-Term Effect of Mergers and Takeovers' (1996).

The management development requirement is therefore two-fold: to identify and develop a body of expertise; and to be able to apply it in whatever situation or environment required.

The body of expertise

This may be broken down as follows:

- **Behaviour:** integrity, equity, respect and value; respecting and valuing the opinions and capabilities of others; openness, honesty; transparency; visibility.
- **Attitudes:** positive, enthusiastic, dynamic; concerned; flexible and responsive.
- **Skills:** in developing the next generation of managers; in identifying and developing skills, qualities and aptitudes of all. Specific skills development is also required in the areas of: leadership, decision-making, delegation, performance measurement. In the specific case of employee and organisation development, a part of management development must consist of identifying and engaging in organisation, departmental, divisional, collective, group and individual development activities.
- **Knowledge:** keeping abreast of developments; reading; awareness; lessons from everywhere (see Summary Box 15.3).

SUMMARY BOX 15.3   Knowledge and understanding

A key feature of management knowledge is a full understanding of the environment in which managerial work takes place. For example:

- It is not necessary for managers to be able to type, file or make bookings if they have secretaries to do this. However, they must understand the pressures, constraints and volumes of work that secretaries have to undertake in these areas.
- It is not necessary for hospital managers to be expert doctors, surgeons or nurses. However, they must have a full understanding of the organisational and operational pressures and constraints of the professional staff under their direction (failure to ensure that senior and middle NHS managers do indeed have this full understanding of clinical and nursing practice is a major cause of NHS under-performance at the beginning of the 21st Century).

There may also be cultural pressures that have to be accommodated. For example, many sales executives need, behaviourally and culturally, to work for someone who already has a proven track record as a sales executive. The view is therefore taken that the best sales executives should be promoted into the managerial position. This must be accompanied by thorough and rigorous management training if the move is to be effective from everybody's point of view.

- **Expertise:** establishing targets and priorities; planning; organising; motivating; measuring performance; communication; integration; accepting responsibility, authority and accountability.
- **Technological proficiency:** understanding the capacity of technology; understanding its use, value and application; maximising and optimising output; scheduling maintenance; developing expertise in its usage; supporting those who use it.

It is important to understand that all of this can be developed – and this includes the behavioural qualities of integrity, respect and value. This is of especial importance to those who have been in organisations for a long time where these qualities are not apparent.

Otherwise, the concern for all managers is to be able to take an enlightened and responsible view of each of these, and to identify their own strengths and weaknesses. Both require building on – strengths in order to become expert; the weaknesses in order to become at least proficient.

Organisations also need to take a strategic or collective view of their own pool of managerial expertise for the same reasons. Managerial audits (needs analyses and appraisal) identify areas of overall strength and weakness. A view can then be formed of what should be developed internally, and what needs to be brought in from outside (see Summary Box 15.4).

SUMMARY BOX 15.4   Grow your own or buy in?

This is another issue on which easy or universal answers are sought – and for which no rules exist. The principle is a balance of giving every possible opportunity to develop and enhance existing expertise, with the need for fresh blood, ideas and talents coming in from outside to prevent introversion.

There are problems with each. Too much emphasis on internal development leaves organisations vulnerable to inability to accept ideas from elsewhere. Known or perceived over-emphasis on buying in from outside leads to feelings of frustration on the part of those who believe (rightly or wrongly) that they should be given their chance.

Buying in expertise is of greatest value when directors and senior managers come to a strategic and supportable view that the development of management now requires fresh talent and expertise; and that this will give those presently in the organisation a positive and effective surge of energy. If this conclusion is genuinely arrived at, it must be publicly stated. The justification is then clear to all and the reasons understandable – even if there is some short-term disgruntlement and turnover.

Developing expertise in-house demonstrates commitment to existing staff and their capabilities, determination and motivation. This should never be ignored or forgotten whatever the need for fresh talent and impetus. Most people understand this once it is explained to them provided that it is clear that their own value and worth is being recognised also.

Management qualifications

As yet, there exists no statutory minimum management qualification. This does not prevent an ever-increasing number of organisations and those who aspire to managerial positions from undertaking a wide variety of nationally recognised qualifications as follows:

- HND/C and undergraduate business studies courses; and an increasing number of more traditional courses with a business or management element (e.g. civil engineering with management; construction management; information management).
- NEBSM/CMS and foundation courses in professional practice: similar in coverage to much that is taught in universities and colleges of higher and further education though the approach is certain to differ. This is because such courses are normally pitched at those (with and without previously acquired academic or vocational qualifications) who already have several years work experience. People take these courses as the result of their own drives and ambitions, those of the organisation, or as one result of performance appraisal and needs analysis.
- DMS and diploma courses in professional and occupational expertise: these courses are invariably pitched at either those who have done a foundation course as above; or at those in professional occupations (e.g. marketing, technology, teaching, nursing) who now wish to enhance their professional employability or (with DMS) look for opportunities to go into management.
- MBA and other Masters/postgraduate level qualifications: normally offered to those who already have substantial occupational experience, at least a diploma, and preferably undergraduate qualifications also. Best value is served by those wishing to acquire a substantial body of organisational, economic, behavioural, functional and environmental knowledge as a precursor to advancement into senior positions.
- Doctorate: attained by those with a combination of high-quality managerial experience and substantial academic achievement, as the result of extensive research and write-up of a major problem or issue.
- The vocational qualification route: those who prefer may undertake management development by attaining a set of work-based competencies and having these accredited through the production of a written portfolio of experience, evidence and workplace testing and observation (see Summary Box 15.5).

The process of gaining formal qualifications and having expertise and achievement credited and recognised serves as:

- an accepted and understood level of achievement;
- a behavioural and perceptual benchmark of progress and opportunity;

National Vocational Qualifications (NVQs) are now available for most occupations in the UK including the work of managers where the Management Charter Initiative (MCI) has had the responsibility for developing a set of management qualifications. NVQs, including the management qualifications, differ from academic qualifications by focussing on performance at work and outcomes that can be assessed against standards defined as performance criteria. NVQs are provided at different levels starting at Level 1 for work which is composed of routine and predictable activities, through to Level 5 for work involving application of complex techniques in unpredictable contexts. This allows people to build up qualifications from the time they complete formal education to the end of their career. NVQs have also become a key part of government initiatives to improve the skill base of the UK economy and an important means for many people to progressively achieve higher qualifications.

Areas covered by management NVQs include:

- managing own performance;
- planning, decision-making and controlling;
- financial awareness;
- organisational awareness;
- performance appraisal;
- managing staff performance;
- managing customers.

Source: J. Bratton and J. Gold, *'Human Resource Management'*, Palgrave (2000).

- a springboard for the next step;
- a measure of value, respect and worth.

Additionally, all management qualifications are now available on open, distance and flexible bases as well as traditional teaching, so that they are much more open to everyone than in the past. They can also be much more closely harmonised with organisation and collective development, as well as individual enhancement. Many of these (especially certificate, diploma and Masters) bring project and secondment opportunities with them.

Organisational and environmental expertise

Managerial expertise, whether supported by qualifications or not, is required by all organisations whatever their size, location, sector or remit. A key management development problem remains ensuring that this expertise is used successfully and effectively in any given set of circumstances. Those who have managerial expertise therefore require environmental knowledge, understanding and capability as much as those who have worked in the particular situation for years who nevertheless still need to develop managerial capability (see Figure 15.1).

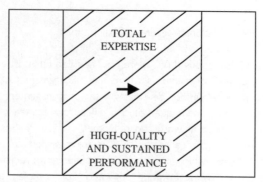

MANAGERIAL
EXPERTISE

ENVIRONMENTAL
EXPERTISE AND
UNDERSTANDING

Figure 15.1   The environmental–managerial expertise mix

Fully effective performance is only possible in the hatched area. If there is a high level of both managerial and environmental expertise, there is a sound basis and high expectation of effective performance. If there is a low level of either, this means that:

- those with managerial expertise have no knowledge or understanding of how it should be applied in the particular organisation, environment or situation;
- those with environmental expertise have no knowledge or understanding of what it takes to manage activities (though they will clearly understand how to carry them out, and what the pressures and constraints are).

Whichever the gap, those involved are much more likely to be successful if they are:

- prepared to learn and be receptive;
- supported by their organisation;
- open to suggestions and ideas from elsewhere rather than only being prepared to stick to what they know (see Summary Box 15.6);
- prepared to modify their own preconceptions and, where necessary, change their own attitudes and behaviour.

SUMMARY BOX 15.6   Managerial openness

A survey conducted of managerial attitudes found that:

- 76 per cent of managers surveyed believed themselves open, approachable and sympathetic to ideas and suggestions from elsewhere;
- 74 per cent of the staff of managers surveyed stated that their managers were aloof, inaccessible and unreceptive to ideas and suggestions from elsewhere.

Clearly, there is some overlap! The core problem arises from ensuring that attention to managerial or environmental learning and development has a high priority both while it is being achieved and also afterwards. Those in the situation require a mechanism which automatically asks the question *why* when rejection or a blinkered view is being offered. Another survey found that 90 per cent of managers and supervisors that adopted an adversarial, aggressive, confrontational or absentee management style did so either because it was how they had been treated themselves in junior positions, or because it was perceived or understood that this was the way to behave, or because they perceived or understood that this was the style to adopt if they wished to make further progress.

Source: C.B. Handy, *'Understanding Organisations'*, Penguin (1995).

Core managerial expertise can then be applied to the particular organisation, situation and environment as follows:

- developing this expertise in ways acceptable and applicable to those working in the environment and the pressures and constraints present;
- developing behaviour, attitudes and values in ways which contribute to the positive development of the organisational and operating culture;
- developing a state of visibility and access that promotes mutual confidence without being intrusive;
- building on past positive experiences that professional, functional and operational staff have had with managers and supervisors;
- rescuing past negative experiences that professional, functional and operational staff have had with managers (see Summary Box 15.7);

SUMMARY BOX 15.7   Rescuing the past

Part of the management development effort in these circumstances must be to understand why and how bad relations arose in the first place and to develop the environment, approach and standards of confidence necessary to rescue them and make them productive and effective for the future.

The keys to this are:

- regular visibility without intrusion;
- short, regular, formal meetings with collectively agreed agenda;
- asking staff for their priorities, issues and problems;
- delivering early, positive and recognisable results.

This is then reinforced by:

- levels of integrity, enthusiasm, ambition and drive exhibited by the manager on behalf of their staff;
- specific lobbying, cheerleading and advocacy when required;
- always supporting staff in public and resolving problems and issues privately and quickly.

This set of conditions and activities is a precursor to any attempt to rescue the past. It is a key feature of all management developments in large complex organisations, both public and private. Without it, little organisational, professional and occupational cultural or behavioural development is possible, and effectiveness of performance is always diluted.

- maximising the opportunities for staff, production and service development that arise as the result.

Management development and product and service enhancement

The contribution of management development to product and service enhancement arises only as the result of understanding the nature of the working environment and the products and services delivered. The contribution then becomes:

- identifying, addressing and removing barriers to effective product and service performance;
- gaining staff commitment to new approaches through demonstrating the benefits and addressing any problems or issues inherent;
- consulting with a view to gaining active involvement and participation;
- addressing key staff priorities including pressures of work, periods of overload and underload;
- ensuring that the jobs that nobody wants to do are either subcontracted are else shared around equally;
- setting and reinforcing absolute standards of behaviour and performance that apply to everyone regardless of profession, status, occupation, length of service or hours of work; and developing problem-solving capability and routes of access for staff so that when these issues occur, they are raised, dealt with and nipped in the bud (see Summary Box 15.8).

SUMMARY BOX 15.8   'I must be seen to be impartial'

In the overwhelming majority of cases, managers that use this phrase when confronted with serious behavioural problems are understood to be avoiding the issue. Overtly, the word 'impartial' implies 'fair' or 'equitable'. The whole phrase implies: 'I would love to help but I cannot'. In practice, therefore, this means that the issue will not be confronted.

If an employee makes an allegation about a colleague, the manager must develop a format that allows the employee to state their case and the alleged offender to respond on a basis of fairness and equality. This must be conducted face-to-face with each.

Once the two sides are heard, then the required action becomes apparent. Above all, if malicious and false allegations are being made, these are dealt with severely and may lead to disciplinary action or dismissal if proven.

Dealing with anything raised quickly in this way normally means that such incidents are kept to a minimum. Where it is known or believed that the manager 'must be seen to be impartial', there are widely held perceptions that nothing will be done.

This part of management development is therefore concerned with creating the conditions in which effective and sustainable high-quality product and service delivery are possible. In directly operational and functional matters, effective development is concerned with knowing the jobs, tasks and outputs required, observing and analysing them either to ensure that the present effective steady-state is maintained and to see where improvements can be made. These can then be discussed with the staff concerned and either implemented if truly practicable, or else killed off if those carrying out the activities come up with overwhelming operational reasons as to why they are bad ideas.

Management development must be concerned with understanding and improving customer, supplier and community relations. This involves creating the conditions in which all contacts with each of these groups are dealt with as a priority, and addressing specific issues, especially complaints, from the point of view of finding out what truly went wrong and why, and putting them right in ways that satisfy those who first raised them. If staffing or internal issues then become apparent they can be addressed separately.

Management development must be concerned with the operational details of the particular domain. This means knowing and understanding the following:

- **Tasks, occupations and work:** required and desired outputs, and the expertise and conditions necessary for these to be achieved; problem areas and blockages, and what causes these; deadlines and priorities.
- **Technology:** the influence of this on work patterns and behaviour (especially alienation); the consequences of breakdown or inability to recruit the required expertise.
- **Information:** availability and accessibility; quality, volume and value; contribution of information availability to effective, positive and productive decision-making and activities.
- **Organisation:** formal structures and reporting relationships; cultural and behavioural issues that these may raise; the nature and expectations of those present (see Summary Box 15.9).

SUMMARY BOX 15.9   Toward flexible and open organisations: MMRC

MMRC was a small but highly expert and profitable London advertising agency. It employed 50 staff on strictly traditional lines and reporting relationships. Everyone had clear job descriptions. From the most positive point of view, it was a role culture.

The company was taken over by a large firm, JWT. The new owners immediately destroyed the prevailing structure, culture and reporting relations. They brought in open-plan accommodation, hot-desking and fully portable technology and a flat operating structure.

Within six months all of the 50 MMRC staff had left. The senior partner at JWT commissioned a firm of consultants to contact the former staff and find out why. The key reasons given were as follows: (continued)

- The role culture had grown up over many years and was orderly and familiar. People had expectations and knew what could be achieved, and under what circumstances.
- The role culture was destroyed, and the hot-desking introduced, without consultation, and by people who were self-evidently working to a prescription rather than genuine understanding.
- Existing staff were given no idea of what was expected of them. It was clear to them that the new owners did not understand **how** the work was carried out, or the constraints and opportunities of the existing ways of working, technology or structure and culture.

- **Primary activities:** establishing aims, objectives and priorities; coordinating activities; integrating staff; communication and decision-making processes; planning for the present and future.
- **Key factors:** motivating staff; addressing individual and group needs, including development needs; knowing and understanding when and where to go for help when required; accepting and using power, influence, responsibility, authority and accountability; understanding the priorities, demands and constraints of the particular situation.

Self-development

The increasing professionalisation of management requires that those in these positions take an active and personal commitment to their own development. The rewards for expert managers are now extremely high. In return for these, it is increasingly necessary to demonstrate and be able to engage genuine capability in the areas of: leadership; decision-making; strategic awareness and strategy design; market knowledge; organisational behaviour; and understanding people. The conflicting and divergent interests of organisation stakeholders have to be balanced and accommodated. High and increasing value products and services must be delivered to evermore demanding customer and client groups. Self-development therefore requires a commitment to:

- read widely about all organisations, industries and sectors, to learn from their managerial practice and approaches;
- meet with other managers at cluster groups and professional body gatherings;
- engage in continuous professional development and enhancement activities, whether at the behest of professional bodies, or self-directed;
- search constantly for areas where both individual management practice and also organisation capability and output can be improved.

Of particular value are 'back to the floor' and 'action learning' approaches (see Chapter 5). More generally, managers must be prepared to go into other organisations at any time with a view to picking up ideas. They must be willing to try things out against their own self-generated and preset criteria. Some ideas and initiatives will succeed – others will fail or fall short of full success. So long as there was a genuine pre-evaluation of what was intended, failure and success can both be used as part of the learning process. This approach also tends towards instilling attitudes of self-development in the rest of the staff.

Succession and transformation

The role of management development in succession and transformation is:

- to ensure that there is a steady flow of ever-improving expertise and quality available to organisations to secure a future;
- to identify potential capability and motivation in existing staff and to develop it for the present and future;
- to recognise succession in its broadest terms.

This means addressing it from the point of view of:

- having a fund of staff to promote when required;
- having a fund of expertise and understanding as the organisation goes through its own succession and transformation from one set of occupations, activities, markets, products and services to the next, including the ways in which these are delivered as well as what is delivered;
- taking a broader view of succession and transformation so that expertise and commitment are both available should they be required;
- looking for derived opportunities especially those that present themselves as the result of following one path of activities.

Traditionally, succession simply meant training the next generation of staff for supervisory, managerial and senior functional positions. Now it is essential that this includes attention to attitudes and behaviour so that qualities of positiveness, flexibility and willingness are instilled and developed. Clear lines of progression through hierarchical organisation structures are much less prevalent and subject to restructuring in any case. However, succession opportunities are, in practice, at least as widely available in terms of:

- rotation and progression through departments, divisions, functions, locations, projects and centres of activities;
- moving into a new job and being given the space, opportunity, resources and support to develop it in new ways;
- identifying potential in existing situations and ranges of activity.

Succession therefore, becomes broadened into progression and transformation. It is dependent on a positive view of the opportunities presently available, as well as those apparent for the future. Organisations that reflect and encourage this approach are certain to get much more out of their staff so long as they commit themselves to offering enhanced salaries and other rewards (which were always the key drives of those on structured promotion paths).

It is important to be able to offer genuine prospects of advancement and development. This approach, conducted properly, ensures that individual drives

Table 15.1   Costs and benefits

Costs	Benefits
• Variable – in paying for courses and other support activities and periods of formalised training (on- and off-the-job) • Fixed – in terms that management development requires a substantial amount of otherwise salaried and occupational time • Priorities – again a fixed cost – because managers must be able to block off periods of their time in order to *walk their job* and learn and understand their domain and environment	• High-quality, enduring management–staff relations • Early identification of problems • Full organisational, environmental and operational understanding

for progress are harmonised with organisational drives for greater effectiveness of resource utilisation and maximisation of staff capabilities.

Costs and benefits

The costs and benefits of effective management development activities are as summarised in Table 15.1.

Conclusions

Effective management development depends on organisations recognising the enhanced contribution and value that expert managerial staff deliver, as well as the derived benefits of generating motivation, commitment and capability in present occupations. It is fully dependent also on attending to the full range of behaviour, attitudes, skills, knowledge, expertise and technological proficiency, and respecting personal, professional and occupational, as well as organisational, drives.

Effective management development has a knock-on effect on attitudes to training across the rest of the organisation. Professional, occupational, technological and 'unskilled' staff are much more likely to be given opportunities if these are available to those for whom they work. This enhances collective, group and organisation development.

Highly developed and expert managers are also much more likely to understand and value the importance of induction, core programmes and initial job training. As stated above (see Chapter 4) these make major contributions to establishing the required levels of attitudes and behaviour, as well as performance, at the outset, and in subsequently reinforcing these. Conducted effectively, management development is therefore all-pervasive making a positive contribution to every aspect of performance.

QUESTIONS

1. Produce an outline management development programme for a new hospital manager who has previously held a managerial position at a supermarket chain. What elements are you going to include and why? Remember to include aims, objectives, timescales and monitoring, review and evaluation.

2. What training should be made available for an individual who is proposing to move from being a Royal Mail postman, to sorting office supervisor?

3. What are the costs and benefits of companies such as McDonald's insisting that all management development trainees conduct an initial period of work at the frontline?

4. Following an organisational restructuring, it has become apparent to those in junior and middle positions that promotion paths are no longer to be offered. What can the particular organisation put in place, and how, in order to ensure that alternatives are made available, and motivation and morale is maintained?

5. 'I knew the company was looking around for a new managing director. They were wondering who to ask. I was at the meeting only as note-taker. Suddenly, I heard myself say: "*I would like to have a go*"' (Elaine Vaughan, then a tour operations manager for Sandals Resorts, 1998). Identify the general issues that have to be considered. If Elaine is to be promoted from a functional position to that of Chief Executive, what development must she go through?

6. How would you develop the qualities of effective visibility, communication skills and decision-making in someone who is known to have good managerial capability, but is otherwise shy and diffident? What benefits would you expect to accrue, and how would you measure this for success/failure?

■ Ṽ **16** Government training and development policy

'*We need industrial training in all sectors, and someone will have to pay for it.*'

> P.J.C. Perry, Chairman of the British Association for
> Commercial and Industrial Education (1961)

'*We need to give greater opportunities for commercial and industrial skills training to everyone, and we need to work out who is going to pay for this.*'

> Stephen Byers, general election campaign (June 2001)

Introduction

Over the past fifty years or so, the UK government has been largely successful in designing, implementing, delivering – and, when thought necessary, changing – a national framework for education and training in primary and secondary schools, colleges and universities. In each of these cases, there are serious shortages of staff, expertise, resources and equipment; however, the outputs – GCSEs, A-Levels, Diplomas, Degrees, occupational and professional qualifications and certificates – are overwhelmingly recognised, accepted and valued (see Summary Box 16.1).

The same cannot be said for industrial, pre-vocational and vocational education and training (see quotes at head of chapter).

SUMMARY BOX 16.1   Nationally recognised qualifications

These are:

- **School attainment testing standards:** taken at regular intervals throughout the school career.
- **GCSEs and A-Levels (and latterly AS-Levels):** taken in a variety of understood, recognised and accepted subjects.
- **Diplomas:** in a variety of technical, occupational and professional subjects and expertise, including marketing, human resource management, management and supervisory studies, nursing, teaching, midwifery; in many of these cases, foundation and pre-diploma courses are also available at certificate level.

- **RSA and City and Guilds qualifications:** in technical and occupational skills, including hairdressing, building, catering, cookery, secretarial work, finance and accounting.
- **Degrees:** in a variety of academic, vocational and technical subjects – many of which include business and management studies.
- **Advanced qualifications:** postgraduate, post-experience, either accredited by universities or professional bodies.

Problems

The enduring problems include the following:

- Lack of overall value compounded by constant changes to the name, content, quality and delivery of programmes (see Summary Box 16.2).

SUMMARY BOX 16.2   The acronym approach to industrial training

The first attempts to make vocational training effective were carried out by Industrial Training Boards (ITBs). Their role was subsequently taken over by the Manpower Services Commission (MSC). The MSC introduced a number of initiatives including: 'The Training for Skills Programme for Action' (TOSPA); and the 'New Training Initiative' (NTI). This was then developed into Unified Vocational Preparation (UVP).

The MSC also introduced specific programmes for:

- young people: the Youth Opportunities Programmes (YOPs); Youth Training Schemes (YTS); Young Worker Schemes (YWS);
- those wishing to return to work or change occupation: Training Opportunities Programmes (TOPs); Adult Training Schemes (ATS).

The MSC was subsequently abolished. The Department for Education had its remit changed to include employment and became the Department for Education and Employment (DfEE). The DfEE introduced various initiatives including 'New Deal' and General National Vocational Qualifications (GNVQs). **Only at this point was some evidence of harmonisation and standardisation of industrial, vocational and pre-vocational training apparent** (see Chapter 15).

It should also be noted that one of the programmes introduced by the MSC was called 'Work Experience on Employer's Premises' (WEEP).

- Lack of recognised contribution to employability.
- Perceptions and beliefs that everything that was produced was politically expedient rather than practical and sound.
- Unwillingness of government or industry to pay for it.
- Continued higher value placed on the other qualifications and attainments listed above (see Summary Box 16.1).

- Perceptions and beliefs that industrial and vocational training was a last resort rather than a serious or substantial alternative to more recognised qualifications.
- Concentration on inspection and administration rather than substance and delivery.
- Lack of overall cohesion and authority in statutory bodies.

Lack of value and consistency

This may be considered from the following points of view:

- Those leaving school with recognised qualifications and who went on into work have never been required also to take industrial or pre-vocational courses. There remains a belief and perception that this form of training is for low achievers. The consequence has been that standards have been set low, written in general terms, and subject to constant change, with the quality of delivery left very much in the hands of individuals carrying out the work.

  School leavers who go into this form of government programme believe that they are being dumped because nobody can think what else to do with them. They have gained this impression from the past experience of those who undertook YT and YW schemes, as well as understanding that they are in any case only on the scheme because they cannot get anything else. This was compounded by the fact that employers were under no obligation to retain them once the scheme had ended.

  The government to date has so far refused to address this through substance of programmes, adequate funding or consistency of delivery. The rest of the education provision is designed, underwritten and, to a great extent, funded by central government (though top up fees are now required in some areas). School leaver and pre-vocational training has always carried a debate concerning who pays, how much and for what; and this remains unresolved at present.

- Adults returning to work have a variety of general opportunities especially in service work, information technology and computers, and other 'new industries' such as retail, call centres and production/assembly. There are also well marketed and presented opportunities to return to teaching and nursing.

  Again, the quality of support offered is varied. Most retail and production/assembly work is well managed and the responsibility for this falls fully on the particular organisations. Grant support and other public funding is available for organisations providing IT and computer training, though the quality of delivery and qualifications achieved remain inconsistent and variable. Those wishing to return to nursing or teaching are entirely dependent on the quality of support that individual hospitals and schools are prepared and willing to provide.

  Branded programmes such as those outlined in Summary Box 16.2 have never been allowed to gain currency, consistency or value. Neither has the quality of content ever been resolved. This will only be achieved when statutory bodies take full account of the substance and content required of all general industrial, commercial, pre-vocational and into work training, and require that it is formalised and delivered under the same conditions as school, college and university education; or that a statutory obligation is placed on all employers to take a proportion of trainees dependent on the size of their workforce.

Political expediency

Many of the problems indicated above have been compounded by the fundamental dishonesty with which the programmes were devised and structured. Industrial and prevocational training becomes a serious issue only at times of high unemployment. This especially applies to young people because it is perceived to be politically unacceptable to have children leaving school with little or no prospect of work (the moral, social and economic aspects have never been genuinely considered).

More recently this has come to be the case with medical, nursing and teacher training. High-profile advertising campaigns have gained serious and enduring interest. However, the structure for both on- and off-the-job training and also the professional education and support required, itself requires substantial investment in expertise, resources and technology (see Summary Box 16.3).

SUMMARY BOX 16.3   Political expediency

Governments address the issue of political expediency by stating that they are engaged in 'pump priming' and 'seed corning' activities only – and that once programmes have a life of their own, the government can withdraw. More generally, it should be noted that government response to national training needs tends to be driven by media coverage.

In the past, efforts were made to try and get people interested and into training for building and civil engineering (1970s and 1980s) because otherwise work would have to be awarded to foreign contractors.

Conversely, decisions were taken to reduce the numbers of teacher and nursing training places because:

- There were projections of reductions in the school population, and therefore not so many teachers would be needed. However, nobody considered that particular subjects would nevertheless need to be taught, however much class sizes may reduce.
- The strategic decision was taken to reduce hospital bed numbers, and the introduction of the waiting list as an NHS management technique. Fewer nurses would therefore be required.

In the latter case, however, nobody ever considered that adverse media coverage would cause outcry, and real attention to be paid by the community at large to the enduring quality of health service provision.

Who pays?

The long-term government position is that industrial training is a tripartite activity in which the national interest, employers and employees' representatives have a legitimate interest as follows (see Figure 16.1):

- the national interest requires absolute standards of substance, content and delivery of programmes;
- the employer interest requires a steady flow of educated and aware staff of all ages;
- the employee interest requires education and training for employability as well as job specific skills and expertise.

With different emphases and priorities, everybody clearly states that they want the same thing. Differences in delivery arise as the result of:

- the unwillingness of government to research, evaluate, design, prescribe and deliver an agreed body of skills, knowledge, expertise and technological proficiency;
- the extent, prevalence and effectiveness of employers' lobbies in skewing the process of their own particular ends;
- the loss of influence of the employee interest especially where represented by trade unions (see Summary Box 16.4).

These problems have further been compounded by collective employer unwillingness to pay for industrial training for anything other than their own narrow purposes. For a time, government tried to get over this by applying a training levy. This was then used to provide organisational, sectoral and generic industrial training. This was successfully lobbied against and eventually

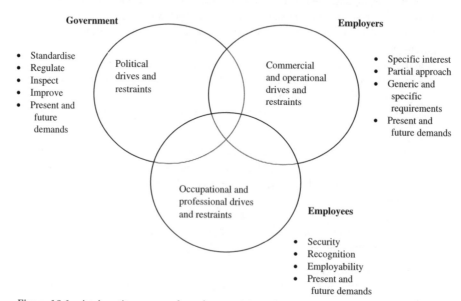

Figure 16.1 A tripartite approach to the provision of national, industrial and vocational training

The unvalued and inconsistent outcome of the approach is further diluted by the particular influences that are present at given times when industrial training is 'reformed'. At various different times therefore, industrial training has been given undue emphasis towards:

- engineering as the result of the involvement of the electrical and engineering trade union leaders Frank Chappell and Hugh Scanlon;
- telecommunications as the result of the involvement of David Young, Chief Executive of Cable and Wireless;
- retail, as the result of the involvement of John and David Sainsbury.

This last was carried to further extremes in 1986 where, as the result of an industrial training initiative, David Sainsbury stated that hospitals would be much better managed by those trained in retail, than by healthcare experts.

abolished. No government has so far seen fit to pay for this out of central funding and increase taxation accordingly, or generate windfall revenues from highly profitable companies. The problem is, in any case, of lesser political consequence at the beginning of the 21st Century because of lower numbers of people out of work and high levels of vacancies.

Status of industrial and prevocational training

It follows from all this that anything that is treated in these ways is certain to carry believed and perceived low quality and value. From this point of view, it is easy to understand employers' reluctance to pay for it (though it is harder to understand their unwillingness to insist that quality, value and content are raised). It is certain to remain a low government priority all the time that this view persists, and until its value to both organisations and individuals is proven and substantially raised (see Summary Box 16.5).

Inspection

Government inspections may be statutory or voluntary and have a number of implications for organisation and employee development.

Statutory inspections

Most public service institutions are subject to government inspections. This also applies to many industrial, commercial and other private sector organisations. Overtly, inspections have the following purposes

- **Public sector:** concentration and emphasis on quality assurance, standards of performance, value added and enhanced to the customer, client or social group expected, anticipated and recognised outputs (see Summary Box 16.6).

Ideally, there should be clear and positive staff and organisation development outcomes from these exercises. In practice, the approach is often punitive,

SUMMARY BOX 16.5   Boots

The status of pre-vocational training is always further emphasised when organisation histories reinforce general perceptions.

Boots, the pharmaceutical and department store chain, employ school and college leavers every year. The company also takes on a cohort of young workers on government schemes paid for, and supported by, the Department for Education and Employment. The company makes it absolutely clear that this group is to be treated differently from anyone else at the end of their period of training. The position of individuals is guaranteed only so long as there is government funding, and it is up to everyone to find a 'real' job during their period of pre-vocational training. Self-evidently therefore, those on the government scheme are being treated as having lesser value to the company than other school and college leavers, even though at the outset of employment, they are doing exactly the same work. They also follow exactly the same induction, job training and NVQ accredited initial development plan.

SUMMARY BOX 16.6   Inspection: some public sector examples

Schools

The emphasis with schools' inspections is on:

- the production of league tables so that people can see how well children and students are doing at each school compared to others in achieving standard attainments, GCSEs, A-Levels and other exams;
- the paperwork and administrative systems that support teaching, syllabi, schemes of work and classroom delivery;
- quality of classroom delivery.

It is clear from this that direct service forms only one part of the inspection and that emphasis is therefore going to be given to the other areas when required.

Prisons

Prisons are inspected for quality of environment and facilities, and relations between staff and inmates. Little attention is paid to rehabilitation, re-offending rates, education, training or the transition from prison to society.

Hospitals

Plans exist to inspect hospitals and grade them according to mortality rates. The format for this is not yet agreed.

adversarial and confrontational. The staff involved are therefore required to work towards target attainment rather than developing professional and expert practice.

- **Industry and commerce:** many sectors have their own statutory inspection bodies. For example, transport and travel organisations are inspected for quality of service, expertise of staff, durability and safety of equipment. Manufacturing, chemicals, oil and gas all have statutory inspections to ensure standards of safety, environment management, waste and effluent disposal. Industrial and domestic equipment manufacturers are required to be able to demonstrate that safety features and cut-outs on their products do indeed work as designed. Where problems in any of these sectors are found as the result of statutory inspection, there are normally organisation and employee development implications – for example, tightening up procedures and staff training in practices.
- **Statutory health and safety inspections:** the Health and Safety Executive (HSE) is the statutory body responsible for ensuring that all work premises are healthy and safe so far as is reasonably practicable. HSE may inspect any premises at any time; they always inspect those premises where serious accidents or incidents occur. They may order premises to be closed altogether, shutdown a particular process, or ask for staff, supervisory and management training to ensure that particular procedures are tightened and followed.

Attention to behaviour, attitude and performance is normally much greater following an accident or disaster, than a general inspection. Problems normally only endure following such incidents where organisations are determined as a matter of policy to do nothing to develop procedures, practices, staff or management whatever the consequences (see Summary Box 16.7).

SUMMARY BOX 16.7 'The world's worst organisations'

As part of a research project into the extent, prevalence and effect of accidents and disasters on organisation performance, Tom Mangold studied HSE reports of companies that have been prosecuted.

The UK's worst company was Tarmac, with 73 prosecutions in the past five years. Of the worst ten companies, six were from building and civil engineering (Costain, Amec, Balfour Beatty, Mowlem, McAlpine and Tarmac). The others named were British Steel, Rentokil (chemicals), British Gypsum (quarrying and building products), BICC (engineering).

Rentokil and British Gypsum produced staff and behaviour and attitude development programmes to address some of the issues. Tarmac and British Steel took the view that they were no worse than anyone else in their sectors, and simply did nothing.

The problem therefore clearly lies in getting those with influence to accept that there are problems and to commit to, and invest in, staff and organisation development approaches to address issues raised by statutory inspections.

Source: T. Mangold, '*The World's Worst Organisations*', Channel 4 Books (1999).

The HSE is allowed to prescribe training and development. However, it will not normally carry this out, but rather leave it in the hands of organisations and their managers to arrange.

- **Other statutory inspections:** the fire brigade, police, environmental health are all allowed statutory access to workplace premises in order to inspect from their own particular points of view. Each has the power to recommend and insist on organisation and employee development, as well as other matters.

Voluntary inspections

Each of the statutory bodies indicated above may be called in by organisations to act as consultants, experts and advisers. Inspections such as for Investors in People (IIP), ISO 9000 (the EU quality assurance mark) may also be undertaken by organisations for a variety of reasons:

- knowledge, belief or perception that the accreditation will enhance customer, client, supplier and sectoral perceptions;
- enhancing attractiveness as an employer both to employees, and in terms of corporate citizenship;
- as a catalyst for further attitude, behaviour and performance change;
- as a lever to break up existing comfortable and declining ways of working;
- as a more general means of generating collective and individual abilities to think beyond what is currently feasible.

Support for these initiatives is provided by government in terms of the standards required, though organisations must pay for the actual inspections. Conducted properly, this form of inspection and certification brings organisation and employee development demands and opportunities. Problems arise among professional, occupational and work groups within organisations when it is known, believed or perceived that the inspection is for hidden or expedient reasons – for example, shake-ups of powerful groups, the present inability to tackle structural or operational problems without some prior form of disruption.

Inspections require evidence that:

- organisational and employee development strategies are in place;
- opportunities are available to all;
- performance appraisal processes exist and are used;
- there are systems for the monitoring, review and evaluation of organisation and employee development.

The inspection process works as shown in Figure 16.2.

The difficulty faced by both organisations and the implementing bodies is the concentration on paperwork evidence rather than quality of delivery. So long as this is recognised, addressed and overcome the inspection process can give effective emphasis and impetus to organisation and employee development strategies, priorities and delivery.

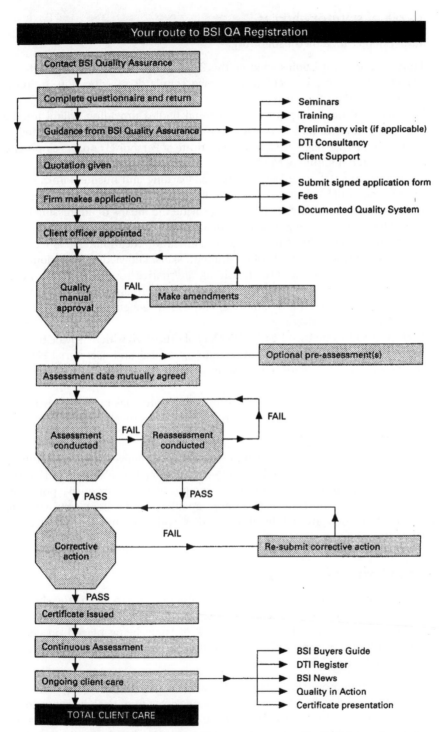

Figure 16.2 A standard procedure for government accreditation and assurance (applied to IIP/ISO 9000)

The role of statutory bodies

Statutory bodies include the following:

- Fully independent bodies such as the British Medical Association and Law Society which set and regulate their own standards of education, training, behaviour and performance.
- Occupational bodies or quasi-professional bodies providing syllabi for the teaching of known, understood and agreed bodies of professional knowledge, skill and expertise (e.g. the Chartered Institute of Personnel and Development, the Chartered Institute of Marketing).
- Non-governmental organisations such as learning and business links which analyse industrial, commercial and public service learning and training needs on a localised basis, and then seek to provide the means of addressing these through self-generating and self-financing initiatives.
- Umbrella bodies such as the National Council for Vocational Qualifications, which sets overall standards of attainment, skills, knowledge, behaviour and performance in specific jobs, providing alternative routes to initial, intermediate and high levels of recognition, achievement and expertise for those who have not gained more traditional and widely recognised qualifications at school, college or university.
- Technical bodies such as the Royal Society of Arts (RSA) which provide training and education in business administration, clerical and secretarial skills at elementary, intermediate and advanced levels, with nationally recognised certificates and exams.
- The City and Guilds of London Institute which provides more technical and skill-based training and education in trades such as mechanics, engineering, catering and hairdressing.

At their best, these bodies are extremely effective in delivering, demonstrating and verifying extensive capability and – at advanced levels – expertise. The process is compromised when it requires the production of extensive portfolios of evidence to demonstrate elementary capability, and where conflicting or divergent standards are set by those bodies with whom organisations and individuals may be working.

Skills and expertise shortages

One of the enduring problems that all governments have to face is the shortage of specific skills and expertise. This arises as the result of over-demand in booming sectors, or else because of a lack of value being placed on certain activities and occupations. At present, for the foreseeable future in the UK, the priorities in this area are the following:

- Public services professions, especially medicine, nursing, teaching and social work. These shortages have arisen partly because of political decisions to cut salaries and increase workloads on frontline staff, and partly because forward planning tended to be linear and one-dimensional rather than fully contextual (see Summary Box 16.8).

There are no simple or expedient enduring solutions. Investment is required in resources and equipment, as well as salaries and terms and conditions of employment, if public professions and occupations are to be made attractive and competitive to what is available to people with equivalent qualifications in industry and commerce.

It should be noted that the problem has been compounded in nursing and teaching by attempting to buy in the expertise from overseas. Because of the shortages, capable and expert non-UK staff have been able to pick and choose their jobs, and move on elsewhere once they have a basic knowledge of the country.

It should also be noted that an intended by-product of the privatisation of social services and healthcare for the elderly, vulnerable and at risk members of society was to shift the responsibility for training in these occupations to the private sector. By and large this has not happened. The private sector have either bought in the expertise, or else shifted the emphasis of their activities into areas where full professional expertise is not required.

- Building, construction and civil engineering which have arisen because of the 'boom and bust' cycles prevalent in the sector over the past twenty years. Again, the problem is compounded because better opportunities are open elsewhere to those with qualifications in this area. Those with degrees in these subjects can choose to go into research, finance and environmental development activities as well as construction, management and civil engineering. Those with City and Guilds can choose to work self-employed as subcontractors anywhere in the EU where the pay, and terms and conditions of employment, are much better than in the UK.
- Computer and IT skills and expertise which is identified by the government as its current priority at all levels – schools, colleges, universities, vocational, into work and back to work. It is undoubtedly true that there is heavy demand. However, the experience of silicon valley in California over the period since 1999, and present UK experiences in IT strongholds such as the Thames Valley, south Wales and Scotland, indicate that this too is a volatile sector, and skills and expertise development has therefore to be carefully managed if the experience of public service professions, building construction and civil engineering is not to be repeated in this sector (see Summary Box 16.9).

It is necessary to be clear about the complexities surrounding shortages of skills and expertise. Clearly, in the areas indicated above, there are people with expertise seeking work. However, pay and terms and conditions of employment have to remain attractive or else people will simply change occupations. Indeed, a major problem with shortages in public professions is that pay levels are not high enough to enable those coming in to get housing mortgages in many parts of the country (some banks will not lend to nurses, teachers or social workers at all because they have no confidence that those in these professions will be able to keep up repayments for the total mortgage period).

So the assessment, delivery and implementation of strategies to tackle skills shortages have to be fully understood and evaluated if it is to be managed successfully. It is also necessary to sustain and in-build continuous professional and occupation development so that people can keep up-to-date whether in or out of work.

Cultural and social factors

The other elements of industrial, occupational, vocational and prevocational education and training that have to be addressed by government is the overall respect and value in which it is held. In the UK, there is an enduring cultural perception that these areas are a last resort – only to be considered after all other options have failed. In terms of status and perceived value, academic qualifications take precedent over professional, occupational or vocational.

Successive UK governments have failed to address this. They have failed to raise the value of practical, vocational, education and training as an equivalent and alternative to 'the education route' of GCSE, A-Level and degree. They have put emphasis on this only when politically expedient. They have gone to a lot of trouble not to have to face the consequences of particular courses of action that have had the result of downgrading and undervaluing particular professional and occupational groups over the years (see Summary Box 16.10).

The management of these factors has therefore to include marketing and public relations campaigns supported by investment and resources, and underpinned by demonstrating that the full range of opportunities is open to everybody regardless of whether they take a professional, occupational, academic or vocational route. To be fully effective, vocational and occupation-based qualifications have to be raised in content, substance, profile and universal

Except where there is over-demand for particular expertise, an enduring derived problem that governments have to face is how to make attractive specific areas of shortage. Alan Clark, a former Industry Minister, acknowledged that there was no solution except to put up wages and salaries to a point where these were overtly attractive in their own right. Approaching the matter from the particular point of view of public services professions, he stated that nobody of calibre or quality will be attracted until the myth that it is a vocation is dispelled. At times of economic uncertainty and volatility, people are drawn to instant high levels of reward rather than the illusion of long-term job security. The only recommendation for a career in public service is that pay levels are so low that nobody who is truly ambitious will want it. Careers only endure when there is long-term economic stability.

Source: A. Clark, 'Diaries: Volume 1', Weidenfeld & Nicholson (1998).

recognition to the point where they are held in equivalent esteem in their own right to those who follow academic and professional training.

Costs and benefits

The costs and benefits of effective government training and development policies are as summarised in Table 16.1.

Conclusions

The main problem faced by government is the ability to respond to short-term political pressures that are certain to be generated if long-term investment is placed in all aspects of national training and development policy. All areas

Table 16.1   Costs and benefits

Costs	Benefits
• Taxation – financial and political costs	• Employability
• Quotas – suffer from lobbies and vested interests acting against them	• Higher levels of expertise
	• Higher levels of expectation
• Responsibilities and obligations – investment in attitude and responsibility changes	• Increases total capability of national and sectoral workforces
• Job security for trainees – based on a combination of perception and reality	• Enhances attractiveness
	• Long-term (not short-term) political gain

require resources, expertise, equipment and technology, as well as enduring good levels of salary and reward, if they are to be made effective, and this is certain to increase taxation and public finance demands in the short to medium-term. This is a problem that is not easily addressed by political institutions.

The other issue that has to be faced is the content of vocational and prevocational programmes. No increases in recognised output and substantial skills development will ever become apparent until agreement is reached on what constitutes the essential content of these programmes. This is reinforced by the belief and perception that such programmes are (as stated above) only to be contemplated by individuals when everything else has failed or become closed to them.

Overall, national education and training policy requires constant professional and expert attention to ensure that standards are maintained and raised. Again, this requires investment, and again, there are political pressures against this. Problems will only be resolved when hard decisions are taken, and presented to the population at large, that this is a necessary and enduring investment, for which everybody must be prepared to pay.

QUESTIONS

1 Design a public relations campaign that has the purpose of encouraging people in public professions such as medicine, teaching and nursing, and that builds on the great value of these services. What else is necessary in order to ensure that there is substance as well as presentation?

2 Under what circumstances would you recommend individuals to go into prevocational education and training, if there were no social and cultural stigma attached?

3 What should organisations gain from total quality management and investors in people inspections?

4 Produce an induction and core training programme for:
(a) a school leaver;
(b) an adult returning to work after many years' break;
(c) the organisation of your choice.
Remember to include aims and objectives, learning outcomes, and measures of success and failure.

5 Produce a format for inspection for the organisation, department or section of your choice. Identify aims and objectives, the overall purpose, and the means by which you are going to inspect. What are the implications for:
(a) the inspection itself?
(b) the organisation to whom you are going to report?

6 Your organisation has just had a serious fire. The Health and Safety Executive have been called in. Their recommendations are awaited with trepidation. What actions can the organisation itself take in the meantime? Why are these essential and desirable?

■ Ṽ 17 The future of organisation and employee development

'Without knowledge, expertise, experience and awareness we are nothing.'

Nubar Gulbenkian

Introduction

Rationally, the future of employee development ought to be assured. The speed of change in technology, expertise and markets, ever-greater customer demands and expectations, and the globalisation of many activities, should provide sufficient incentive for governments, organisations and individuals to establish absolute priorities in training and development. It is true that many organisations do now take a much greater and more active interest, though there still remains an attitude of 'someone should do this – but not us' in many areas.

Major influences on the future are certain to include:

- the European Union;
- continued demands for continuous professional and occupational development;
- managing across cultures;
- the role and function of specialists and experts.

The European Union

So long as the UK remains a member of the EU, the following influences are certain to apply:

- Greater emphasis on security of employment. This means that training and development in order to redeploy, rather than lay-off or make redundant, are to be required as the first response to market, technology and competitive changes.
- Greater emphasis on staff and worker consultation, participation and involvement. This raises the staff interest in organisations to the same level of influence as that of shareholders. This means, in turn, that staff are to have ever-greater access to information and an active say in decision-making. This, in turn, requires development of attitudes and behaviour towards full commitment and specific training in reading, using and analysing information (see Summary Box 17.1).
- Harmonisation of professional and occupational qualifications so that

A valuable lesson in this can be learned from Semco, the Brazilian engineering and white goods manufacturer. Jointly with its recognised trade unions, Semco puts on financial management and business performance courses and classes for all of its staff. It reinforces this learning with the production of weekly, monthly and quarterly balance sheets as well as annual accounts – and these have to be approved by the staff.

Following on from this, the company has an attitude development programme aimed at creating full flexibility of working hours and work group responsibility for output, volumes, quality and deadlines.

The company has used this fully open and participative approach to grow turnover, market share and profit margins net of inflation in spite of the following:

* annual inflation rates in Brazil as high as 5000 per cent;
* recession in four of the past ten years (during which the company has had no compulsory redundancies);
* serious problems in the supply of raw materials and the capability to distribute the finished product.

The full employee development programme concentrates all efforts on making, selling, billing and collecting. The company has no support staff or 'people in dead-end jobs that feed ego but hurt the balance sheet'. Everything is directed at product effectiveness, and customer and client satisfaction.

Source: R. Semler, 'The Maverick Solution', BBC Television (1998).

eventually a particular qualification gained in one country will be recognised in all the other Member States. Persons from any part of the EU will therefore be free to ply their expertise or trade anywhere subject only to language barriers (see Summary Box 17.2).

There are problems with this and it is certain to take many years to resolve. For example, industrial training is of the highest quality in Germany where it is accorded the same priority and status as any other further and higher education. Everybody has the right to attend work school (arbeitschule) and employers must support and pay for it.

Some professional training is to different levels of expertise. While medical training is broadly similar, the highest quality nursing training is in France, Sweden and Finland.

There are issues surrounding the education schemes run by UK professional bodies and associations (e.g. those of the Chartered Institute of Personnel and Development, Institute of Civil Engineering). This is because there are no equivalents elsewhere. This level, quality and standard of training is carried out elsewhere in the EU at a postgraduate or post-experience stage at universities and colleges.

- There is also certain to be further development of existing ERASMUS and TEMPUS programmes which seek cross-border cultural, social, occupational and professional awareness. At present, largely offered to university students and within certain professions, plans exist to make these opportunities much more widely available.
- The requirement to respond to EU Directives on working hours and health and safety at work implies the need for greater capability among all staff so that their operational efforts are maximised and optimised and in order to keep specific problems to a minimum.
- There is certain to be increased demands for language training in the medium to long-term as people gain an ever-greater awareness of the opportunities open to them in different parts of the EU. This reinforces the collective and individual responsibility to enhance employability referred to elsewhere. Handy (1992) refers to this as the 'portable career'.

Continuous professional and occupational development

This is a stated requirement in many occupations as a condition of being able to continue to practice or retain membership of the particular profession or occupation. It is certain to spread to other areas in the interests of sustaining and developing employability. It is increasingly required as a condition of employment in many organisations as they strive for full flexibility of working, multi-skilling and multi-capability.

In many cases, this is becoming formalised into training and learning agreements and contracts. Individuals are formally required by their organisation to commit themselves to a certain amount or type of training, and completion of this is a condition of continuing employment, pay rises, promotions and other opportunities. It also forms an effective written and formalised summary of what employers expect of employees, and vice versa. Learning, capability, performance, responsibility and outcomes are all specified and dates and deadlines established.

Some organisations take this a stage further and include training and learning contracts in their basic terms and conditions of employment. The process and emphasis is discussed and agreed at the selection stage so that new employees fully understand what is expected of them. This then commences at induction, core and initial job training on an agreed and formalised basis.

Other organisations still, ensure that continuous professional and occupational development requirements of professional body membership and continued ability to practice are written into learning contracts. This ensures that everyone involved continues to take an active interest in what is required. It also helps to ensure that organisations benefit from professional and occupational development in these circumstances (see Summary Box 17.3).

Continuous professional and occupational development as required by professional bodies covers a wide variety of activities. This includes the following:

- project work;
- professional updates and seminar attendance;
- postgraduate and post-experience study and project work;
- computer-based training and expertise development (e.g. architecture, building, planning, surgery);
- specific activities followed in an orderly and prescribed manner (e.g. Institute of Civil Engineering logbooks).

This builds up the total body of expertise and capability available to organisations. Project work and research activities required on postgraduate and post-experience courses can invariably be conducted using work-based problems and issues allowing the organisation to derive specific benefits at the same time as their staff are enhancing their quality and expertise.

Managing across cultures

The importance of understanding how things are done in organisations (as well as what is done and why) was first identified as a separate issue by Handy in 1973. It was subsequently popularised by Peters and Waterman (1980) as a key contributor to enduring excellent levels of performance.

It has therefore come to be widely established that while being able to understand, accommodate, accept and work within the constraints of different organisation cultures is a key management quality, it is one part of the answer only. The ability is also required to 'manage across cultures'. This means:

- setting standards of attitude, behaviour, skills, expertise and performance that transcend local, social, professional and occupational differences;
- recognising the presence, prevalence and influence of subcultures – professional, occupational and social, and also negative aspects such as group-think, *canteen* cultures and *bunker* mentalities;
- setting and delivering over-arching, shared and positive attitudes and values in multinational and international organisations, and public service bureaucracies, so that these are acceptable wherever in the world activities are conducted (see Summary Box 17.4).

The organisation and employee development implications here concern the following:

- Active and positive training in ethics, integrity and openness; and in cultural, social and behavioural awareness as a precondition of understanding how and

Learning from the experience of Japanese companies when they first set up manufacturing operations in the West is critical. The companies are located as a matter of policy in areas of high structural unemployment. They then set about transforming the collective attitude to work in these communities.

The companies promised high levels of pay and job security in return for 'doing things our way'. The companies, in turn, made 'doing things our way' acceptable to all as follows:

- extensive induction and familiarisation programmes;
- extensive initial and continuing job training;
- fully developed core training programmes;
- commitment to continuous development and full flexibility of working;
- commitment to organisational funding for all employee development activities;
- full trade union involvement;
- full consultation and participation;

The success of the approach can be illustrated by the following examples:

- The Nissan UK factory at Washington, Tyne and Wear has the highest level of output of any car factory in the world; and it has achieved this through the transformation of the skills, qualities and expertise of 'failed' dockers, miners and shipyard workers.
- The Honda factory at Swindon, Wiltshire produces the perceived highest quality cars of any factory in the UK through having transformed a skilled, semi-skilled and largely unskilled workforce with its traditions and roots in the railway industry.

why people behave in the ways that they do. This means that misapprehensions, preconceptions and national and social stereotyping are transcended. Steps can then be taken to design the behavioural and operational aspects of organisations so that effective performance *in context* is achieved. This often means cultural and social immersion in which managers and key figures live in particular communities and locations, and are required to undertake a specific set of tasks and activities so that they become familiar with the ways in which the people think, behave and act, their beliefs, and their hopes, fears and aspirations.

- Within organisations, managing across departmental, divisional, functional, professional and occupational cultures is also being increasingly seen as important. This reinforces the need for environmental awareness and understanding (see Chapter 13) and recognising and understanding the quite legitimate range of loyalties that people have – to their peers, occupation, profession, other colleagues, union, professional bodies as well as organisations and managers. Overall standards of attitude, value, behaviour and performance must be capable of acceptance and achievement.

- Where barriers between occupational and professional groups exist, they can only be broken down through communications, meetings and facing up to the operational consequences of what exists at the present and why. Managerial expertise and priority in these cases is in the creation of conditions in which the different groups and individuals are going to want to address the difficulties (see Summary Box 17.5).

SUMMARY BOX 17.5   Breaking down cultural barriers

There is no easy solution. The principles on which any successful attempt to do this are based on the following:

- knowing and understanding the environment;
- knowing and understanding the hopes, fears and aspirations of each group;
- knowing and understanding that the barriers have gone up for reasons, and recognising and accepting these as a prerequisite to tackling them;
- creating a series of meetings with substantial agenda and required tangible outcomes, and imposing compulsory attendance.

The keys to successful application of these principles are:

- continued visibility;
- high-quality effective communications;
- leading by example;
- taking a hard, honest line with malcontents, recalcitrance and non-attenders;
- having the energy, stamina and commitment to persist if things do not immediately or quickly work out.

There are clear implications for both management and staff development. Above all, where attitudinal barriers and professional and peer group-think are allowed to persist, there is always a negative effect on product and service performance.

Managing across *canteen* cultures and *bunker* mentalities requires all of the above, especially understanding why and how they have been allowed to form and become influential. They additionally require confrontation, breaking up and the acceptance by those involved of the organisation's standards of attitudes, behaviour and performance rather than their own. This invariably means underpinning with understanding and, where necessary, applying relocation, redeployment and, in some cases, sanctions including disciplinary and dismissal procedures.

The prerequisite to the effective application of all of this is that the organisation's own standards of attitude, behaviour and performance must be capable of acceptance by all so that existing prevailing professional, occupational and social standards, hopes, fears and aspirations can be accommodated and integrated rather than rejected.

Consultants and specialists

In organisation and employee development, understanding is required from the following points of view:

- It is essential to understand the organisation and employee development aspects and implications of organisation, production, technological, market, structural and cultural change much more deeply. Most ventures, investments, mergers, takeovers, overseas activities, new product and market initiatives fail or fall short of full success because little or no account is taken of the attitudinal and behavioural aspects, and because insufficient weight is placed on the development of new skills, knowledge and expertise or the application of existing capability in new ways. All those hiring business process re-engineering, total quality management and other business development consultants should in-build an automatic reaction that questions the staff development implications wherever such proposals are being considered.
- The contribution of training consultants and specialists should also be the subject of constant review and evaluation so that this continues to be effective. A balance has to be struck between the advantages and benefits of building long-term, effective and mutually profitable relationships with providers and ensuring that this is not simply a corporate habit. If delivery requirements change or performance appraisal and needs analyses produce changing implications then present providers must adjust their service accordingly; or it may be an opportunity to bring additional providers in to freshen up the existing programme as well as addressing new needs levels.
- Value for money is also critical. Effective employee development functions should always be looking at the balance of costs and benefits for every activity. The use of good quality consultants and specialists normally means paying premium costs and charges, and enduring value needs constant monitoring, review and evaluation. The benefits, when effective, are always to boost behavioural, attitudinal, performance and expertise elements.

This must be kept under constant review to ensure continuity. No organisation should ever become dependent on outsiders (for employee development or anything else). Consultants, specialists and advisers are a resource to be brought in and used when required, and to support and develop organisation capability, not replace it.

Costs and benefits

The costs and benefits of considering organisation and employee development implications for the future are as summarised in Table 17.1.

Conclusions

Each of these elements can be seen either as an opportunity or a threat. The first requirement for the future is therefore to take a positive view of organisation and

Table 17.1   Costs and benefits

Costs	Benefits
• Opportunity costs – fixed costs involved in staffing requiring greater emphasis on organisation development • Behavioural – managing across cultures and the active management of consultants requires degrees of self-development and discomfort, and investment in changes in professional and occupational attitudes • Some variable costs – in resource gathering and individual expertise development	• The relationship between professional and occupational harmony and effective product and service delivery • The questioning approach is likely to lead to much more effectiveness in the use of consultants, specialists and outsiders • Everything contributes to the development of attitudes, values and behaviour, and therefore collective cohesion and harmony, as well as expertise in product and service output and delivery

employee development, and to recognise that provided that the basic conditions are right, everyone benefits. So long as this is maintained, organisation and employee development constitute a major contribution to professional and occupational success and performance effectiveness. Continuing efforts enhance this and the collective and individual capability and willingness that are necessary as a prerequisite in all organisations that do not have captive or relatively assured markets. Viewed in this way, EU regulations, legislation and directives are as much an opportunity as a threat.

Organisation and employee development must be tied to business performance much more directly and in ways capable of being clearly understood and accepted by all concerned. The implication here is for greater overall levels of understanding on the part of directors, senior managers and public sector governors and fund holders. In turn, there is a requirement for the greater professionalisation of the organisation and employee training and development function, all those who work in it, and the expertise required to be effective. It is an active responsibility of all organisations to enhance their own operational and competitive capability and capacity, and the employability and value of their staff.

QUESTIONS

1 For the organisation of your choice, identify six collective and individual development priorities that are apparent to you. Outline the means by which these should be addressed, and include cost, benefit and resource implications.

2 Your organisation is required to conform with the EU Working Hours Directive. Produce a short report outlining the organisation and employee development implications to be addressed to your Chief Executive. Remember to include cost implications.

3 Identify the cultural, behavioural and performance implications of taking on professionally qualified staff from elsewhere in the EU to work in the UK. Outline

an induction programme that will (a) highlight any particular difficulties; (b) ensure that the new staff become effective and productive as quickly as possible.

4 Outline the costs and benefits inherent in developing an organisation and employee awareness and change programme in a merger or takeover with which you are familiar.

5 Why do the senior managers of organisations pay so little attention to the human aspects of investment and ventures? Produce a briefing paper that addresses these shortcomings for the benefit of directors and senior managers.

◼ ◪ Bibliography

M. Armstrong (1999) *Human Resource Management*, Kogan Page.

M.K. Ash (1985) *On People Management*, MacDonald.

D. Biddle and C. Evenden (1990) *The Human Side of Enterprise*, CIPD.

R. Blake and J. Mouton (1986) *The New Managerial Grid*, Gulf.

J. Bratton and J. Gold (2000) *Human Resource Management*, Macmillan (now Palgrave).

D. Buchanan and A. Huczynski (1997) *Organisational Behaviour*, Prentice Hall.

R. Cartwright (2001) *Mastering the Business Environment*, Palgrave.

R. Cartwright and G. Green (1996) *In Charge: Managing Yourself*, Blackwell.

A. Clark (1998) *Diaries: Volume 1*, Weidenfeld & Nicholson.

P.F. Drucker (1986) *The Practice of Management*, Prentice Hall.

P.F. Drucker (1988) *The Effective Executive*, Fontana.

P.F. Drucker (2000) *Management Challenges for the 21st Century*, HarperCollins.

W. Goldsmith and D. Clutterbuck (1990) *The Winning Streak*, Penguin.

G. Hammel (2000) *Leading the Revolution*, HarperCollins.

C.B. Handy (1973) *Understanding Organisations* (1st edn), Penguin.

C.B. Handy (1992) *The Future of Work*, Penguin.

C.B. Handy (1993) *The Age of Unreason*, Penguin.

C.B. Handy (1997) *Understanding Organisations* (4th edn), Penguin.

J. Henry (1990) *Creative Management*, OU Press.

G. Hofstede (1980) *Cultures' Consequences*, Sage.

P. Honey (1986) *Learning*, UMIST.

P. Honey and A. Mumford (1992) *Preferred Learning Styles*, Peter Honey.

R.M. Kanter (1983) *The Change Masters*, HBS Press.

R.M. Kanter (1990) *When Giants Learn to Dance*, HBS Press.

J. Kenney and R. Reid (1992) *Training Interventions*, CIPD.

D.A. Kolb (1985) *Experience as the Source of Learning and Development*, Prentice Hall.

R.S. Lessem (1989) *Managing Corporate Culture*, Gower.

B. Livy (1990) *Corporate Personnel Management*, F.T. Pitman.

F. Luthans (1993) *Organisational Behaviour*, McGraw-Hill.

M. Marchington (1998) *Organisational and Individual Training and Development*, CIPD.

L. Mullins (1999) *Management and Organisational Behaviour* (5th edn), F.T. Pitman.

A. Mumford (1997) *Management Development*, CIPD.

M. Pedler, J. Burgoyne and T. Boydell (1997) *The Learning Company*, McGraw-Hill.

T. Peters and R.H. Waterman (1980) *In Search of Excellence*, Macmillan (now Palgrave).

R. Pettinger (1998) *Managing the Flexible Workforce*, Cassell.

R. Pettinger (1998) *The European Social Charter: A Manager's Guide*, Kogan Page.

R. Pettinger (1999) *The Future of Industrial Relations*, Cassell.

R. Pettinger (2001) *Learning Organisations*, Capstone.

R. Pettinger (2001) *Mastering Management Skills*, Palgrave.

M.E. Porter (1980) *Competitive Strategy*, Free Press.

M.E. Porter (1985) *Competitive Advantage*, Free Press.

R. Revans (1974) *Action Learning in Practice*, John Wiley.

A. Roddick (1998) *Body and Soul: The Body Shop Story*, Ebury.

R. Semler (1992) *Maverick*, Century.

P. Senge (1992) *The Fifth Discipline*, Century.

R. Tannenbaum and W. Schmidt (1958) *How to Choose a Leadership Pattern*, HBR.

D. Torrington and L. Hall (1998) *Human Resource Management,* Prentice Hall International.

P. Wickers (1992) *The Road to Nissan,* Macmillan (now Palgrave).

P. Wickers (1997) *The Ascendant Organisation,* Macmillan (now Palgrave).

A. Williams, P. Dobson and M. Waters (1997) *Changing Culture,* CIPD.

Index

A-Levels   192
absence   44
    costs   6, 7
academic/vocational divide   204–5
acceptance of culture   167
accountability   134, 135
action learning   66, 81–2
activist learning style   17–18
ad hoc contribution   152, 154–5, 158–9
administration-based organisational
    training function   152, 155–6, 159–60
administrator role/function   150–1
advanced qualifications   182, 193
adviser role/function   150
agreements, training   147
aims   89, 99–101
'alsos'   92
anxiety   172
appraisal   28–30, 39–40, 144–6
apprenticeship   68
architecture   19
attendance   44
attitudes   25, 45, 86–7, 180
    difficult and event design   108
    organisation development   165–8
attitudinal barriers   119, 143, 212
authority   134, 135

'back to the floor'   82–3
banking   58
barriers to change   171–3
BASF   204
BASKET approach   25–6
behaviour   25, 45, 86–7, 180
    managers and behaviour problems   186
    quality of learning environment   120–1
behaviourist approach   19–20
beliefs   165–8
beneficiaries   89, 169–71
blackboards   112
Blake, R.   132
blame   30, 31, 134, 135, 167
Body Shop   6, 11, 147, 169, 170

Boo.Com   160
Boots   38, 198
Borg, B.   127
brainstorming groups   85
branded material   114
Bratton, J.   183
British Gypsum   199
British Medical Association   202
British Steel   199
BSI quality assurance   200–1
building   195, 203
bunker mentality   210, 212
bureaucracy   172
    bureacratic organisational training
        function   152, 155–6, 159–60
business studies courses   182
buying in expertise   11, 181

Cadbury's chocolate   115
Canon   6
canteen cultures   210, 212
capability   13–14, 69–70
Care in the Community   81
case studies   65, 117–18
change
    barriers to   171–3
    coping with   169–71
Channel Tunnel   171
characteristics, personal   134–5
charges   5–8
Chartered Institute of Marketing (CIM)   68,
    202
Chartered Institute of Personnel and
    Development (CIPD)   7, 67, 68, 202
City Communications   128
City and Guilds of London Institute   193,
    202
civil engineering   195, 203
Clark, A.   205
classroom-based training   64
clients   169–70
Clough, B.   129
CMS/NEBSM   182

coaching *see* mentoring, coaching and counselling
cognitive approach 20
collective review 146
commerce 199
commitment 15
  generation of 168–9
common sense 178–9
communications 36
communities 170–1
community awareness training 155
competencies training 64
complaints 45
computer-based training 65, 94
  equipment and resources 115–17
  opportunities of 9–10
  see also internet
computer skills 203, 204
conditioning 21
conflict management 173–5
consistency, lack of 194–5
construction 195, 203
consultant role/function 151
consultants 6, 7, 213
  see also trainers
consultation, process 101–2
content 89, 107
context
  employee development 2–5, 9–11
  mentoring, coaching and counselling 124–6
  projects and secondments 76–7
  training events 90
continued job training and development 44
continuous professional and occupational development 10–11, 61, 106, 148, 209–10
contracts 147
core training programmes 42–50
  costs and benefits 48
  programme purposes 45–8
  universal programmes 42–5, 55–6
cost–benefit analysis 8–9
cost leadership 139–40, 158
Co-Steel Sheerness Plc 49
costs 5–8
counselling *see* mentoring, coaching and counselling
courses, taught 64, 66, 106
critical incidents 33–5
criticism 48
cultural barriers 119, 212
culture
  managing across cultures 210–12

organisation culture 45, 121, 165–8
and practical/vocational training 204–5
customers 169–70

day release 68
debrief 114, 115
defeatist attitudes 172–3
degrees 193
delivery 89
Department for Education and Employment (DfEE) 193
design 19
designer role/function 150
designing training programmes 99–110
  aims and objectives 99–101
  costs and benefits 108–9
  group mixes 107–8
  group size 106–7
  process consultation 101–2
  target audience 102–4
  use of time 104–6
development strategies 138–49
  collective review 146
  continuous professional and occupational development 148
  contracts and agreements 147
  costs and benefits 148
  generic strategies 139–40
  inspections 147
  peer review 146
  raising expectations 141
  training environment 142–4
  training needs analysis and appraisal 144–6
differentiation 139–40, 159–60
difficulty 33–4
dilution of training function 151
diplomas 182, 192
direction 39
directors 102
discussion 105
distance learning 65
DMS 182
doctorate 182

emergency procedures/programmes 43, 100
empathy 134, 135
employability 25, 209
employees
  difficulty of retaining after development 94
  filming 114–15
  as primary beneficiary 170
  role in training provision 196

see also under individual types of employee
employers   196
empowerment   3, 57–9
end-of-the-day sessions   104
engineering   195, 197, 203
environment   71, 92, 93, 119–21
  behavioural   120–1
  development strategies   142–4
  physical   119–20
environmental expertise   183–6
equality   16–17, 43, 144
equanimity   134
equipment   6, 111–23
  costs and benefits   121
  quality of learning environment   119–21
  types of   112–19
ERASMUS   209
Ernst & Young   6, 154
European Union (EU)   207–9
Eurotunnel   171
evaluation   *see* monitoring, review and evaluation
evening classes/sessions   104, 105
event leaders   91–2
exclusivity, occupational   143, 212
expectations   107
  of on-the-job training   54–5
  raising   141
  and rewards   15–16
  unreasonable   1–2
experience   26
  planned   61
expertise   26
  body of   180–2
  high expertise/low influence training functions   152, 154–5, 158–9
  keeping up-to-date   153
  management expertise   180–2, 183–6
  organisational and environmental   183–6
  organisational training functions   150–1, 152
expertise shortages   202–4

facilitators   91–2, 101
  see also trainers
failure   77, 171
fear   172
feedback   19–20, 23, 47–8, 105
feedback sheets   91
figureheads   179
financial services   152–3
flexibility   59–60, 69
flipcharts   112
focus   139–40, 158–9

Ford UK   173
frequency   33–4
frontline organisation development   83–5
frontline staff   56–7
functions of training   150–1, 160–1, 162
  see also organisational training functions
future of employee development   207–15
  consultants and specialists   213
  continuous professional and occupational development   209–10
  costs and benefits   213, 214
  EU   207–9
  managing across cultures   210–12

GCSEs   192
generic programmes   42–5, 55–6
generic strategies   139–40
  and training function   158–60
Gold, J.   183
government policy   192–206
  costs and benefits   205
  cultural and social factors   204–5
  inspection   197–201
  lack of value and consistency   194–5
  political expediency   195
  problems   193–204
  role of statutory bodies   202
  skills and expertise shortages   202–4
  status of training   197, 198
  who pays for training   196–7
graveyard shift   104
groups   140
  mixes   107–8
  size   106–7
  training needs analysis   37
guidance   52–4
Gurley, S.   83

Handy, C.B.   184–5, 209, 210
happy sheets   91
harmonisation of qualifications   207–8
Harvester Restaurants   3, 58
health and safety   43
  inspections   199–200
Health and Safety Executive (HSE)   199–200
high-cost seminars   65, 67
history   165, 171
  rescuing the past   185
HND/HNC   182
Honda   211
Honey, P.   17–18
hospitals   198
human resource management   34–5, 43–4

impartiality 186
implementation costs 6
importance 33–4
in-house expertise vs buying in 11, 181–2
individuals 140
  performance appraisal 28–30
induction programmes 42–3, 56, 68
industrial relations 118
industrial sectors 199
industrial training 193, 194
  paying for 196–7
  status of 197
Industrial Training Boards (ITBs) 2, 193
influence
  high expertise/low influence training
    functions 152, 154–5, 158–9
  mentoring, coaching and counselling
    134, 135
  organisational training functions 151,
    152
information 150, 187
information technology (IT) skills 203, 204
  see also computer-based training
initial job training programmes 44, 68
inspections 147, 197–201
Institute of Administrative Management
  (IAM) 67, 68
Institute of Chartered Accountants 67
Institute of Management open management
  programme 85
Institute of Training and Development 150
internet 1, 65, 115–17
  opportunities of internet training 9–10
Investors in People (IIP) 200–1
ISO9000 200–1
ivory towers 4

Japanese companies 167, 211
  core training programmes 43–4, 44
job assessment and evaluation 32
job training 44, 68
John Jarvis 113
Johnson Matthey 204
Joynson, S. 84–5
junior management 119
junior staff 103–4, 126–7

Kanter, R.M. 3–4, 25, 178–9
Kent County Council 81
knowledge 25, 180

laboratories 64, 112–13
Law Society 202
leadership
  models and mentoring 129–34

training 114
leadership grid 130
learning 13–27
  behaviourist approach 19–20
  cognitive approach 20
  conditioning approach 21
  conditions for 13–17
  contracts and agreements 147
  costs and benefits 26
  factors affecting 23–6
  how people learn 19–23
  open learning 65, 68
  preferred learning styles 17–19
  rate of and on-the-job training 52–4
learning cycle 21–2
learning organisation 152–3
Ledward, R. 146
libraries 113
lifting 51
Livy, B. 33
location 166, 171
long-term timescales 106
Lucas CAV 6, 11

Management Charter Initiative (MCI) 183
management development 61, 178–91
  body of expertise 180–2
  costs and benefits 190
  management qualifications 182–3
  organisational and environmental
    expertise 183–6
  product and service enhancement
    186–8
  self-development 188–9
  succession and transformation 189–90
management style 166
manager role/function 150
managerial grid 132
managers 45, 172
  designing training programmes for
    102–3
  junior managers 119
  and monitoring, review and evaluation
    90–1
  performance assessment 32–6
  senior managers see senior managers
managing across cultures 210–12
Mangold, T. 199
Manpower Services Commission (MSC)
  193
Marchant, A. 128
Marconi 204
marketing 35
maths tests 72
MBA 103, 182

McKersie, J. 118
mentoring, coaching and counselling 65,
    77, 124–37
    characteristics 134–5
    context 124–6
    costs and benefits 136
    nature of relationship 129–34
    outputs 127–9
    qualities 126–7
MMRC 187–8
monitoring, review and evaluation 40,
    88–98
    basis 88–94
    costs and benefits 97
    criteria 89
    exchange of views 93–4
    post-testing 95–6
    pre-evaluation 95
    producing reports 96
    when to evaluate 92–3
    who evaluates 89–92
Mouton, J. 132
multi-skilling 57, 58
Mumford, A. 18

National Council for Vocational
    Qualifications 61, 202
national interest 196
national training framework 2
National Vocational Qualifications (NVQs)
    183
NEBSM/CMS 182
need 89
    training needs analysis see training
        needs analysis
negative feedback 19–20
networking 67
NHS 143, 195
    see also nursing
Nissan 6, 11, 58, 211
non-punitive/non-adversarial approach
    134
Northern Ireland 155
nursing 2, 19, 60, 143, 167, 195, 202–3
    unvalued employee development 157

objectives 89, 99–101
occupation-based training 23–4, 68
    see also continuous professional and
        occupational development
occupational groups 119, 143, 212
occupational libraries 113
occupations 74, 187
off-the-job training 64–75
    consequences 66–8

costs and benefits 73, 74
    key factors 69–72
    opportunities 65–8
    process 73
    specific programmes 68–9
    support 72–3
on-the-job training 51–63
    continuous professional development
        61
    costs and benefits 62
    empowerment 57–9
    expectations 54–5
    flexibility 59–60
    frontline staff 56–7
    generic programmes 55–6
    guidance and supervision 52–4
    multi-skilling 57, 58
    planned experience 61
    technological training 61–2
    time serving 60
open learning 65, 68
Open University 116
openness, managerial 184–5
operations
    management development 187–8
    procedures and practices 44
opportunity costs 7
oral presentations 79–80
organisation
    context and projects/secondments 77
    cost of use of facilities 6
    culture 45, 121, 165–8
    management development 187–8
    performance assessment 32–6
    policy and direction 9
    strategy see strategy
organisation development (OD) 164–77
    barriers to change 171–3
    conflict management 173–5
    coping with change and uncertainty
        169–71
    costs and benefits 175–6
    culture 165–8
    frontline organisation development
        83–5
    generation of commitment 168–9
organisational development needs 23, 24
organisational expertise 183–6
organisational libraries 113
organisational training functions 150–63
    ad hoc contribution 152, 154–5, 158–9
    administration-based 152, 155–6,
        159–60
    balance of expertise and influence
        150–1, 152

costs and benefits 161
learning organisation 152–3
relating organisation strategy to 158–60
roles, functions and resources 160–1, 162
strategic position 151–8
unconsidered and unvalued functions 152, 157–8, 158
output 35
concern for 132–3
mentoring, coaching and counselling relationships 127–9
outside expertise 11, 181–2
outward-bound activities 65
overhead projectors 112

PADIMAC 150–1
Panasonic 77
participation 207, 208
approach to mentoring, coaching and counselling 129–32
paternalism 127
patience 134
Patten, C. 155
peer assessment/review 30, 146
people, concern for 132–3
perfection 172
performance appraisal 28–30, 39–40, 144–6
performance gaps 32–3
personal characteristics 134–5
personal development 24, 25
personalities 108
Peters, T. 99, 121, 210
physical environment 119–20
pilots, airline 13, 19
planned experience 61
plenary sessions 105
police training 138
policy 39
government policy see government policy
political drives 172
political expediency 195
Porter, M.E. 106–7, 139
positive feedback 19–20
post-testing 95–6
Power-Point 112
practice, theory and 70
practitioner role/function 150
pragmatist learning style 17–18
pre-evaluation 95
preferred learning styles 17–19
pre-occupational courses 71
pre-preparation 95
pre-qualification 13–14

prescriptive approach 129–32
presentation formats 79–80
presentation skills 119
pre-vocational training 194
status 197, 198
primary activities 188
Pringipas, C. 79
prisons 198
private study 68
procedures 156
process 73
process consultation 101–2
production 35
concern for 132–3
enhancement 186–8
professional development 24, 74, 127
see also continuous professional and occupational development
professional education schemes 65, 67, 68
professional libraries 113
proficiency 69–70
projects 64, 76–87, 94, 106
action learning 81–2
context 76–7
costs and benefits 86
demands of project work 78–81
self-interest and self-starting 86
sources of project work 77–8
promotion 189–90
paths 178–9
public sector 197, 198
public services 172, 202–3
public transport driving 19
punishment 134

qualifications 103
harmonisation 207–8
management 182–3
nationally recognised 192–3
quality
of training programme 46–7
of working relationship 133–4
quality assurance 200–1

recommendations 82
recruitment and selection 55
redeployment 172
redundancy 172
reflector learning style 17–18
reinforcement 22
rejection of culture 167
Rentokil 199
replacement costs 6
reports 96
reputation 71–2

resources   6, 77, 111–23
  costs and benefits   121
  quality of learning environment   119–21
  roles, functions and   160–1, 162
  types of   112–19
responsibility   134, 135
retail   197
retention   22
returners to work   194
Revans, R.   66, 81
review   see monitoring, review and
  evaluation
rewards   15–16
role plays   65, 118–19
roles, and functions   150–1, 160–1, 162
Rolls Royce   204
Royal Society of Arts (RSA)   193, 202
Royal Ulster Constabulary (RUC)   155
rules   39

sales   35, 118
Sandals   83
Sanyo UK   170
scapegoating   30, 31, 134, 135, 167
schedule, project   78–9
Schmidt, W.   129, 130
school attainment testing standards   192
schools' inspections   198
secondments   64, 76–87, 94, 106
  'back to the floor'   82–3
  brainstorming groups   85
  context   76–7
  costs and benefits   86
  frontline organisation development
    83–5
security of employment   207
self-assessment   30
self-development   188–9
self-interest   86
self-starting development projects   86
Semco   208
seminars, high-cost   65, 67
Semler, R.   164, 208
Senge, P.   167, 174
senior managers
  designing training programmes for   102
  mentoring, coaching and counselling by
    126–7
  sending junior managers on courses for
    3–4
  360 degree appraisal   31, 145–6
service
  enhancement   186–8
  output   35
shareholders   170

Sid's Heroes: Stena Cross-Channel Ferries
  84–5
simulators   112–13
skills   25, 180
  demonstration sessions   105
  multi-skilling   57, 58
  updates   65
skills shortages   202–4
slide shows   112
social work   202–3
Society of Chief Police Officers   138
specialists   6, 7, 213
  see also trainers
specific programmes   68–9
sponsors   101
spotlighting   30
Sprite Soft Drinks   54
staff   see employees
staffing mixes   11
standard programmes   see core training
  programmes
standards   45
statutory bodies   202
statutory inspections   197–200
Stena Cross-Channel Ferries   84–5
strategy
  development strategies   see development
    strategies
  generic strategies   139–40, 158–60
  relating to training function   158–60
  strategic approaches to training needs
    analysis   37–40, 144–6
  strategic position and organisational
    training functions   151–8
strengths   47
structure, project   78–9
student nurse   157
  see also nursing
subordinates, appraisal by   31, 145–6
success   77, 171
succession   189–90
supervision   52–4
supervisors   119, 172
  designing training programmes for
    103–4
  development   see management
    development
  process consultation   101
suppliers   170
support   69, 72–3
sympathy   134

tainted characteristics   135
Tait's Greetings Cards   143–4
Tannenbaum, R.   129, 130

target audience 102–4
Tarmac 199
tasks 187
  concern for task 132–3
taught courses 64, 66, 106
teacher training 72, 195
teaching 202–3
technological experts 102–3
technology 26, 68
  management development 181, 187
  on-the-job training 61–2
  organisation development 165, 172
telecommunications 144–5, 197
television programmes 114
TEMPUS 209
tennis coaches 125
theorist learning style 17–18
theory, and practice 70
360 degree appraisal 31, 145–6
time
  extended time periods 106
  monitoring, review and timescale 89
  use of 104–6
time serving 60
tradition 165, 171
trainees
  expectations 54–5
  filming 114–15
  monitoring, review and evaluation
    89–90, 92
  off-the-job training 70–1
  process consultation 101–2
trainees' manager 90
trainers
  expectations 55
  future of employee development 213
  hiring costs 6, 7
  monitoring, review and evaluation
    91–2
  process consultation 101
training and development
  context 2–5, 9–11
  cost and charges 5–8
  priorities 45
  process 73
training expenses 6
training and learning contracts/agreements
    147
training levy 2, 196–7
training needs analysis 28–41
  costs and benefits 40

group contributions 37
individual performance appraisal 28–30,
    39–40, 144–6
job assessment and evaluation 32
organisational and managerial
    performance assessment 32–6
peer assessment 30, 146
self-assessment 30
strategic approaches to 37–40, 144–6
structured approaches 38–40
subordinate assessment 31, 145–6
training programmes, designing see
    designing training programmes
transformation 189–90
tutors 101

uncertainty, coping with 169–71
unconsidered and unvalued development
    functions 152, 157–8, 158
understanding 134, 180
Underwood, T. 112
Unilever 145
universal programmes 42–5, 55–6
universally applied framework 39–40
uselessness 4–5

value
  lack of 194–5
  perceptions of 71–2
values 45, 165–8
vested interests 172
victimisation 30, 31, 134, 135, 167
videos 113–15
Vilas, G. 127
vocational/academic divide 204–5
vocational qualifications 182, 183
voluntary inspections 200–1

Walton, D. 118
waste and effluent disposal 45
Waterman, R.H. 121, 210
weaknesses 47–8
web@WORK survey 116
website-based learning see internet
whole person, developing 23–5
willingness to learn 14–15, 69–70
wipe-boards 112
work 187
working relationship, quality of 133–4
workshop-based training 64
written presentations 79–80